DEFEND YOURSELF!

ALSO BY MARK GREEN

*Losing Our Democracy: How Bush and the Far Right Are Sabotaging Our
American Democracy* (2006)

What We Stand For: A Program for Progressive Patriotism (ed., 2004)

The Book on Bush: How George W. (Mis)leads America
(with Eric Alterman, 2004)

*Selling Out: How Big Corporate Money Buys Elections, Rams Through
Legislation, and Betrays Our Democracy* (2002)

Mark Green's Guide to Coping in New York City (2000)

The Consumer Bible (with Nancy Youman, 1998)

Changing America: Blueprints for the New Administration (ed., 1993)

America's Transition: Blueprints for the 1990s (ed. with Mark Pinsky, 1989)

The Challenge of Hidden Profits: Reducing Corporate Bureaucracy and Waste
(with John Berry, 1985)

Reagan's Reign of Error: The Instant Nostalgia Edition
(with Gail MacColl, 1987)

Who Runs Congress? (with Michael Waldman, 1984)

The Big Business Reader (ed. with Robert Massie Jr., 1980)

Winning Back America (1982)

Taming the Giant Corporation (with Ralph Nader and Joel Seligman, 1976)

Verdicts on Lawyers (ed. with Ralph Nader, 1976)

The Other Government: The Unseen Power of Washington Lawyers (1975)

Corporate Power in America (ed. with Ralph Nader, 1973)

The Monopoly Makers (ed., 1973)

The Closed Enterprise System (with Beverly C. Moore Jr.
and Bruce Wasserstein, 1972)

With Justice for Some (ed. with Bruce Wasserstein, 1970)

DEFEND YOURSELF!

How to Protect Your Health, Your Money, and Your Rights in 10 Key Areas of Your Life

Mark Green

with

Kevin McCarthy and Lauren Strayer

A New Democracy Project Book

Newmarket Press • New York

To the memory of a great fighter, Harry Chapin

This book is published in the United States of America.

First Edition

ISBN-13: 978-1-55704-716-8
ISBN-10: 1-55704-716-2

10 9 8 7 6 5 4 3 2 1

Library of Congress Cataloging-in-Publication Data

Green, Mark J.
    Defend yourself : how to protect your health, your money, and your rights in 10 key areas of your life / by Mark Green.— 1st ed.
        p. cm.
    ISBN-13: 978-1-55704-716-8
    ISBN-10: 1-55704-716-2 (pbk. : alk. paper)
    1. Law—United States—Popular works. 2. Life skills—United States. I. Title.
    KF387.G699 2005
    349.73—dc22
                                        2005031127

QUANTITY PURCHASES
Companies, professional groups, clubs, and other organizations may qualify for special terms when ordering quantities of this title. For information or a catalog, write Special Sales Department, Newmarket Press, 18 East 48th Street, New York, NY 10017; call (212) 832-3575; fax (212) 832-3629; or e-mail info@newmarket-press.com.

www.newmarketpress.com

Manufactured in the United States of America.

CONTENTS

Talking Back and Fighting Back to Vindicate Your Rights

Some of our roles in life—such as those of patient, client, employee, consumer, and taxpayer—make us feel like a cork bobbing in an ocean of big interests and institutions. Small and helpless, we are forever figuring out how to navigate that vast ocean.

And the situation is getting worse. Much of the large middle class in this country is slipping back into a kind of near-poverty: real income for the average worker has essentially stagnated over the past thirty years, as it often takes two incomes in a family to maintain a quality of life that one income supported in 1956 or 1976. It's like trying to run up an ever-accelerating down escalator.

Ever since the time of President Franklin Delano Roosevelt, the struggling middle class (and those attempting to enter it) has looked to the federal government for a safety net of Social Security and minimum wages and for vigorous consumer, environmental, and labor regulation. But in this era of Bush and Co.—when the operating philosophy seems to be laissez-faire, or you're-on-your-own, fella—government protection is becoming less and less reliable.

So it's time to defend yourself! Why tolerate an HMO that won't pay for your emergency surgery because you didn't give notice beforehand? Why accept a higher insurance rate because you live in a low-income community? Why lose custody of your children because of judges who tilt in favor of "the monied spouse" (i.e., high-income men)? Instead, you should take advantage of the large body of laws, rights, and strategies available to workers, consumers, and citizens in order to talk back and fight back. In a world where the Internet can instantaneously provide you with much of the information you need to negotiate confidently with the powers-that-be, nothing is stopping you from getting what you deserve.

For nearly forty years—as a young public interest lawyer in the 1970s and as a public official in the 1990s—I've been trying to organize people to vindicate their rights. Or, as one federal regulator put it decades ago, "The way to keep government [or business] upright is to lean on it from all sides."

So in 1967, I persuaded 178 other summer congressional interns to send a petition to LBJ opposing the Vietnam War (leading to the elimination of the House intern program for two years). In 1978, when Congress was balking at enacting our proposed Consumer Protection Agency because it was "just more big government," I organized The Nickel Campaign and got 40,000 people to inundate members with actual nickels—since that was the exact annual cost per citizen of the agency. In 1996, upset at how tobacco ads were targeting kids, I launched "Kick Butts Day" (with President Clinton and Garry Trudeau), and now every April some 800 cities engage young students in a day of pro-health/anti-tobacco activities. And when Mayor Rudy Giuliani tried to change the NYC Charter in 1999 so that the elected Public Advocate (then me) wouldn't succeed him if he left to run for the U.S. Senate, I put together a large labor and civic coalition that defeated him in a referendum, 74 percent to 26 percent.

Defend Yourself! is my best effort to convey some of the lessons I've learned to others who feel aggrieved by some abuse of power. It's a one-stop guide to preserving your money, your health, and your rights in a world of powerful big business and ineffective big government. Give yourself, in effect, a pay raise by having a copy of

Defend Yourself! by your side to help you exercise your rights the next time some retailer or lawyer or boss tries to unfairly separate you from your money. If you're not interested in getting a 1000+ percent return on your $16.95 investment, then please don't read this book.

MARK GREEN
FEBRUARY 2006
NEW YORK CITY

CHAPTER 1

THE RIGHTS OF PATIENTS

By reserving the right to decide what is—and what is not—
medically necessary, managed-care plans can now practice medicine
without a license and without the same accountability that physicians
face every day.
—John Nelson, American Medical Association President

W hile being injured or ill can be a frightening experience for
anyone, skyrocketing medical bills and prescription drug costs
can be especially terrifying for those without health coverage. Even
those with a health care plan are at the mercy of insurance companies, HMOs, for-profit hospitals, and pharmaceutical companies, all
out to profit from your pain. Nor has the federal government done
much to make the system more effective and affordable. At any given
moment, 45 million Americans have no health coverage at all, while
some 82 million—approximately a quarter of all Americans—go
without it at some point over a two-year period and over 65 million
have no prescription drug benefits.

Meanwhile, the cost of health care is again rising far faster than
wages or other prices. According to the advocacy group Families
USA, workers' premiums increased 35.9 percent between 2000 and
2004, while wages rose by only 12.4 percent. At the same time, the
health care industries are reporting record profits: HMOs had a 52
percent profit increase in 2003 and pharmaceutical companies continue to be among the most profitable in the world. Employers, once
the proud providers for millions of working Americans, are increasingly cutting back on coverage to reduce costs, leaving more of their
employees to fend for themselves. The result of this crisis: the
Institute of Medicine estimates that 18,000 people die prematurely
each year due to lack of health care. Until our health system is

significantly overhauled—unlikely, since President Bush derided John Kerry's reasonable plans as just more big government if not socialism—you'll have to know the current laws and rules to help you get the health care you need at a price you can afford.

KEY HEALTH LAWS

ERISA, COBRA, and HIPAA The *Employee Retirement Income Security Act* of 1974 (*ERISA*) is a federal law that sets standards on private sector heath care plans and pensions. No employer is required to offer health benefits, but the many that do must follow *ERISA*'s minimum standards. Health plans are required to provide its participants with detailed information on benefits and funding. *ERISA* helps consumers by requiring health plans to have an internal review system and allows participants to sue for benefits and breaches of fiduciary duty. This law was expanded by the *Consolidated Omnibus Budget Reconciliation Act* of 1985 (*COBRA*), which allows you to continue benefits after you've lost eligibility, and by the *Health Insurance Portability and Accountability Act* of 1996 (*HIPAA*), which offers protections to people with preexisting conditions or people with an existing health condition who might lose coverage when they change jobs. While *ERISA* offers some valuable protections for consumers, it also offers important protections to health care providers and limits your ability to sue managed care organizations for malpractice.

Patients' Bill of Rights Some individual states have taken it upon themselves to guarantee their patients' rights, while most hospitals have signed on to the American Hospital Association's standards on patient rights since the 1970s. These limited provisions, however, do not offer the full rights and protections that a federal Patients' Bill of Rights would—for example, the right to use an emergency room without prior approval; the right to access specialty care; the right to appeal a plan's decision; and the right to hold a plan accountable when it withholds needed care. Furthermore, the Supreme Court has weakened some state laws, as when it struck down laws in ten states in mid-2004 that allowed health care consumers to sue HMOs for malpractice when they refused to provide needed medical care. But the Court did, at least, uphold laws in forty-two states that provide independent review boards that can overrule decisions of HMOs. Federally, Congress is deadlocked on the issue: the House and the Senate have each passed different patient rights bills, with HMO malpractice liability still a major barrier to passing a comprehensive law.

EMTALA   The Emergency Medical Treatment and Active Labor Act of 1986 (EMTALA) ensures your right to emergency medical care. Also known as the Patient Anti-Dumping Law, EMTALA outlaws the once common practice of refusing emergency treatment of patients without insurance and pregnant women in labor without insurance by passing them on to other hospitals.

Medicare/Medicaid   The Social Security Act of 1965 created both Medicare and Medicaid. Medicare assists seniors and disabled persons with health care services, regardless of their income; every American who is over sixty-five or eligible for Social Security disability benefits qualifies. Medicare has multiple plans that cover different health care needs, including Part A, which covers hospital needs, and Part B, which covers medical needs. Part B costs its enrollees a yearly deductible ($110 in 2005) and a monthly premium ($78.20 in 2005). Medicare patients may also be able to expand their coverage by purchasing Medigap insurance or a Medicare Advantage plan. Beginning in 2006, Medicare will expand its coverage to offer Plan D, the first prescription drug benefit for seniors.

Medicaid is a health care program that aids the poverty stricken. It is funded jointly by the federal government and states and varies greatly by locale, but generally covers at least the basic medical needs for families who qualify. Health care for children was expanded in 1997 by the *State Children's Health Insurance Program (SCHIP)*, which provides additional funds for states to cover uninsured children. Millions of children, unemployed adults, and low-wage workers, however, continue to fall through the cracks in coverage.

HEALTH INSURANCE

Understanding Insurance: The ABC's of HMOs, PPOs, POSs, Indemnity, and Other Aspects   There are two basic variants of insurance coverage. With indemnity "fee for service" health insurance, you may see any doctor and then pay a separate fee for each service, which the insurer reimburses after you complete a claims form. In many cases the insurance company pays the provider directly—but you're ultimately responsible for the payment. In an HMO, all your medical care is overseen by a primary care doctor who must approve visits to specialists. At the time of treatment you pay only a token copayment (typically around $15) and you don't have to file all the claims.

Indemnity insurance was the standard insurance provided by employers until the rise of managed care in the 1990s. Generally, an indemnity policy consists of three distinct types of coverage. Surgical/medical insurance is basic coverage for doctors and other health professionals such as physicians, ambulatory technicians, anesthesiologists, and home care workers. Hospitalization insurance covers the bills incurred during a hospital stay, such as a hospital room, operating suite, nursing care, and intensive care unit. Major medical or "catastrophic" insurance covers you once your insurance has paid out its maximum in medical and hospitalization bills. Most indemnity insurance policies have an annual deductible—a minimum amount that you pay out of pocket before insurance coverage kicks in. They also have "co-insurance" rates (generally around 20 to 30 percent of the bill) that you pay until you hit your annual cap, after which the insurance company pays the rest.

Rather than choosing your own provider, paying co-insurance, and assuming responsibility of your medical bills, HMOs offer insurance plans in which participating providers agree to take care of your health needs for a set, prepaid fee. In these plans, you must use primary care physicians, specialists, laboratories, and hospitals from a prescribed network. Preferred Provider Organizations (PPOs) and

Point of Service (POSs) are hybrid plans. When you choose a doctor in these plans' networks, you pay only a small copayment, but you have the option of going outside the network and paying a deductible plus a percentage of your bills. HMOs have proven themselves a valuable cost-saver for the young and healthy, especially when they live up to their name of "Health Management Organization" by promoting preventative medicine. But illnesses and emergencies can spell trouble when a cost-cutting bureaucrat has control over your treatment.

Choosing a Plan   Most Americans who do have health insurance get their coverage through their employers, who pay either all or a portion of their premiums. Some three-fifths of employees with health insurance are now given a choice of plans. Carefully consider your family's needs when looking at your options and read the plans thoroughly. Does the HMO require special preauthorization before you can get the care you need? Can your doctor get authorization, or will you have to call the plan yourself? Will you have to get a referral every time you want to see a specialist? Can you get a referral over the phone or do you have to make an appointment with your primary care provider? What kind of prescription drug benefits does the plan offer? What does your plan charge for out-of-network care?

For more information on picking a plan, check out *Consumer Reports* at www.consumerreports.org. The publication and its parent organization, Consumers Union, publish frequent reports on the health care industry and offer ratings on health plans. A recent report from 2003 found that their readers were equally satisfied with HMOs and PPOs—or dissatisfied, since the average score was a tepid 73 out of 100. These results held even for readers with chronic diseases such as high blood pressure and diabetes, but respondents preferred the freedom of a PPO for ailments with trickier treatments such as back pain and arthritis. You can also consult the National Committee for Quality Assurance, which offers report cards on health care plans and can be found online at www.healthchoices.org.

CASE STUDY

In 1995 Debra Moran of Winfield, Illinois, began feeling pain shooting from her hand to her neck. She later found that it was caused by a nerve condition in her shoulder. Eventually, the pain grew so bad that Moran, a speech therapist, could no longer work or even do basic household chores such as cooking or cleaning. Searching in vain for a treatment, she tried doctors in her HMO's network. "I went to orthopedists, rehab doctors, and physical therapists but the pain would always come back," she said. All failed to alleviate the pain, which grew so debilitating she eventually had to be hand-fed by her husband. "We've put off having a family until we know this whole thing is over," Moran told the *Chicago Daily Herald*. "It was to the point where I couldn't hold a child because my arm hurt so much."

While Moran began looking for a specialist, her HMO, Rush Prudential, gave her the runaround. She eventually found a specialist outside her network named Julia Terzis in Virginia. Terzis had a successful track record with similar patients and recommended a specialized microneurological surgery to repair the damaged nerves in her shoulder. Moran got support from her primary care physician, but Rush refused to cover the care, arguing that the $95,000 operation was not medically necessary. Instead, they recommended a cheaper surgery by one of their own doctors. Their surgeon predicted only a one in three chance at improvement and admitted it was just as likely to make the condition worse and carried a risk of paralysis.

Moran appealed the HMO's decision and was turned down multiple times. She then went to the Illinois independent review board, which declared that the procedure was indeed medically necessary and should be covered by her HMO. But Rush refused to budge. In 1998, Moran paid for the surgery herself, maxing out credit cards and taking a personal loan to pay the bill. The surgery was successful and Moran took Rush Prudential all the way to the U.S. Supreme Court to recover the cost. In June 2002, the Court decided in Moran's favor by requiring Rush to reimburse her for the surgery. The Supreme Court's decision secured the right of 60 million Americans, who get their health care through employee sponsored plans, to an independent review of HMO denial of coverage decisions.

Talk Back/Fight Back

If you have a dispute with your health care provider, defend yourself. You have the right under *ERISA* to an internal review and, depending on where you live, an external review. While appealing to your HMO seems like a losing defendant appealing to the plaintiff, you should always take advantage of this option. A well-prepared case can get results; according to a recent Kaiser Family Foundation study of four states, patients won 52 percent of the time in the first internal review. Even if your internal grievance is unsuccessful, most states now have some form of external review, but you generally have to go through the HMO's process first.

You can find the detailed review procedures in your manual that you get when you join up. Carefully prepare the best possible case. When you call, ask the HMO for a complete clinical explanation of their determination. You also should get a copy of the plan's complete policies. Get your doctor's active and written support. Ask your plan administrator or human resource manager for help and talk to nurses and office managers who work in your medical offices. Always keep detailed records of your conversations along with other important documents.

Be aggressive with your HMO. Demand the names of the utilization reviewers and their supervisors—and get their credentials. What kind of clinical experience do *they* have? Are they a specialist in the field? You may be surprised to find that some of the people you speak to have a limited medical background, or worse, none at all. Be sure to get their names and a direct line to reach for a follow-up—and always ask what the next step is and when you can expect a result. Your HMO will take your grievance more seriously when you engage in such thorough research and then back it up with a formal complaint to your state's insurance or health department.

If your dispute is about urgently needed medical care, make it clear that you need an immediate response. Most health plans have a filing period that can vary from sixty days to a year, but ERISA employer-sponsored plans must give you at least 180 days to file and cannot require more than two reviews or charge a fee. Usually health plans have a rapid process for appeals involving needed emergency or urgent care. You have a right under federal law to get a decision in these cases within seventy-two hours.

If you don't win, you may have to file another appeal before you can get an independent external review. Plans have unique processes for second reviews, some of which may benefit you by including a panel of physicians and/or consumers. But others might just use representatives from your HMO who weren't involved in the original decision. Some plans may also require you to enter into or offer voluntarily an arbitration program. Because the same federal rules apply to this process, those with employer-sponsored health plans can appeal the arbitration rulings, and you have the right to challenge a decision in court. Whether or not you choose arbitration, your health plan cannot use your choice against you in an appeal or in any other decision involving your benefits.

If you still haven't received the services you need after the internal review, forty-two states give you the option of filing for an independent external review. The external review board made up of specialists is the final word on health care disputes.

But don't be shy about appealing if you believe a corporate bureaucracy has made a wrong medical decision. A 2002 study of the Texas independent review process, one of the country's first, found that 55 percent of consumers received additional treatment, overturning, at least in part, the HMO's original ruling.

You Can Take It with You   The loss of a job is stressful enough without the added weight of losing your family's health insurance. Fortunately, the *Consolidated Omnibus Budget Rehabilitation Act* (*COBRA*) allows you to retain your coverage by paying for the same coverage yourself at up to 102 percent of the group rate paid by your previous employer—given the company had at least 20 employees. Your past employer must notify you about your right to continue your group insurance under *COBRA* within fourteen days of losing your benefits. From that point, you have sixty days to claim your *COBRA* benefits, which will cover you up to eighteen months if you lost your coverage due to employment status. For coverage lost for other reasons, such as losing insurance through your spouse's plan due to death or divorce, *COBRA* may cover you up to thirty-six months. And for people with disabilities, *COBRA* can last up to twenty-nine months but may cost up to 150 percent of the original group plan. Because *COBRA* does not require a billing process, it's up to you to know who to pay and to get your check in on time. If a family member loses benefits due to separation or divorce or if a child becomes ineligible, you need to notify your plan administrator within sixty days.

COBRA coverage can be expensive. So if you're young and in good health, with no preexisting conditions, you might find a better option on your own. But for people with health problems, *COBRA* is likely the best bet. Private plans often turn down individuals with a serious health condition or exempt any preexisting conditions from coverage. Plus, even after your *COBRA* benefits run out, under the *HIPAA* you may be able to waive the preexisting conditions clause in private health care if you've maintained continuous coverage under *COBRA*.

Portable Insurance From the flames of President Clinton's attempted health care reform package came the *Health Insurance Portability and Accountability Act* of 1996 (*HIPAA*). This law offers important rights and protections for consumers of health care. It outlaws discrimination of employees and their dependents based on health status and preexisting conditions. Employees changing jobs and entering new group coverage must be covered for their preexisting conditions. It also allows employees who have exhausted their *COBRA* benefits a chance to be covered without a waiting period or preexisting conditions clauses. Your employer must provide you with a certificate of creditable coverage after you've become ineligible—make sure you get it to preserve your rights. And don't let your insurance lapse for more than sixty-three days, or your *HIPAA* rights may lapse along with your coverage.

Medicare/Medicaid There are other options available for those who can't afford insurance. Medicare covers you if you're over sixty-five or disabled and eligible for Social Security benefits. Medicaid is available for America's poorest individuals and families. Qualifications and benefits for Medicaid vary from state to state but always include a very low income threshold. Those who receive Medicare have an appeals process for grievances similar to the process for HMOs. For more information on Medicare appeals go to www.medicare.gov, or call (800) MEDICARE. Medicaid recipients are entitled to a hearing of their grievance. Because the exact policies again differ from state to state, you should look up your state's Medicaid office in the government pages of your phone book and give them a call to find out.

Last Resort If you are uninsured with a serious health problem and do not qualify for Medicare or Medicaid, your state may offer you health insurance through a "high-risk pool." Thirty states have set up such emergency risk pools that take care of about 150,000 Americans who have health conditions that prevent them from getting individual health insurance. These pools are usually for the sickest of the uninsured who have been denied insurance for needed health care. Risk pools are not cheap. They often have low lifetime maximums, high premiums, and long waiting periods. However, some states have more open enrollment policies and lower rate caps, making risk pools an option even for healthy people. Minnesota, for example, has a low rate cap, no annual limit on benefits, and no enrollment caps, allowing it to cover about 30,000 of its citizens, the highest number of any state-sponsored risk pools.

Talk Back/Fight Back

If you are unexpectedly turned down for health insurance, make sure the insurer provides a reason for the decision. Insurers can check your medical records to verify that the information you give them is correct. The Medical Information Bureau (MIB) is a private organization that provides a medical history on people with serious conditions or other high risks to prospective insurers. If you have applied for health, life, or disability insurance, you may have a file. Like a bad credit report, an MIB file can severely limit your ability to get reasonable insurance; consequently you have the right to know if you have one and to see what's in it. Call (866) 692-6901 for access to your free, annual report.

HOSPITALS

Know Your Rights Most hospitals have signed on to the American Hospital Association's new patient bill of rights, called "The Patient Care Partnership: Understanding Expectations, Rights and Responsibilities." Ask for a copy whenever you're getting hospital care. In addition to discussing home care and billing information, this document describes your rights to:

- know the identity of doctors, nurses and others involved in your care, and…know when they are students, residents or other trainees;
- a clean and safe environment;
- discuss and understand:
    - the benefits and risks of each treatment,
    - whether your treatment is experimental or part of a research study,
    - what you can reasonably expect from your treatment and any long-term effects it might have on your quality of life,
    - what you and your family will need to do after you leave the hospital,
    - the financial consequences of using uncovered services or out-of-network providers;
- consent to or refuse a treatment;
- protect the privacy of your medical information.

Don't stop there! Since the pamphlet gives you general information on your rights, make sure you understand your treatment fully before you sign admission and consent forms. It's important to know that while hospital consent forms appear formal and authoritative, it's a document that both parties must agree to. If you disagree with something on the form, discuss it with your doctor and see if you can negotiate a change. Be wary of clauses that say your surgeon *or his or her associates*, can perform the operation.

The Institute of Medicine estimated in 1999 that 44,000 to 98,000 people die in hospitals each year due to medical errors. That's more than the amount that die from AIDS, breast cancer, or auto accidents. A study by the Agency for Healthcare Research and Quality suggests that at least one factor in hospital errors is miscommunication between doctors and patients. Doctors don't always provide enough information for patients to make a wise decision. Don't be afraid to question your doctors—it's *your* health at stake.

If you are the victim of a medical error, get a personal injury attorney immediately. But before you end up filing a malpractice suit, remember that your best weapon to prevent medical mistakes is to know your rights and your treatment and ask questions *first.* Be especially vigilant in making sure you're taking the right drugs at the right dose. And if anything seems unusual, investigate. Most hospitals have patient advocates who will take up your cause if you have a problem. You also might want to get your own advocate, such as a knowledgeable friend or family member, who can help you make decisions while you're getting care or discussing treatment with your doctor.

Before going to the hospital, call your insurance company to find out what treatments they will cover—it will help you understand your financial obligations when considering options. Also, call ahead to find out if the hospital charges for incidentals such as toothpaste and mouthwash, tissue paper, extra pillows—and consider bringing your own to avoid the big hospital markups. While you're at it, see if you can bring your own prescription medications, which could save you a lot of dough.

Hospital Bills   The health crisis has turned medical billing into a war zone. Hospitals regularly overcharge patients and insurers, insurance companies systematically down-code bills (paying for a cheaper service than was delivered) from physicians to save money, and the consumer is always caught in the crossfire. Hospital billing errors can turn a molehill of a bill into a mountain of debt. Billing errors include women being charged for the removal of a prostate or receiving a bill for their daughter's circumcision. Even if you only pay a small portion of a bill, or your insurance company picks up the whole tab, go over it carefully and make sure you can account for every charge. Overcharging hurts no matter who pays. When the insurance company is overcharged, it affects the premiums for everybody and it counts against your yearly and lifetime spending caps.

Talk Back/Fight Back

It's not always that easy to determine a billing error. Hospitals use a computer code instead of the name of the procedure to tabulate your bill. One wrong keystroke can be the difference between an aspirin and major surgery. But Pat Palmer, a longtime patient advocate, doesn't believe these errors are always innocent mistakes. She wrote in her *Medical Bill Survival Guide* that the "system [is] so convoluted that it actually discourages accuracy and encourages error." And the billing system in place "seems to profit everybody...except the patient."

Hospitals are required to provide an itemized bill on request. Make sure you get one that includes a description of the charges or ask the billing department to explain the codes. If you're up to it, keep a notebook of each procedure, test, and medication you are given in the hospital to compare when you get the bill. You can also request copies of your medical records and your doctor's and nurse's notes after you're released. A *Consumer Reports* survey found that people who reviewed their medical records were four times more likely to find an error in their bill.

When you get your bill, check it against your records. If you spent time in an operating room or delivery room, find out how the hospital charges for the time and verify that your bill is correct. Make sure that the dates are correct, that the procedures are accurate, and that you aren't being double-charged. "I often see charges for supplies like sheets, towels, and gloves that should be included in the room charge," says Palmer.

If you suspect an error in your bill, you can ask the hospital or your insurer for an audit. They might warn you that it could increase the bill, but Nora Johnson, a hospital bill auditor, reports that "only one bill out of thousands that Medical Billing Advocates has looked at through the years has had charges added to it."

If you don't have the time to investigate your bills yourself, seek an outside auditor. Pat Palmer founded Medical Billing Advocates of America to help people sort out their hospital bills. They have affiliates nationwide; find one near you at www.billadvocates.com. There also may be an organization in your community that provides free help with your medical bills, such as The People Organization in Cleveland.

Price-Gouging the Uninsured   If you're uninsured and make it out of the hospital in good health, you may still be at risk of a cardiac arrest when you get your bill. It's common practice for hospitals to charge the most to those with the least ability to pay. Because insurance companies and government services can negotiate discounted group rates, hospitals jack up their list prices and the uninsured get stuck with the bill—sometimes four or five times what insurance or Medicare pays for the same procedure. If you're uninsured, there are ways for you to defend yourself.

Most hospitals, particularly nonprofits, have some kind of financial assistance program offering free or discounted care for the uninsured and indigent. That's because nonprofits receive a tax-exempt status that comes with a "community benefit obligation." These programs commonly cover people who make from around 100 to 200 percent of the federal poverty level—some 60 percent of the uninsured have incomes below 200 percent of the federal poverty level—but there might be other qualifications as well.

Surprised? That's because a lot of hospitals don't want you to know about it.

A 2003 study by the health advocacy group Community Catalyst revealed that many hospital employees don't even know these policies exist, or even worse, hide them from the people they were created to help. The group studied hospitals in nine cities across the United States and found that "callers to the hospitals were invariably told that free care was not available." A participant in the study describes a Washington, D.C., hospital's policy: "If the person calls up and says I can't pay, then the hospital tries to work out a payment plan and does not necessarily offer the option of financial assistance unless the person specifically asks." Another staff member at a Columbus, Ohio, hospital refused to disclose the income scale for assistance, telling Community Catalyst that "patients tend to lie."

CASE STUDY

Daisy Makeupson was a part-time home health aide in Cincinnati. The fifty-nine-year-old, who was suffering from heart disease, high blood pressure, diabetes, and arthritis, was charged $1,159 for outpatient services by Cincinnati University Hospital. Makeupson's income was below 200 percent of the federal poverty level, which qualified her for free care under the hospital's financial assistance policy. However, when she couldn't pay the bill, the hospital gave her not assistance but a subpoena.

Her lawyer, Trey Daly, accompanied her to the courthouse. "The courtroom was jammed with other people who owed money to University," Daly recalled. "I looked around at the people waiting with us, and my guess was that many of them also had incomes low enough to qualify for free care. It made me mad, so I shouted, 'Has anyone heard of the Hospital Care Assurance Program?'" Daly explained to them that Ohio law requires hospitals to provide free care for people with incomes under 100 percent of the federal poverty level, and that University's policy provides free care for people up to 200 percent. "Right away people started coming up to me to ask where they fit....[H]ere was a group of people who probably were qualified for free care, but the hospitals had done nothing to help them apply, let alone tell them it was available." One Texas hospital administrator told *Time* magazine why hospital collections departments are so relentless in pursuing the poor: "The driving force is to badger them so they don't come back."

When K. B. Forbes discovered this gross inequity, he dedicated himself to fighting the hospitals. He began his career as an advocate for the uninsured in 2001 when he heard the story of a friend's sister who had been injured in a car accident and was hospitalized for a couple of days, then charged over $23,000. The son of an Irish American union organizer and a Chilean immigrant, the thirty-three-year-old Forbes founded his own group, the Consejo de Latinos Unidos (Council of United Latinos), to document and combat hospital overcharging in the Southern California Latino community. Forbes found again and again that hospitals charged the uninsured far more than other patients and followed up the bills with brutal collection practices such as garnishing wages and putting liens on homes. Before long Forbes was investigating hospital bills all over the country and found the same behavior by hospitals everywhere he went. The organization that he formed to defend Southern California Latinos became a national advocacy group for the uninsured.

Forbes has traveled the country taking on the cause of people like Carlos Colon, a Home Depot employee in Chicago who had the misfortune of needing a cyst removed from the back of his head before his health benefits kicked in. Colon spent a week at the Lady of Resurrection Medical Center and was billed $74,396, "more than ten times what an insurance company would pay," according to the *Chicago Sun-Times*. The hospital sued Colon for wage garnishment and now walks off with $300 out of his monthly pay—about 20 percent of his income. With interest, Forbes estimates it will take twenty-five years or more for Colon to pay off the debt.

In June 2003, Forbes negotiated a settlement on behalf of ten uninsured patients of Tenet Healthcare Corporation, the nation's second biggest hospital company. Along with that settlement, Tenet announced its new "Compact with Uninsured Patients," which promises insurance-rate discounts and charity care for the indigent and an end to its collection practices of suing unemployed patients and putting liens on their homes. After the Tenet agreement, which the *Wall Street Journal* called his "biggest success," Forbes set his sights on reforming America's biggest for-profit hospital chain, HCA (Hospital Corporation of America), which acknowledged in 2004 that its charity plan—which he characterizes as a "sliding scale of discrimination"—had "failed to reach at least half the people who qualify."

Until 2004, the hospital companies defended their brutal

billing and collection practices by saying federal laws governing
Medicare prevented them from offering discounts to the uninsured. Forbes has an analogy for that: "Like the segregationists in
the 1950s who hid behind Jim Crow laws to justify their egregious
and immoral behavior, some hospitals have attempted to hide behind phantom regulations to justify their egregious and immoral
conduct." The "phantom regulations" argument collapsed in 2004
when Health and Human Services Secretary Tommy Thompson
declared that there is no regulation that "prohibits a hospital from
waiving collection of charges to any patients, Medicare or non-
Medicare, including low-income, uninsured or medically indigent
if it is done as part of a hospital's indigency policy."

Talk Back/Fight Back

Whether you are in need of hospital care or are managing bills for care
you already received, make sure that you know what kind of financial assistance your hospital offers. There are hundreds of hospitals nationwide that
are still governed by the *Hill-Burton Act* passed by Congress in 1947 to aid
hospitals in modernizing their facilities. These hospitals and nursing homes
are required to dedicate a percentage of their budget to free and discounted
care. For a state-by-state list of Hill-Burton hospitals—and for more information on how to qualify—see the U.S. Government's Health Resources and
Services Administration site at www.hrsa.gov/osp/dfcr/obtain/obtain.htm, or
call their toll free hotline at (800) 638-0742. If you are unfairly denied free or
low-cost care at a Hill-Burton facility, you can file a complaint.

Most states also have laws governing free care for uninsured patients.
State laws, however, offer vague guidelines for hospitals, have little oversight,
and rarely include a grievance procedure for people who have been denied
financial assistance. For a state-by-state overview on financial assistance laws,
see Community Catalyst's report "Free Care: A Compendium of State Laws,"
which can be downloaded at www.communitycat.org/index.php?fldID=219.

It may be helpful for you to know the American Hospital Association's
guidelines for billing and collections. Among them are the following:

• Hospitals should respond promptly to patients' questions about
  their bills and their requests for financial assistance.

• Hospitals should make available to the public information on hos-

pital-based charity care policies and other known programs of
financial assistance.

- Hospitals should ensure that all written policies for assisting low-income patients are applied consistently.
- Hospitals should have policies to offer discounts to patients who do not qualify under a charity care policy for free or reduced cost care and who, after receiving financial counseling from the hospital, are determined to be eligible under the hospital's criteria for such discounts....Policies should clearly state the eligibility criteria, amount of discount, and payment plan options.

Rx Drugs

Duped by Drug Companies   Americans spent about $200 billion a year on prescription drugs in 2004, a staggering figure that rises sharply each year. And we pay about twice as much as Europeans and Canadians pay for the same drugs. But often it's *our* tax dollars that develop the bulk of important new treatments, not the pharmaceutical companies'. The Medicare drug benefit scheduled to begin in 2006, while providing an important new service to Americans who need it most, actually prohibits the government from negotiating with the drug companies for lower group rates.

The pharmaceutical companies take us for suckers over and over again. They first earn monopoly profits by patenting drugs developed over years by federally subsidized medical institutions like the National Institutes of Health and university research laboratories. Then, when the patent expires, they sue to extend monopolies and continue charging obscene prices for drugs, many of which are "me too," or "copycats" that offer few or no benefits over older, less expensive drugs already on the market. And now, with the newly passed Medicare drug benefit, these corporations can once more bilk taxpayers for seniors' medications.

Seniors make up the largest share of the prescription drug market and suffer the most from rising drug costs. Though only 13 percent of the population, seniors account for about 42 percent of all drug spending according to Families USA. Tragically, one in four seniors has reported skipping prescribed doses to stretch out their medications or has failed to get them refilled at all. While the new Medicare drug benefit is a necessary help to many aged Americans, their out-of-pocket spending on drugs will continue to rise, and taxpayers will continue to pay the drug companies' ransom, if there's no effective way to control prices. Families USA estimated (based on figures from the Congressional Budget Office) that a typical senior with average drug expenses will spend $2,087 out of pocket on prescription drugs in 2006 under Medicare's Plan D, accounting for 8.8 percent of her or his income. By 2013, unless the law is changed, a typical senior can expect to pay $3,455 out of pocket, or 12.3 percent of her or his income, on medication alone.

No wonder millions of Americans are now importing their drugs from Canada, where drugs are anywhere from 30 to 80 percent cheaper. People like Elizabeth Riems, a retired teacher from Sandusky, Ohio, find that a yearly pilgrimage to Canada is the only way they can afford the prescriptions they need. The *St. Louis Post-Dispatch* reported that the octogenarian Riems has been making the two-hour trip every year since 2001 and has saved about $2,500 a year on heart medications and prescriptions for high cholesterol and acid reflux. Other Americans use popular online pharmacies like www.canadarx.com to access cheaper prescription medications.

The issue of Canadian importation is coming to a head. In 2000 Congress passed a law allowing reimportation of drugs from Canada, but both the Bush and Clinton administrations, under an advisory of the FDA (which relies on the pharmaceutical industry for much of its funding), blocked it, saying that the safety of imported drugs couldn't be verified. However, the Government Accountability Office has now reported that Canadian pharmacies meet and sometimes even surpass American safety standards.

A few states and municipalities are pressing the issue. Minnesota, Wisconsin, North Dakota, New Hampshire, Rhode Island, and Illinois along with a number of cities have launched programs to help their residents import drugs from Canadian pharmacies. In 2004, the FDA responded to the trend by occasionally seizing shipments of imported drugs at the border. That same year Vermont sued the FDA to give its residents the right to buy Canadian.

Cutting Rx Drug Costs You don't have to get your drugs from Canada to be a smart consumer. There are ways to save in the United States as well. Prices for prescription drugs vary wildly from place to place. A survey conducted by the NYC Department of Consumer Affairs found that 30 pills of the blood-thinner Coumadin cost $21.88 at a large chain drugstore and $89.85 at an independent pharmacy across the street. Some drug retailers take advantage of the necessity of prescription drugs and count on you not to compare prices. Many large chain drugstores use bulk buying to offer lower prices to customers. Additionally, national chains like Wal-Mart, Kmart, and Rite Aid, and even some independents, have policies to match the lowest advertised price. Kmart has even been known to meet the prices of mail-order and Internet pharmacies according to *Consumer Reports*. Look around for the lowest price and then see if your pharmacy will match it.

For a listing of verified Internet pharmacies, go to the National Association of Boards of Pharmacy. They certify online pharmacies with the VIPPS (Verified Internet Pharmacy Practice Sites) seal of approval; don't buy from a site without one. Other popular prescription services include the American Association of Retired People's (AARP) mail-order service, which they offer even to non-members, and Costco's mail-order program.

For short-term medications like antibiotics, ask your doctor for free samples. Don't be seduced, though. The pharmaceutical industry keeps an army of some 88,000 sales reps and spends hundreds of millions of dollars giving free samples to doctors to lure them—and you—into the newest, most expensive treatments. If you're going to be taking a drug for a sustained period, don't get hooked on an expensive treatment if a less expensive or generic drug would be equally or more effective.

Cheap generics are one benefit U.S. consumers have over the rest of the world. And even more of them will be hitting the market in the next few years as an unprecedented number of exclusive patents run out. According to Dr. Marcia Angell, in her book *The Truth About Drug Companies*, seventy-one of the seventy-eight new drugs released in 2002 were "me too" drugs devised by pharmaceutical companies to continue a patent, a high price, and an exclusive market share. Sometimes these drugs will be the best or only treatment for you, but more often generics would be just as effective and far less expensive. In 2002, for example, the National Heart and Blood Institute of the NIH released the results of the largest high-blood-pressure clinical trial ever undertaken, concluding that the fifty-year-old, generic diuretic outperformed the blockbuster new drugs Norvasc, Cardura, Zestril, and Prinivil. It was equally effective at lowering blood pressure, and even better at preventing heart disease and strokes. The report found "that diuretics are the best choice to treat hypertension, both medically and economically."

Ask your doctor if your pills can be prescribed at a double-dose and then halved with a pill-splitter. Some drugs can't be split without losing quality, but *Consumer Reports* cites the hypertension drug Prinivil as an example of one that can be. Both the 10 mg and the 20 mg doses run about $30 a month. Cutting the larger dosage in half would save $130 a year. Also, if the cost of needed medications is prohibitive, ask your doctor to look into the patient assistant programs offered by drug companies.

Drug Safety   Public Citizen's Health Research Group stresses the importance of planning a "brown bag session" with your doctor as the most important drug safety step you can take. Bring in all of your prescription and over-the-counter drugs, even occasional cold medicines or cough syrups, and review them with your doctor. This will help you prevent any dangerous drug interactions and make sure your treatments are working as intended. Public Citizen's prescription drug site, www.worstpills.org, offers helpful worksheets you can use to keep track of your drugs.

This is also a good time to reevaluate your prescriptions. Ask your doctor if there's anything that you no longer need or if any expensive brand-name prescriptions can be substituted with lower priced generics. Not only are generics less expensive and equally effective, but they're often safer than the newest drugs. New drugs have only limited clinical testing behind them, while generics often have a track record spanning decades. Once a drug hits the market, it could have side effects or risks that weren't discovered during the initial testing, and unfortunately for consumers drug companies aren't exactly forthcoming about the risks of their products.

CASE STUDY

Take the example of Vioxx, the pain reliever pulled by Merck in 2004 after the firm learned that it caused heart attacks and strokes in thousands of users. While Merck insisted that it had taken "prompt and decisive action," it's clear that as early as 2001 studies suggested that Vioxx increased the risk of heart attack and strokes in some patients. Dr. Eric J. Topol, who wrote the first study that linked the drug with an increased risk of heart disease for the *Journal of the American Medical Association (JAMA),* told the media that Merck scientists had tried to stop him from publishing the study. Dr. Gukirpal Singh, another Vioxx critic, said that Merck officials told him that they could "make life very difficult for me."

The FDA monitored the drug and required Merck to include a strong warning label for people with heart problems, but never required Merck to do more testing. In August 2004, Dr. David Graham, an FDA safety reviewer, got the results of a Kaiser Permanente study of Vioxx underwritten by his office, which concluded that the drug nearly quadrupled the risk for heart disease in high doses. While the FDA argued internally about the results in September, Merck pulled the drug itself.

Graham estimates that at least 88,000 Americans may have suffered a stroke or heart attack from taking the drug, and as many as 55,000 may have died. He told Congress that, "faced with what may be the single greatest drug safety catastrophe in the history of this country or the history of the world," federal regulators are "virtually incapable of protecting America."

Vioxx is just one of many new drugs with unknown risks. In his testimony, Graham spoke out about other potentially harmful drugs including Accutane, the acne medication that causes birth defects; Bextra, a painkiller similar to Vioxx that is suspected of increasing blood pressure and heart attacks; Crestor, the cholesterol medication that has caused kidney failure in some patients; Meridia, the obesity drug that raises blood pressure; and Serevent, the asthma medication about which Dr. Graham starkly warned, "we have case reports of patients dying clutching their Serevent inhalers."

One of the most tragic elements of the Vioxx catastrophe is that the drug itself apparently worked no better than traditional painkillers like aspirin or ibuprophen, which can be purchased easily and safely over the counter. Its added benefit was for people with intestinal and stomach disorders, which can be worsened by traditional painkillers—a substantial number to be sure, but far from the huge number of patients who were taking the drug.

In the end, Merck's all-out promotional blitz turned a marginal and dangerous drug into a blockbuster best seller with tragic consequences. A National Institute for Health Care Management study revealed that Vioxx was the single most advertised drug, as Merck spent $160.8 million in a single year—more than Pepsi or Budweiser—to make sure that consumers would beg their doctors for Vioxx. It worked—the drug quadrupled its sales the very next year.

Don't believe the hype! Drug companies spend far more on marketing than they do on research. TV commercials that promise wonder drugs with few or no side effects are not to be believed. Many people assume that drug commercials are thoroughly examined and vetted by the FDA. In reality, the agency has only 30 employees to view the roughly 30,000 ads each year.

While most doctors have your best interest in mind when prescribing a drug, it's impossible for them to be familiar with every study on every drug available. Furthermore, doctors are the targets of the millions of dollars the pharmaceutical industry spends on drug propaganda each year, much of it disguised as scholarly research. It pays to be skeptical when considering new treatments. So do some research on your own, which even laypeople can plausibly do in the Internet/Google era. You can also find the venerable *Physicians Desk Reference (PDR)* at most libraries or look up their online subscription service at www.pdr.net. The trusted advocates at the Public Citizen Health Research Group also put out an excellent reference guide, *Best Pills, Worst Pills*, which is available at bookstores, or go to their website, www.worstpills.org, to see their online version; they had Vioxx on their "Do Not Use!" list in 2001, three years before it was removed from the market. *Consumer Reports* has also started a prescription drug site, which you can visit at www.crbestbuy-drugs.org.

FIX IT: HEALING THE HEALTH CARE SYSTEM

Universal Health Care   Ultimately, the only way to provide a decent standard of health care to all Americans will be to adopt a universal health care system. The Institute of Medicine has urged the government to do just that by 2010. The fact is Americans pay more per capita for our health care than people of any other industrialized nation. And what do we get in return? A quarter of the population without health insurance at some point during a two-year span; 9 million American children without health insurance; over 18,000 premature deaths a year due to lack of care; about half of all bankruptcies caused by medical debt; among the lowest age expectancy and the highest infant mortality rate of industrialized nations.

Since the failure of President Clinton's broad attempt at health care reform, Washington has shied away from universal coverage. Indeed, with Republicans in control of each branch of the federal government—and staunchly opposed to universal health care—the chance of passing such federal legislation is remote in the near future, even though a 2004 survey found that 69 percent of Americans said they would trade higher taxes for universal health coverage. In fact, the Bush administration has been backsliding on American health care policy and has even floated the idea of eliminating tax incentives for businesses that provide insurance to their employees.

For broad health care reform, concerned citizens can turn to their state and local governments and push for universal coverage along with other forms of health care reform. A ballot initiative in Massachusetts, for example, requiring a universal health plan was narrowly defeated in 2000, failing to pass by only 1 percentage point despite an expensive campaign waged against it by health care corporations. But Massachusetts will have another chance—a ballot question in 2006 will ask for a constitutional amendment requiring the state to ensure health care for all its citizens. Additionally, Hawaii and Maine have both enacted some kind of universal health system. Legislators in California, Illinois, Maryland, Michigan, and North Carolina have all attempted broad health care reforms, and other states are studying universal coverage options. It will take strong and dedicated local movements to transform the nation's failing health care system.

Helping Health Care Consumers   At the federal level, there are still a number of important incremental reform battles to be won. *ERISA*, the broad law covering employee-sponsored health insurance (written in the 1970s before the rise of HMOs), makes it difficult for states to regulate the modern health care industry. As a result, state laws protecting patients' rights have either been challenged or struck down, creating the need for federal legislators to reconcile emerging conflicts between state and federal regulations. The first step in protecting health consumers is to enact a federal Patients' Bill of Rights. The Senate passed a bipartisan bill introduced by John Edwards (D-NC), Edward Kennedy (D-MA), and John McCain (D-AZ) that would (1) hold HMOs accountable by allowing patients to sue for malpractice when their HMOs make a negligent decision that harms a policyholder; (2) guarantee emergency care; and (3) allow access to specialty care. The House passed a patient rights bill that stripped a number of important consumer protections. If you want to support the rights of health consumers, urge your representatives to pass a Patients' Bill of Rights that does just that.

Improving Access   In an essay from the New Democracy Project book, *What We Stand For: A Program for Progressive Patriotism,* Ron Pollack, executive director of Families USA, suggests a number of reasonable incremental proposals for improving access to health care. Pollack demonstrates that Medicaid's eligibility standards differ so much from state to state that they resemble a "crazy quilt" and are in desperate need of modernization. Children are covered for public health if their family's income falls below 200 percent of the federal poverty level (thanks to Medicaid and SCHIP), but the median eligibility threshold for their parents across the United States is just 71 percent of the poverty level, which represents an income just over $10,800 for a family of three. For adults without children, Pollack depicts the federal safety net as "almost all hole and no webbing." Adults with no children, in most states, "can literally be penniless and still fail to qualify for Medicaid or any other public health coverage."

If all Americans who fall within 200 percent of the federal poverty level, regardless of family status, were eligible for public health coverage, the figure of 45 million uninsured would be more than halved. Senators Edward Kennedy and Olympia Snowe (R-ME) have already introduced legislation that would extend eligibility to parents of children who receive public health coverage, which would reduce the ranks of the uninsured by about 7 million.

Controlling the Cost of Rx Drugs   If our legislators refuse to control the prices that pharmaceutical companies charge for prescription drugs as a condition of their monopolies—as Canada and most European nations do—then they should at least allow savvy consumers the right to buy safe drugs from other countries. It seems absurd to import drugs from other countries when many of them are made right here in the United States, but forcing drug companies to compete with the prices they charge non-Americans may be the most feasible way to bring down exploding drug costs here at home. Millions of Americans are already pushing the issue by filling their prescriptions at Canadian pharmacies. Urge your representatives in Congress to overrule the FDA's block on drug importation, and remind them that many state and local governments are making Canadian drugs an option for their citizens.

To help those hardest hit by rising drug costs, we need to fix the Medicare drug benefit, Plan D, so that it benefits our seniors more than pharmaceutical companies. In 2003, the year Medicare Plan D became law, pharmaceutical interests spent an unprecedented $108.6 million lobbying the federal government on drug policy, mobilizing a total of 824 lobbyists, according to Public Citizen's Congress Watch. They got what they wanted. Preventing Medicare from bargaining for group rates, as the Veterans Administration and private businesses do, will only add to the industry's already overflowing coffers.

Once Medicare secures the ability to bargain for seniors, the enormous savings can be used to fill in the huge holes in the Medicare benefit coverage. As it stands, seniors who qualify will pay about $420 in monthly premiums and the first $250 in expenses before getting any coverage at all. After that initial $670, Medicare beneficiaries will pay a quarter of the next $2,000 in prescription drugs: a total of $500. At this point a senior will have paid $1,170 out-of-pocket and Medicare will have covered $1,500. After recipients reach the $2,250 threshold, they will have to pick up the tab for the next $2,850 in expenses before catastrophic coverage kicks in at $5,100 and pays the rest, meaning that many seniors will fall through the Medicare "doughnut-hole." This bizarre coverage gap will hurt seniors even more as drug costs continue to rise.

Drug Safety   The Vioxx withdrawal in 2004, along with other controversies, from the Phen-Fen fad to the flu-shot shortage, have raised questions about the FDA's ability to oversee drug safety maintenance. Many experts have called for a new watchdog agency independent of the FDA to conduct surveillance of drugs after they have gained FDA approval. A December 2004 editorial in the *Journal of the American Medical Association* (*JAMA*) makes a good argument for an independent drug review board. "It is unreasonable," the editors write, "to expect the same agency that was responsible for approval of drug licensing and labeling would also be committed to actively seek evidence to prove itself wrong."

Under the current system, the FDA's MedWatch program allows pharmaceutical companies to police themselves. This is a clear conflict of interest, as drug manufacturers are responsible for conducting research, analysis, and reporting data on their own products. Dr. Alastair Wood, a drug research and regulation expert from Vanderbilt University, recently described the system to the *New York Times*: "When we have a drug problem, it's analogous to a plane crashing off the coast of New York City, and being investigated by the air traffic controllers who controlled the flight and the airline flying the plane. They're not bad people, but it's not the way we do things in this country."

The FDA itself may also have a conflict. From 1993 to 2001, the agency collected about $825 million in fees from pharmaceutical companies. During that span, the median time it took for a standard drug to gain FDA approval was cut in half; not surprisingly, as the approval times were reduced, the recall rates for approved drugs more than doubled. Furthermore, when *USA Today* investigated eighteen FDA expert advisory boards, it found that more than half of its members had financial ties to the field in which they offered expert advice. In 2003, the industry committed $200 million to the FDA under conditions that specified a significant amount to be spent toward drug approvals rather than monitoring.

An independent drug review board would greatly improve consumer safety and should be implemented. The drug review board, which would have to be created by Congress, should be completely free of pharmaceutical industry influence. And, as the editors of *JAMA* suggest, the "agency should be given full authority to ensure compliance with regulations and sufficient funding to establish an effective national active surveillance system with a prospective, comprehensive, and systematic approach for monitoring, collecting and analyzing, and reporting data on adverse events."

CHAPTER 2

THE RIGHTS OF CLIENTS

Ninety percent of our lawyers serve ten percent of our people. We are overlawyered and underrepresented.

—President Jimmy Carter

Over a lifetime we all invariably encounter disputes in the various roles we play—at work, at home, and in the marketplace. Hopefully, this book will help you solve most of them yourself. Sometimes, however, justice comes at a price and we have to hire a lawyer to represent us. And all too often the price of justice is outrageously high. An American Bar Association survey from 2002 found that 71 percent of Americans had "some occasion during the past year that might have led them to hire a lawyer," but just half of them said they would—high costs being the leading reason why. In fact 38 million poor and middle-class Americans find the doors to justice slammed shut because they can't afford to hire a lawyer.

According to Stanford Law professor Deborah Rhode, "Equal Justice under Law…should not just decorate our courthouse doors; it should guide what happens inside them." And when you go to court, know your options. You may be able to do it yourself in small claims court, in an alternative dispute resolution program, or as a pro se litigant, but knowing how to use a lawyer when you need one is yet another way to defend yourself. Hiring a lawyer may seem like a daunting or unpleasant task for a majority of Americans—beyond the continuing appeal for lawyer jokes, a 2003 *CNN*/Gallup survey showed that 84 percent of Americans do not believe that lawyers have "high ethical standards." But remember, when you hire a lawyer, they're working for you.

KEY LAWS FOR LEGAL CLIENTS

Right to Attorney/Legal Services Corporation Act   The Sixth Amendment of the U.S. Constitution guarantees the right to an attorney for those facing criminal charges and possible jail time: "In all criminal prosecutions, the accused shall enjoy the right…to have the Assistance of Counsel for his defense." While the Bill of Rights expresses the right to counsel, it was not until the *Gideon v. Wainwright* decision in 1963 that the Supreme Court interpreted this right to extend to those without the means to pay for representation. Think about it—until 1963, an indigent defendant could be put to death or incarcerated for life without counsel representing him in a court.

Civil cases are another story. The U.S. government began providing some legal aid to the poor under President Lyndon Johnson's "War on Poverty" in the 1960s. Then the *Legal Services Corporation Act* of 1974 established a foundation to provide legal services to the poorest Americans. However, only a fraction of those who qualify for assistance actually receive legal aid, and many political concessions (including budgetary) prevent the program from taking on some of the structural causes of poverty.

Federal Arbitration Act   In 1925 Congress passed this law to allow merchants in contract disputes an alternative to litigation. The new law made arbitration agreements binding and enforceable contracts. For businesses and individuals who agree to solve their disputes out of court, arbitration and other forms of alternative dispute resolution are a reasonable alternative. Originally, both parties had to agree to the contract to make a binding agreement. But since 1983, the Supreme Court has expanded the power of the *Federal Arbitration Act* in a way that has forced consumers to abdicate their right to court justice when corporations sneak mandatory arbitration clauses into the small print of consumer contracts and bill stuffers.

Model Rules of Professional Conduct   Most rules governing lawyers and clients' rights are taken from the American Bar

Association's Model Rules of Professional Conduct. Implemented in 1983 to replace the ABA's Model Code of Professional Responsibility, and occasionally modified, the Model Rules have been adopted by each state in some form, though minor differences exist between the states. The ethical guidelines oversee attorney behavior and provide the basic principals for malpractice, breach of contract, conflict of interest, professional negligence, and financial misconduct claims. State courts and bar associations oversee attorney discipline, and clients can sue for compensation when a violation occurs. See "Statement of Client Rights" on page 42.

BEING YOUR OWN CLIENT: DO IT YOURSELF

CASE STUDY

Too many people, facing a dispute with a corporate giant, give up before the game is played. How can we match the resources of these companies? For inspiration, take the story of Kevin Schmerling from Havertown, Pennsylvania, who fought Ford Motor Company in small claims court—and won.

Schmerling bought a Mercury Cougar in 1999 and by June 2001 he began to have trouble starting the vehicle. He hadn't driven the Cougar much early on, so by the time the problem was diagnosed, Schmerling's three-year, 36,000-mile warranty had run out, though his odometer had logged just 21,224 miles.

Replacing the faulty flywheel and starter cost $1,200, yet Ford refused to help out. Schmerling wrote letters to the dealer, the regional representative, and even the CEO, William Clay Ford Jr., to no avail. A spokesperson for Ford said, "We'll review if a customer is a loyal customer....Have they bought our products before? Do they buy our parts? Do they maintenance at a Ford dealer? Do they finance through Ford Motor Credit? In this case none of those things existed." Apparently, spending $18,000 on a car is not enough to qualify for Ford's "good will assistance."

Kevin B. Schmerling v. Ford Motor Co. was filed in Pennsylvania's small claims court in 2004. Schmerling showed the judge two technical service bulletins that Ford had issued in 1999 addressing the problems in the Cougar and proved that his vehicle had begun to falter in 2001, while still under warranty. Siding with Schmerling, the judge ordered Ford to pay $1,200, which he received in March 2004.

How to Win in Small Claims Court   If you have not been able to solve your dispute by negotiating with the person or business that wronged you, or by appealing to a local, state, or federal regulator, you may still be able to handle it yourself in small claims court. These courts are the place to settle disputes involving breach of contract, negligent behavior, property damage, minor personal injuries, and various consumer disputes involving relatively small sums of money. Additionally, some courts allow you to settle other types of legal disputes such as the restitution of property or eviction cases. More complex cases, such as bankruptcy or divorce, generally cannot be handled in small claims court.

The requirements vary from state to state and sometimes by city or county. The maximum amount you can claim in these tribunals can be as low as $1,500 in Kentucky or as high as $15,000 in Georgia and Tennessee, but most states fall somewhere in between $3,000 and $8,000. Recently, due in part to the work of HALT—a public interest legal reform group—states have been raising their limits. Be sure to check with your court clerk to get your county's current rules. You usually have at least a year to file and often much longer depending on the statute of limitations for the applicable law in your state.

Small claims courts are set up to be friendly to nonlawyers. While civil courts require you to prove your case based on legal precedent and knowledge of applicable laws, small claims courts allow you to present just the facts of your case, in plain English, to a judge with specialized knowledge of the law, who then applies the principles of justice to the facts of your case. In rare instances there might be a jury. Often there is little paperwork to fill out and a short hearing will be held within a month or two. The decision is either announced at the hearing or the judge may mail it in a letter shortly afterward.

While legal training is not necessary for small claims court, your case can only be stronger if you understand the applicable laws. You won't need to cite laws and precedents in your claim, but it will help you to know what the judge is looking for.

Some states, like California and Michigan, ban lawyers altogether. Others only allow counsel if both parties are represented. In any case, most courts will try to level the playing field to keep trained lawyers from intimidating nonlawyers with objections and legalese, but should you feel that you need professional help, you may be able to hire a lawyer to help you prepare or even to represent you in court. Furthermore, state and local consumer offices may be able to help locate low-cost legal advisors and some courts have self-help programs. A few states, including California and Washington, D.C., have advisors who offer personalized help throughout the process. There are also a growing number of self-help books and computer programs to walk you through the process.

Before filing a claim, make every effort to resolve the dispute outside of court. In doing so, you will create a paper trail of attempts that you've made to correct the problem. Failing to make an effort to settle the dispute beforehand might lose you the judge's sympathy. To avoid appearing eager to sue, send a final letter (return receipt requested) alerting the other party that you will reluctantly be forced to take further action unless they settle the dispute within a given time frame—indeed, some states mandate that you send a letter before filing suit. You can attempt to settle the claim right up to the day of the hearing.

Filing a Claim   In most states, filing a small claim is simple and easy. Fees are relatively low—around $50 to $100—and can often be waived for persons with low incomes. Usually, all you have to do to initiate your claim is provide a statement, name the defendant, and state the dollar amount you are suing for. Your statement should be short and to the point—you'll have a chance to elaborate in court.

Deciding how much to sue for will depend on the claim limits in your court. If your loss is higher than what you're allowed to sue for, you can either sue for the full amount in civil court (where you will likely need a lawyer), or claim your state's maximum and waive the rest of the debt. To figure out the amount you should sue for, calculate your total loss or debt owed. Then make a complete itemized list of expenses and fees you've spent on the ordeal, including court costs, and add them all together. Include interest if it was part of the contract, but you can't tack it on if it wasn't agreed to in the first place. Finally, when evaluating damaged or lost property, aim high. The judge can award you less than you ask for but will not be able to give you more, even if you deserve it. A small claims court study in California found that of the 27.5 percent of claimants who filed for the $5,000 maximum, the judgments were reduced to an average of $2,719. But be careful not to inflate your claim unreasonably, or your credibility could suffer.

When deciding whether to make a small claim, two questions should be carefully considered above all others.

- Do you have the evidence to win your case? No matter how valid your claim is, you will need to prove it with documentation.
- Will you be able to collect from the person you are suing? Unfortunately, small claims court does not automatically enforce the judgment should you win.

If the person or business that owes you money can pay, you may be able to take further legal action to collect the debt, such as garnishing wages or placing a lien against their property. However, some debtors are "judgment proof," meaning that they have no way to pay the debt, even if you win. Carefully consider whether or not you'll be able to collect before you file suit. Judgments may be valid for many years after the decision, so you may be able to wait until the debtor can afford to pay—but waiting for justice can be painfully frustrating.

Making Your Case   Throughout this book, we stress the importance of keeping a file of all your disputes. When you go to court, the evidence that you've kept will make or break your case. You should have a complete file of the transaction in question, any documents related to it, and a file of your correspondence with the defendant or company representatives you dealt with in trying to resolve the dispute, including a written log of your spoken conversations, with names, times, and dates.

Cases in small claims court are not won on brilliant oratory skills or word wizardry; they're won because one party has the evidence to back up her or his claim. So make a concise timeline of events in the dispute. Think about what your opponent's defense might be and produce evidence to counter it. If visual evidence would be helpful, take some photos. Try to line up witnesses or speak to experts such as doctors or get professional estimates on damaged property. If a witness or expert can't come to court, get a signed statement.

In court, as your opponent makes her or his case, pay close attention and remain calm. It never does any good to get angry in court—it may cause the judge to think you have a poor argument or to simply lose respect for you. Instead, take notes on any misstatements or misinterpretations of facts or of events and point them out to the judge, again calmly and rationally.

If the judge decides against you, you should be notified of your rights to appeal. Appeal processes vary greatly. The most complicated might require a lawyer's help, but you usually can only appeal on legal grounds, not on the facts of the case. So if you think the judge got it wrong, you must be able to explain how the law was misapplied.

While we've concentrated on using small claims court when you've been wronged, you should be equally prepared to defend yourself in court should someone make a claim against you. The *Hartford Courant* reported in 2004 on the growing trend of collectors buying debt from credit card companies and others for pennies on the dollar and collecting judgments in small claims court. Few people show up to defend themselves, and collectors often win judgments by default. Many defendants don't realize they've lost until their wages are garnished or some other action is taken. According to the *Courant*, one East Hartford firm filed over 8,000 lawsuits in 2004 and more than half of them were won by default. Companies that buy debt second- or thirdhand may not have the documentation to support their claims. Nevertheless, collectors can easily win a judgment if there's no opposition. Remember, the burden of proof is on the plaintiff. If someone makes a claim against you in court that you disagree with, show up and defend yourself. In most jurisdictions you can easily file a countersuit.

Alternative Dispute Resolution (ADR) Litigation, on top of being time consuming, can be divisive. Obviously, if you're taking somebody to court you're probably pretty divided already, but a court battle may open permanent wounds and cause more hardship than the original dispute. To avoid antagonizing people with whom you have ongoing relationships, such as relatives, neighbors, landlords, tenants, business partners, or employers, you might want to try an ADR program. Like small claims courts, these programs can be valuable in other situations as well to save time and cut the costs of litigation.

There are a variety of services to choose from, including conciliation, mediation, and arbitration. Sometimes these programs are offered, or even required, by your local court. Additionally, Better Business Bureaus (BBB) and trade organizations may offer ADR programs for disputes with businesses and manufacturers. Likewise, your employer may have a program to settle workplace disputes.

Some federal agencies offer ADR programs as well; the Equal Employment Opportunity Commission, for example, has a mediation program to settle discrimination cases (see "The Rights of Employees" chapter).

But be wary. Some arbitration firms appear to have special relationships with companies that give them repeat business. Always watch out for mandatory arbitration clauses—corporations don't have your interests in mind when they include them in their contracts. "The whole reason companies have these clauses is so they can avoid any liability for their wrongdoing," said Jon Sheldon of the National Consumer Law Center. And if companies repeatedly use an ADR firm to settle disputes, they may have an advantage over a person using it for the first time. A study of employee arbitration systems found that employers were likely to win five out of six cases.

Conciliation   Conciliation is a relatively informal process in which a neutral party, such as the BBB, seeks the facts of the case from both parties and tries to work out a solution. Conciliation is most effective when your primary problem is communicating with the company you're disputing. Sometimes it can be difficult just to get through the bureaucracy to establish a dialogue.

Mediation   This is a voluntary process in which a trained mediator meets with both parties in a dispute to try to come to a resolution. While you may be required to take part in a mediation process, the mediator usually cannot make a binding decision. Instead, you and the opposing party are encouraged to come to a mutually agreeable settlement. Mediation is especially advisable when you are in a dispute with someone you have an ongoing relationship with. If you cannot come to a settlement in mediation, you can proceed with a court action or arbitration. Any common disagreement can be handled through mediation to see if a reasonable compromise can be made, even if no law governs the conflict.

There are a few things that make this process unique. Caucuses with the mediator allow you to privately discuss the strengths and weaknesses of your case and generate fresh ideas for a resolution. Also, mediation doesn't limit the issues and evidence that can be brought up in discussion. Because everything is fair game, you might find that something completely unrelated to the case at hand is fueling the feud and come up with an innovative agreement to correct it. Most mediation processes, unlike court hearings and trials, are confidential, so you can keep private matters out of the public records.

Studies have shown that mediation is better equipped than civil courts for "nonmonetary outcomes"—like getting your noisy neighbor to turn down the stereo at a reasonable hour. Likewise, mediation more commonly results in an immediate payment (of at least a portion) of the settlement; and because both sides have a hand in shaping the outcome, mediation has a higher compliance rate than adjudicated cases. In studies of court-related mediation programs, the majority found it fair and reported feeling less angry at their opponents afterward—as opposed to trials, which can make people angrier.

In mediation, you should be prepared to give something up as well. It works best when both sides feel like they're meeting their goals. While you need not give up what you believe is rightfully yours, it will probably help encourage a settlement to at least consider the other side's point of view and mediation goals. Before you start, think about what you may be willing to concede and what you absolutely won't.

If you think your case may end up in court, be careful about sharing evidence that may help an opponent prepare a better defense. If you're unsure, you can meet with a lawyer to consider the consequences of revealing your evidence.

Furthermore you might not want to opt for mediation if there is a serious power imbalance between you and your disputant, or if you find the process emotionally disturbing. Court procedures are more likely to even the playing field in these special cases. Similarly, if you feel very strongly about the rightness of your case and want to make a point or establish a legal precedent, maybe you shouldn't mediate a compromise.

Arbitration Arbitration is a private hearing in which a neutral arbitrator is hired to hear the case and render a decision. Usually, it is organized like a court trial, complete with opening statements, evidence, and witnesses, followed by closing arguments. However, the arbitrator might not have to consider all the applicable laws and rules of evidence that a court of law would follow. Arbitration doesn't require the same process of "discovery" as a court of law, which might prevent you from accessing key evidence from the other party.

Arbitration proceedings can differ greatly from one to the next. In some cases lawyers are not allowed, in others it would be hard to succeed without one. An arbitration proceeding may be binding, requiring both parties to accept the decision, or nonbinding, in which case the parties must decide to sign on to the arbitrator's decision before it becomes enforceable.

The costs are also highly variable. In theory, arbitration is cheaper and faster than a court proceeding. But sometimes, in practice, you may be liable for the significant expenses of paying the arbitrator and staff, and for the rooms for the hearings or other charges. On the other hand, if the other party is paying all the expenses, you might wonder about the impartiality of the arbitrator. The best programs for consumers have low fees, neutral arbitrators, fair rules of evidence, and decisions that allow consumers their right to a day in court should they not get justice from an arbitrator.

Choosing an ADR Program When considering your choices for dispute resolution, consider the following important questions:
- Is the program truly neutral?
- Is it cost effective?
- Who pays for it?

- Will you have a say in choosing your arbitrator or mediator?
- Will you be able to represent yourself?
- Is the process confidential?
- Is the decision binding?
- Will you be able to file an appeal?
- Will you have to forego your legal right to file a lawsuit?

Pro Se: Representing Yourself Remember the adage that he who has himself as a lawyer has a fool for a client? Yet more and more people who find themselves priced out of legal representation are forced to defend themselves without a lawyer. Going it alone may be tough, but it's certainly more palatable than abdicating your rights altogether. And some procedures, while mired in technical jargon and legalese, are actually quite simple. Pro se divorce litigants have doubled in recent years, according to the American Bar Association, and in Florida, 65 percent of divorce cases are now filed pro se. The reason is simple: hiring a lawyer to handle a divorce in Florida could cost the unhappy couple $5,000 to $15,000 each. The same procedure, pro se, is less than $350.

Courts are slowly becoming more open to pro se representation. Self-help centers seem to be popping up everywhere, and books and computer programs can also be a big help. The priceless Nolo Press puts out complete step-by-step how-to guides on just about every legal issue you can think of, from small claims court and mediation to defending yourself in a criminal trial or, in their words, "from adoption to zoning." You can visit www.nolo.com for a list of their titles and for free online resources. The legal advocates at HALT also provide self-help resources at www.halt.org.

State governments and bar associations—long the protectors of lawyerly interests—also are opening their arms to pro se help. California has led the charge by providing courts with family law facilitators, who help with cases involving family matters like child support; small claims legal advisors to assist consumers and other small court claimants; as well as general self-help centers to aid pro se litigators and assist with other legal needs. California's self-help site is located on the web at www.courtinfo.ca.gov/selfhelp/. A list of services offered by other states can be downloaded from the website of the National Center for State Courts at www.ncsconline.org/WC/Publications/KIS_ProSeStLnks.pdf or you can call them at (800) 616-6164. Furthermore, law schools offer vast resources for amateur legal scholars. One near you may offer access to a law library, or you may be able to access materials online. Cornell Law School is just one of many that has an excellent online law library, which you can find at www.law.cornell.edu.

Hiring a Lawyer

When the New York City Department of Consumer Affairs began investigating divorce proceedings in 1991, we found a system rife with abusive lawyers preying on trusting clients. So we drafted a *Clients' Bill of Rights* to educate women at risk. The idea caught on and, in 1998, New York State made a posting of clients' rights mandatory for all clients. The advocates at HALT have taken on the cause as well, and similar laws have passed in Florida and Illinois. While the phrasing of these guidelines may change from location to location, the basic principals are based on ethical standards that apply to lawyers everywhere. If your state hasn't passed a clients' rights bill, you should still demand these basic rights, taken from the New York law.

Statement of Client Rights

1. You are entitled to be treated with courtesy and consideration at all times by your lawyer and the other lawyers and personnel in your lawyer's office.
2. You are entitled to an attorney capable of handling

your legal matter competently and diligently, in accordance with the highest standards of the profession. If you are not satisfied with how your matter is being handled, you have the right to withdraw from the attorney-client relationship at any time (court approval may be required in some matters and your attorney may have a claim against you for the value of services rendered to you up to the point of discharge).

3. You are entitled to your lawyer's independent professional judgment and undivided loyalty uncompromised by conflicts of interest.

4. You are entitled to be charged a reasonable fee and to have your lawyer explain at the outset how the fee will be computed and the manner and frequency of billing. You are entitled to request and receive a written itemized bill from your attorney at reasonable intervals. You may refuse to enter into any fee arrangement that you find unsatisfactory.

5. You are entitled to have your questions and concerns addressed in a prompt manner and to have your telephone calls returned promptly.

6. You are entitled to be kept informed as to the status of your matter and to request and receive copies of papers. You are entitled to sufficient information to allow you to participate meaningfully in the development of your matter.

7. You are entitled to have your legitimate objectives respected by your attorney, including whether or not to settle your matter (court approval of a settlement is required in some matters).

8. You have the right to privacy in your dealing with your lawyer and to have your secrets and confidences preserved to the extent permitted by law.

9. You are entitled to have your attorney conduct himself

or herself ethically in accordance with the Code of Professional Responsibility.

10. You may not be refused representation on the basis of race, creed, color, religion, sex, sexual orientation, age, national origin or disability.

Finding a Lawyer   Lawyers in the United States are over a million strong, and the number grew by about 10 percent between 1998 and 2004. So it's not hard to find one. But finding the right one for your needs takes skill—and finding one you can afford may prove even more challenging. No matter how dire your situation, try to avoid rash decisions when looking for a lawyer. "People are usually under emotional trauma of some sort and they are not used to dealing with lawyers," said William Hornsby, of the ABA's division for legal services. "When you combine the uncertainty of it and the fact that people frequently don't know the questions to ask…it creates a series of obstacles for people."

To handle these obstacles, know what you're looking for and what questions to ask. You'll want to find a lawyer who you feel personally comfortable working with, and who has expertise in the area that you need. Remember, *you're* hiring *her* or *him*—treat it for what it is, a job interview, and make sure you get all your questions answered before you sign a contract.

Talking to friends and family for a personal recommendation is the best place to start. Additionally, bar associations offer referral services, which are usually free. Look up your local or state bar association in the phone book, and tell them your problem. They will refer you to a lawyer with expertise in your area of need and/or to another resource. If you don't know whether you can afford an attorney, ask about low-cost and pro bono legal services as well. You can also search online at www.abanet.org/legalservices/lris/directory.html and, depending on where you live, you might be able to do a completely online search with the American Bar Association's iLawyer database at https://abanet.ilawyer.com/client_menu.jsp.

Most bar associations will require their attorneys to carry malpractice insurance—others, such as San Francisco, New York City, and Los Angeles, go so far as to require a lawyer to demonstrate experience in their area of practice. But in general, when taking a referral, you don't really know who they're recommending. Follow up with some questions and find out what the criteria were for making the referral list.

There are also a number of specialty referral services for particular problems and populations. The National Association of Consumer Advocates (www.naca.net) is the foremost resource for consumer lawyers. HALT also has a referral service; contact them by mail, fax, or e-mail with your legal problem and they'll respond with recommendations. AARP members have access to their legal services network, which provides free referrals and reduced fees for services.

Legal Aid   There are a number of legal aid societies and legal service providers set up to help those who otherwise can't afford representation. Legal aid societies have helped the poor with legal needs for over a century, beginning with the New York Legal Aid Society in the late 1800s. Until the 1960s, these organizations relied mainly on private philanthropy for their funds. Federal funds were added during President Johnson's "War on Poverty," which sought to make legal services part of the pantheon of equal rights, guaranteeing access to the justice system for those Americans who had been left out.

In 1974, Congress created the Legal Service Corporation, a nonpartisan, independent organization that distributed federal funds to legal service providers all over the country. In order to get bipartisan backing and the approval of the Nixon administration, limits were put on grantees prohibiting them from tackling abortion, desegregation, the draft, and several other hot-button issues. In 1996, a new Republican Congress further limited the abilities of legal service providers by requiring that they only focus on addressing individual cases rather than dealing with broad institutional problems of inequity—and then Congress slashed the funding by 40 percent for existing programs. Federally funded legal service attorneys no longer participate in class action litigation, lobby on behalf of their clients, or represent most illegal immigrants or prisoners, or challenge welfare reform laws. Since the harsh budget cuts of the 1990s, funding has remained stable, but legal aid services struggle to help only 1.4 million of the 45 million Americans who qualify each year.

The Legal Aid Society of Salt Lake City provided free care for decades, taking on as many as 1,400 cases in a year according to the *Salt Lake Tribune*. But in 2004 it handled only 45 and now charges on a sliding scale of $200–$600 for divorce and custody cases— out of reach for some of the neediest clients. On the bright side, it began running a self-help clinic in 2003 to assist those who would otherwise fall through the cracks. In fact, upward of 75 percent of federally funded legal aid providers include pro se assistance of some kind.

These programs make up an integral part of America's legal safety net. Usually restricted to clients within 125 percent of the federal poverty level, legal service providers protect the rights of the working poor and other needy Americans, such as disaster victims and veterans. Because women make up more than two-thirds of the Legal Service Corporation's clientele, most of them with children, legal service programs also provide our nation's children and families with basic legal protections. To find a federally funded legal service program, go to www.lsc.gov and click on "Get Legal Assistance," or call your local bar association for more help.

Low-Cost Services   If you are having trouble finding a lawyer you can afford and can't qualify for free assistance, don't count yourself out. Lawyers who specialize in personal injury, workers comp, discrimination, and similar areas of law often work on a contingency basis—meaning they are paid a percentage if you win, but take home nothing if you lose.

There are also many programs offered by bar associations, law schools, and community groups that offer pro bono, or low-cost, legal assistance to those who need it. Call your local bar association and law schools in your area to see what services are available. Further, more help is available on the web. Sites like www.lawhelp.org help those with low and moderate incomes find affordable legal services in their area. Many states have legal hotlines for senior citizens; you can download a list at www.aoa.gov/eld-fam/Elder_Rights/Legal_Assistance/SRdirclient.pdf, if you or a loved one is in need.

Other online services allow you to compare attorneys' rates and qualifications. For instance, www.legalmatch.com allows you to present your case, which is then sent out to qualified lawyers in your area. You'll receive e-mails with fees and qualifications and you can pick and choose from the various lawyers. While www.legal-match.com promises to protect your identity, keep in mind that the Internet generally is not a safe place for confidential material. Furthermore, always try to meet with a lawyer and ask questions before you decide to hire one.

CASE STUDY

When Marvin and Margaret Farley of Baltimore needed a lawyer, they found help through an innovative "low-bono" program offered through the University of Maryland School of Law. The program was affiliated with the nationwide Law School Consortium Project, which connects local small-firm and independent attorneys with law-school-supported referrals, training, and assistance to perform low-cost legal services for clients in need.

The Farleys were certainly in need. They had been conned into buying a house for $49,500—a price inflated times six—from a seller who didn't even own the deed. Unfortunately, none of that information was known to them until a problem with the sewage system caused waste to fill the basement. "We were living in sewage, smelling the stench all the time. You couldn't go to the bathroom, because it all went down to the basement," Margaret Farley explained. "Marvin went to clean it up once, and the air was so bad, he ended up in the hospital on the verge of a heart attack."

The home in which these grandparents had planned to live out the rest of their years became uninhabitable and infested by rodents and insects. What's worse, due to the fraudulent deed, the house didn't even belong to them. The lawyers working for the Farleys took the case to court and a jury awarded them $148,250, plus attorney fees, from the fraudulent seller.

The Law School Consortium Project is a promising innovation offering legal assistance to low- and moderate-income clients. "Every day there are more and more people who need legal assistance that don't qualify for pro bono help, so why not combine this incredible demand and need with this incredible supply of lawyers?" says Lovely Dhillon, director of the Law School Consortium Project. It expands the more common pro bono services offered by law schools with a model for helping people who don't qualify for typical assistance. The result is a virtual law firm built by a community dedicated to social justice. The project has been a success, spreading to sixteen campuses in seven states so far, and according to Dhillon they keep growing each day. The project "shows lawyers that you can do well and do good," she said. To find a "low bono" program near you, go to the consortium's website at www.lawschoolconsortium.net and click on "Members."

Public Interest Cases   If your case has the potential to set a precedent or punish some type of wrongdoer—be it corporate malfeasance, discrimination, reproductive rights, access to health care, or environmental protection—you may be able to find a public interest litigation group to take your case.

Here are a few organizations that specialize in public interest litigation, and there are many more both nationally and locally that specialize in a wide range of public interest causes. Look for one that can address your needs.

Organization	Focus	How to contact
American Civil Liberties Union (ACLU)	First Amendment Equal protection Due process Privacy rights	Find your local chapter at www.aclu.org
Legal Momentum	Sex and gender discrimination Civil rights Domestic violence issues	Go to their website at www.legalmomentum.org or call (212) 925-6635
National Association for the advancement of Colored People (NAACP)	Race discrimination Civil rights Access to justice	Go to www.naacp.org or call (410) 580-5790
Public Citizen Litigation Group	Consumers' rights Workers' rights	Go to www.citizen.org or call (202) 588-1000
U.S. Public Interest Research Group (U.S. PIRG)	Environmental justice Public health	Go to www.uspirg.org to find your local PIRG

NEGOTIATING A CONTRACT

Consultation Most referral services offer a free or inexpensive consultation, during which you should go over the strengths and weaknesses of your case and get an idea of what's in store. You may find that you can take care of the matter yourself after speaking to a lawyer and that you don't need representation at all. In any case, be sure to provide a full file of documentation and a chronology of events so the attorney gets a good idea of your case, and be prepared to ask questions. Get their expert opinions on how you should proceed and what your chances are. Will your case likely involve litigation or are there other options?

This is also your chance to get to know the attorney. Find out how long they've been in practice; what kind of experience they have with cases like yours; and what kind of case schedule they have.

Will they be able to devote an appropriate amount of time to your case? Who will really be doing the work on your case? Will much of it be done by paralegals or other attorneys in the firm? If so, find out about their qualifications and the fee structure. Finally, get an estimate for the various possible costs including estimates for pretrial work, a trial, and an appeal. However, the unpredictable nature of legal proceedings can make costs hard to foresee, and unexpected motions and delays can add up. Don't feel like you have to make a deal right then—it's a good idea to speak with multiple lawyers to get different perspectives and estimates.

Types of Fees   Regardless of whether you're hiring a well-heeled litigator or a well-intentioned public interest lawyer, knowing how to negotiate a contract and fee structure will save you money and allow you to better defend yourself. Remember, when dealing with lawyers and other legal professionals, always get it in writing!

Attorneys most commonly charge an hourly rate. While you may be quoted a price for each hour of work, it's important to understand in what increments the contract stipulates the rate will be charged. They may round up to every fifteen minutes, ten minutes, or six minutes. Obviously, the lower the increment the more beneficial to you. Who wants to be charged for a quarter-hour for a three-minute phone call? Furthermore, if your attorney has other employees working on your case, such as legal secretaries, paralegals, or less experienced attorneys, the contract should stipulate a far lower rate for their work. Nolo's guide suggests that $35 to $75 an hour is appropriate for paralegals.

For more simple legal procedures, such as uncontested divorces or bankruptcy proceedings, attorneys may charge a flat rate. But the "flat fee" you're quoted may not be all you'll be charged for. Be sure to get an estimate of court costs or other expenses you'll be accountable for if the case goes that far.

Contingency fees are common for class action, personal injury, malpractice, discrimination, and product liability cases, especially when the defendant is insured or well-financed and it's the only way a nonwealthy plaintiff can bring a promising case. In effect, an attorney may gamble on winning a case and take a percentage of the award; if the case is a loser, however, the lawyer gets nothing. The lawyer's cut is usually about a third of the award, but you might be able to negotiate it lower. You can also negotiate a tiered contingency fee structure that gives the lawyer a greater percentage for any award to a point, and a smaller percentage for any amount over.

Lawyers who work on a contingency basis theoretically take high percentages of awards they win to offset their losses when they lose. You may not be charged any fees if you lose, but you'll likely be on the line for court costs and other expenses. And if you win your case, you might be surprised how little of the award is left after the lawyer takes her or his cut and the expenses are paid. It will save you money to stipulate in your contract that the expenses be deducted from the total award *before* your attorney takes her or his cut.

Legal expenses can add up fast. Simple costs like filing fees, court reporters, transcripts, phone calls, and postage can get quite expensive. More complicated cases may require private investigators and expert witnesses, which can be even more costly. Be sure you understand what expenses you are responsible for and what are included in your fees.

Ensure that your fee agreement, or engagement letter, calls for an itemized monthly bill. You have the right to know what you're being charged for, so make sure your bill spells out exactly everything that has been done on your case, who preformed the work, and how much time it took. Review these documents each month. If any vague language leaves you guessing what you're paying for, be sure to follow up and have it spelled out.

Your contract should also explain how to resolve fee disputes. Like a pre-nup, it may be uncomfortable to go over these issues at the beginning of your working relationship, but nobody should understand the importance of a written contract more than a lawyer. Broach the issue of fee disputes in a professional demeanor and ask your lawyer to agree to fee arbitration or mediation should a dispute arise. Furthermore, make sure you aren't charged for any time spent discussing a fee dispute.

Many lawyers will ask you to provide a retainer at the offset. A retainer may include a bulk advance payment, kept in a trust, from which the attorney can draw funds for services and expenses. You should know how the retainer will be used. Will it be used only for attorney's fees or to cover other expenses as well? Make sure that your contract stipulates a refund for any funds left over. Nonrefundable retainers are illegal in New York and some other states, but lawyers can still charge a minimum fee.

Finally, clients in New York, Illinois, and Florida are required to be notified of their rights in a statement. You can go even further by attaching these rights to your contract. Even if you don't live in one of those states, feel free to attach the New York Statement of Clients' Rights (on page 42), or go to www.halt.org to see their model state law, and attach it to your contract.

CASE STUDY

Personal injuries can be traumatic and frightful experiences. Those who endure them might face prolonged periods without an income while their lawsuit slowly ambles on. For clients in these situations, a number of companies offer cash advances until the lawsuit is settled. These firms can be a lifesaver. Much like a contingency fee, you don't pay if you lose…but if you win watch out for the fees!

Consider the case of Michele Youngblood of the Bronx. On New Year's Day, 2002, a cab dragged her twenty feet down the street, causing serious injuries and permanent disability. Without her job as a manager for a Fortune 500 company, she quickly went through her savings and had to resort to borrowing from friends and family. "I had to see how the other half lives, all of a sudden, to have nothing at all," she said.

Then Youngblood took $12,000 in advances on her lawsuit. "I don't know how I would have lived," she said. But after Youngblood settled her case for an undisclosed sum, she had to pay back the $12,000—plus an additional $11,000 in fees! "It was highway robbery," Youngblood told the *New York Times*.

The usurious sums are legal because the advances don't actually qualify as loans. But borrowers are often blindsided by the high fees. One client, who borrowed $3,000 in 2001, ended up owing $19,000. "These are multipage documents that require a great deal of sophistication to understand," according to New York's assistant attorney general, Stephen Mindell. While these firms need to account for the money that they don't recover in lost lawsuits, there's no excuse for fees so outrageously high.

Using a Lawyer as a Coach / Unbundling If you decide to represent yourself in court, you could hire a lawyer as a pro se (or small claims) "coach." Ultimately, the responsibilities of litigation are yours, but for an hourly fee you can get the backing of an attorney to go over your case and in some cases even make an appearance in court. A lawyer can review your documents and evidence, prepare you for court, assist with legal research, and generally steer you in the right direction.

If you choose this option, it is important to have a written fee agreement clearly outlining the role(s) you and the attorney will and will not play. Additionally, if your case grows more complicated, you have the advantage of having a lawyer who knows the details and who might be able to take over for you.

"Unbundling" allows you to pay for services a la carte rather than allowing a lawyer bill you carte blanche, but it can be a tricky situation for a lawyer. Ethics guidelines require that lawyers do as much as they can to help their client, but those guidelines get tested in cases in which they're selling only certain services because no lawyer wants to face charges of professional negligence. Many lawyers have embraced unbundling, however, especially in states that have tried to define the ethical issues. At a coffeehouse in Los Angeles called the Legal Grind, customers can get a lawyer's hand in document drafting and other legal assistance over a cup of joe.

Nonlawyer Legal Services   While the American Bar Association has spent much of its history and substantial resources protecting the legal establishment's monopoly on legal services, there are increasingly more nonlawyer options available to clients in need. For relatively simple or uncontested legal tasks, you can hire an independent paralegal or legal document assistant. We the People, a national firm, advertises an uncontested divorce at a flat rate of $399, in addition to court costs. Professional nonlawyers can assist you with documents and paperwork for legal needs such as wills, real estate transactions, small business dealings, and the like. Nonlawyers can offer ample knowledge and experience at a fraction of the price. However, the law prohibits nonlawyers from offering "legal advice" specific to your case, which can only be offered by a lawyer licensed by the bar. Nonlawyer services and self-help resources—like this book—offer only "legal information," and the responsibility to apply that information to your case is yours alone.

Despite that distinction, the ABA has continued to attack nonlawyer professionals. In 2003 it lobbied the federal government to make "selecting, drafting or completing legal documents" by nonlawyers an unauthorized practice, against the position of its own antitrust division. That definition would have made it possible to hold professionals like real estate agents, tax preparers, credit counselors, as well as paralegals and others liable to civil and criminal charges, but the FTC and Department of Justice balked, and the ABA took its fight back to the states. The Florida bar has pushed legislation that would make the unauthorized practice of law a felony, and lawsuits against nonlawyers are common all over the country.

The ABA claims that they're protecting consumers (rather than lawyers' wallets), but a study in the *Stanford Law Review* found that just 2 percent of all unlicensed practice of law complaints were filed by consumers. Furthermore, consumer protection laws in most states—which protect consumers of nonlawyer services—go farther than the self-regulated attorney discipline mechanism of those states. When 38 million Americans can't afford legal services, nonlawyer services fill a crucial need. "It really reflects the worst of the profession, which is to assume that lawyers own the law," said Steven Lubet, a legal ethics professor at Northwestern University. "It's anti-democratic. In a democracy, everyone has an interest in discussing the law."

When you hire a nonlawyer professional, it's a good idea to know what training he or she has undergone and how much experience they have with matters like yours. If your state certifies independent paralegals or legal document assistants, check to see that they are properly licensed with the state. Otherwise, see if they are accredited by an independent organization.

Talk Back/Fight Back

If you have a dispute with your lawyer, there's good news and bad news. The good news is that there are multiple avenues for you to defend yourself...the bad news is that they're all bad. A 2002 HALT review of lawyer discipline systems concluded that "this country's lawyer discipline system continues to be irresponsible at best—and in some cases downright antagonistic—toward consumers." Bar association discipline procedures remain, in large part, veiled in secrecy, and most of the time they fail to take any meaningful action against lawyers. Malpractice cases are among the hardest to prove and it is usually difficult to find a lawyer to take a case against a colleague. Fee arbitration systems offer some relief, but a system that relies on lawyers to hear cases of lawyer billing disputes gives at least the appearance of a conflict of interest. If you have a disagreement with a lawyer, try to resolve it amicably. Take notes of your conversation and keep records of your written correspondence. If you are unable to resolve your dispute, take action.

Firing Your Lawyer   Your lawyer works for you, so if something goes wrong it's your right to fire her or him. Your first action in a dispute (assuming you haven't been able to work it out in person or over the phone) is to write a letter to the offending attorney describing your position. If your lawyer did not act according to your wishes or violated the fee agreement, explain your grievance and how you expect the situation to be corrected. Give a time that you expect her or him to comply with your request. As with all disputes, include copies of your contract and other documents that support you and send it return receipt requested; keep the original documents for your records.

If your lawyer fails to respond to your wishes, you can convey to them the signature line of Donald Trump's *The Apprentice*. If you have ongoing legal proceedings, you may want to find another lawyer first. Explain your case to the new lawyer and the problems you're having with the other one. The new lawyer can then assist you both with your ongoing case and with discharging the other attorney. Your discharge letter should include the reason for the termination and the arrangements for a final bill, as well as an arrangement to receive the case files of the work that you've paid for.

In such a dispute, a lawyer may refuse to turn over files that they believe you haven't paid for. A new attorney can take over your file or, if you're pro se, you can demand the files yourself. If you have trouble retrieving them, contact the local bar for help. If you have to pay to get your file back, you might be able to retrieve the funds in court or by fee arbitration. Make sure to include a letter with your payment saying that you believe the charges are unjustified.

If the fees in dispute are less than your state's small claims maximum, you can try to recover them through small claims court. If not, contact your local or state bar association to find out how to arrange for fee arbitration or mediation, which are usually free or have only nominal fees. You can find out what your local bar association offers by calling them, or looking them up online through the ABA's Directory of State and Local Bar Associations on the Internet at www.abanet.org/barserv/stlobar.html or download a list of fee arbitration programs at www.abanet.org/cpr/clientpro/cp-dir_feearb.pdf.

Fee Arbitration   There are two kinds of arbitration. If your state offers mandatory arbitration, the lawyer must appear before an arbitrator when you file. In voluntary arbitration both parties must agree to take part in the process. For the most part, if it is not binding, you can preserve your right to a day in court should you not be satisfied with the results. But before you sign away your legal rights, consider whether you'll get a fair hearing from a neutral arbitrator.

Usually, the bar association appoints other lawyers—and less frequently nonlawyers—to hear your case. While there's little you can do to combat the inherent inequity of lawyers policing themselves, you'll want to be sure to weed out real conflicts of interest. Do some research on the arbitrators. If they have a connection to the attorney at issue, you'll want to challenge their appointment as your arbitrator. Does the arbitrator belong to the same firm or bar?

The arbitration process usually just takes two or three months from start to finish. Once the arbitrators are named, a hearing will be held. You can make your arguments and present your material yourself or get a lawyer to assist you. See if the bar association or arbitration administrator can provide low-cost or pro bono assistance.

Filing a Complaint At the same time you pursue a fee arbitration or court action, you may also choose to file a disciplinary complaint against the attorney. Unfortunately, this option cannot result in a corrective action or get you your money back. Even worse, the likelihood of real discipline is marginal at best. Of the 121,000 complaints filed against lawyers in 2002, only 3.5 percent resulted in formal discipline. Nevertheless, it's important to report bad behavior to protect others from future abuse, and a disciplinary action from a bar association may help you recover your lost fees in arbitration or court.

Your local bar association can give you the formal procedures for filing a complaint. It usually involves a letter or form summarizing your dispute. Describe the attorney's bad behavior as concisely as possible. Attach copies of any documentary evidence you have. From there, the bar will investigate your complaint. They may contact you for further questioning or to participate in a hearing. The bar may decide to publicly reprimand the lawyer by fine, suspension, temporary disbarment, or permanent disbarment. But more likely, the complaint will result in a private wrist-slap that never sees the light of day, or in nothing at all. To find the proper disciplinary agency, call your bar association or look online at www.abanet.org/cpr/regulation/scpd/disciplinary.html.

But if you've been misrepresented by a lawyer, you have the right to sue for malpractice. In fee disputes, you can also sue for breach of contract. If your dispute is for a modest sum, you might be able to recover it in small claims court. But before you file for malpractice, consider that you will have to prove that you would have won your case if your attorney hadn't bungled it—a difficult feat. If it's worth it, and doesn't give you an ulcer to think about, you can hire a new lawyer to sue the other. Use a referral service to find a lawyer that specializes in malpractice cases.

There's another option to recover your money if an attorney has stolen it from your trust, refused to return funds from your retainer, kept a judgment award, or otherwise absconded with your dough. States operate client compensation funds, which are sometimes called "client protection funds" or "client security funds." A survey from 2001 showed that compensation provided relief for over 54 percent of the nearly 4,000 claims that year, for a total of $24.3 million. File a claim with your state's client compensation fund should you find yourself in this predicament. Most states bar lawyers from representing you, but they may allow one to volunteer as a public service. You can download a list of client funds from the ABA at www.abanet.org/cpr/clientpro/cp-dir_fund.pdf.

After you submit a claim with your summary of events and copies of your evidence, a committee will investigate your charges. They may ask you to participate further or supply additional materials to their investigation. If you've filed a disciplinary complaint, they may delay their investigation to incorporate the findings of the disciplinary hearing. If it finds in your favor, the committee can order the attorney to reimburse you, but if they don't, they might not even tell you why, and there may or may not be an appeal procedure.

How to Be a Private Attorney General

If you have knowledge that a company or a local government is defrauding the government, hurting taxpayers and consumers, you have the power to fight back. The *False Claims Act* dates back to the Civil War, when Lincoln used it as a tool to go after ammunition suppliers and other war profiteers who defrauded the government by, for example, providing sawdust in place of gunpowder to Union soldiers. Then known as the Lincoln Law, the *False Claims Act* was revived in 1986 when $600 toilet seats and other fraudulent defense contracts hit the American presses.

The Act encourages whistleblowers to bring forth information relating to fraud against the government, and allows you to file a civil action called *qui tam*, from a Latin phrase that means "who as well for the king as for himself sues in this matter." In a qui tam case, you essentially partner with the government to hold the fraudulent party accountable. The person who brings the suit is called a "relator" and can receive 15 to 30 percent of a successful award—the average cut is usually around 16 percent. Since 1986 the government has won back over $13.5 billion in qui tam cases, and citizens have won about $1.5 billion for their efforts in bringing these companies to justice.

Since 1992, when National Health Laboratories suffered a $110 million settlement and criminal plea for bilking the government, about half of all qui tam cases have been in response to health care fraud. But the law can be invoked for a number of reasons, including to protect: patients from unnecessary procedures and faulty health care devices; consumers from overcharging and shortages; soldiers from faulty equipment; seniors and the disabled from fraud and substandard care; and all of us from misuse of public land and funds, pollution, and exposure to toxic materials. Additionally, a number of states have False Claims Acts to protect state governments and citizens.

One of the largest qui tam judgments came in 2000 when America's biggest for-profit hospital chain, HCA, paid over $730 million for false claims related to fraud. This suit recovered costs for crimes such as billing patients for unnecessary tests, "upcoding" bills to charge for higher-priced procedures, and charging the government for advertising costs under the pretense that they contributed to "community education." The company paid another $631 million in 2003, for charges of defrauding Medicare and Medicaid and paying kickbacks to participating doctors.

Talk Back/Fight Back:

You can file a qui tam suit when you have knowledge that the actions of a company or person costs the government money, either by overbilling, taking fraudulent payments, or depriving it of revenue—though tax violations are specifically excluded from the False Claims Act. Your knowledge must be original, not lifted from the daily paper or other publicly available materials; and in cases where more than one whistleblower comes forward, the first one to file will be heard. You don't have to prove that the fraud was intentional. Government contractors are expected to know what public funds they are entitled to and to refrain from taking any to which they are not—so convenient ignorance would be considered cause for a qui tam case.

To bring a case, you need to file a "disclosure statement" in federal court with the Department of Justice and U.S. Attorney's Office. This claim is kept secret while the government investigates. The government has sixty days to decide if it will join your suit—but almost always requests additional time. A typical qui tam claim may remain under seal for a few years.

If the Department of Justice doesn't join in a qui tam suit, the relator may pursue the case alone. The government can then join in at any time and ultimately has the power to settle or dismiss the case altogether, as long as the relator has a chance to be heard. Obviously, a case that the government joins stands a better chance of winning. The Department of Justice has vast evidence-gathering powers that can't be matched by private attorneys. Attorneys' fees and costs can be recovered from the defendant in a successful suit, and whistleblowers receive protection against retaliation, including twice the amount of back pay, with interest, and other benefits such as reinstatement after a firing. To find out more about qui tam actions and to look for a specialist, go to the Taxpayers Against Fraud website at www.taf.org.

FIX IT: PROTECTING CLIENTS' RIGHTS

The American civil justice system is in need of serious reform. Unfortunately, politicians are pushing in the wrong direction. The so-called "tort reform" movement, which has gained strength in recent years, seeks to make it harder for ordinary people to gain access to civil justice. The proponents of this movement claim that America faces a "litigation crisis" that raises costs for America's businesses. Actually, the civil caseload has been going *down*, not *up*, in recent years—as have jury awards. And businesses that claim they are hurt the most, such as medical malpractice insurers, are actually making a killing. Nevertheless, these "reformers" have gone to great lengths to gut the ability of citizens to (1) file class action suits—pushing them into federal courts where most will be deemed unmanageable by busy federal judges, and (2) bring malpractice and consumer liability suits. The first priority should be to reverse the flawed *Class Action Fairness Act* of 2005 and to prevent further erosion of our system of civil justice.

Real reform should make it easier, not harder, for America's middle- and low-income families to find justice. America's premier legal reform organization, HALT, has made a number of reasonable proposals that should be heeded in Washington and state capitals. Here are several of their simple ideas.

Legal Rights. A few states have passed a Clients' Bill of Rights to ensure that legal consumers are granted and informed of their basic legal rights. This simple measure should be extended to all American citizens. These basic rights (listed previously) should apply to all Americans. Putting them in a contract that both the lawyer and the client must sign will help put predatory lawyers on notice and even the legal playing field.

Small Claims. HALT has had success raising the monetary limits in several small claims courts across the country. Its goal is to get the ceiling in most states up to $20,000. This simple reform allows more Americans to settle relatively small disputes without having to hire a lawyer, which for many Americans is a near impossibility, especially when the payout is a modest sum. Furthermore, small claims judges should be given the power to make court orders, which would greatly increase the ability of consumers to settle more complicated contract disputes and to actually collect the judgments they win. Once again, this is the responsibility of state legislatures.

Legal Aid. When 44 million of the 45 million people who qualify for legal aid are unable to receive assistance, that's a crisis. And it is not trivial cases that are left behind. Mothers are unable to get child support for their children, and women desperate for relief from abusive husbands have difficulty finding assistance. Just listen to Sarah Campbell, director of Kisatchie Legal Services Corporation in Louisiana, who describes having to "pick the women who seemed to be in the most immediate danger" for the scarce legal aid. "If they'd had a gun to their heads, or they'd been severely beaten, we'd squeeze them in no matter what. Or if they had kids, we'd take the case. As awful as it sounds, you'd rationalize that a case where several people were in danger deserved priority over one person who's being beaten up."

Legal scholar Deborah Rhode argues that tripling the federal budget for legal aid would come to less than a billion dollars, a modest amount to enhance democracy in America compared to the hundreds of billions we've spent trying to bring democracy to Iraq. Moreover, simply expanding surcharges on lawyers' revenues and court filing fees, says Rhode, "would be a relatively painless and progressive way to expand access to justice."

CHAPTER 3

THE RIGHTS OF EMPLOYEES

All may dismiss their employees at will, be they many or few, for good cause, for no cause or even for cause morally wrong, without being thereby guilty of legal wrong.
—From the Tennessee Supreme Court 1884 decision
establishing "employment at will"

The history of workplace disputes in the United States has heavily favored employers. For more than a century the controlling legal doctrine, known as "employment at will," has given employers the power to fire a worker at any time for any reason. Since the 1884 precedent legally established this doctrine, much has changed in the workplace to legally reign in abusive employers and provide employees with more rights and protections. The Labor Movement and the Civil Rights Movement have also won hard-fought battles to enact laws that enable you to defend yourself against unfair treatment in the workplace.

KEY LAWS AT WORK

National Labor Relations Act (NLRA) The greatest challenge to "employment at will" has been collective bargaining. The National Labor Relations Act of 1935 gave workers the right to collectively bargain and negotiate contracts that provide job security. As a result, most union workers and civil service employees today can only be terminated for "just cause." However, only about 13 percent of workers are now represented by unions, down from a peak of 36 percent in the 1950s. But the *NLRA* gives *all* workers the right to voice their concerns collectively and be protected from retaliation by management. Yet, because the commissioners of the National Labor Relations Board (NLRB) are political appointees, it has weakened worker protections during anti-union presidential administrations.

Fair Labor Standards Act (FLSA) The *FLSA* guarantees over 100 million workers the basic rights to be paid and treated fairly. It establishes the minimum wage; defines the forty-hour work week; sets requirements for overtime pay; and restricts child labor. The *FLSA* has been updated regularly since its creation in 1938, and now includes a provision that men and women receive equal pay for equal work through the *Equal Pay Act* of 1963. Not all updates to this law have increased worker protections, however. The Bush administration's overhaul of overtime pay rules in 2004, for instance, has millions of workers seeing red—on their paycheck stubs.

Civil Rights Act of 1964 Title VII of this law makes it illegal for employers to discriminate against workers based on sex, race, skin color, religious beliefs, or national origin. Title VII also established the Equal Employment Opportunity Commission (EEOC) to enforce and oversee workplace discrimination law, which includes protection against sexual harassment. Today, discrimination law has been expanded by the *Age Discrimination in Employment Act*, the *Pregnancy Discrimination Act*, and the *Americans with Disabilities Act*, among others.

Occupational Safety and Health Act (OSH Act) This key 1970 law requires employers to maintain a safe and healthy workplace and created the Occupational Safety and Health Administration (OSHA) to regulate the law. While OSHA has produced many important reforms, weak enforcement powers have meant that workplace injuries and deaths persist at an alarming rate.

FAIR PAY, FAIR PLAY

One of the most basic employee rights is the right to be paid fairly. The *FLSA* provides a minimum pay rate (currently $5.15 an hour) and demands that "unskilled" employees be paid at least time and a half for any hours over forty in one week. In addition, states have minimum wages that can be higher, but never lower, than the federal rate and sometimes have overtime rules that go further than the federal standards require.

For instance, in addition to providing overtime for any hours over forty in a given week, a few states provide overtime pay for any hours worked in excess of eight in one day.* Thirty-two states have prevailing wage laws that set minimum wages for particular industries that contract with the state—and likewise, there are federal prevailing wages for businesses contracted by the federal government. In addition, many municipalities have "living wage" ordinances that require any company that does business with the city to pay a minimum "living wage"—and a few even have citywide minimum wages. In 2004, a San Francisco referendum went into effect creating a citywide minimum wage of $8.50 per hour and the city requires a higher "living wage" for companies that have contracts with the city. Employers are required to post the relevant minimum wage in the workplace for hourly employees, but you should take the time to familiarize yourself with your state's standards by calling the Department of Labor, Wages and Hours Division, found in the U.S. Government section of your phone book. You can also look at your state's Department of Labor website to make sure that your employer is paying you what you deserve.

CASE STUDY

While millions of workers toil at or near minimum wage to support their families, some employers compound the insult by cheating them of their hard-earned money. In a 2004 *New York Times*

---

*Alaska, California, and Nevada all have statutes that allow employees to receive overtime after eight hours in one day. Colorado allows overtime to kick in after twelve hours in a day. Additionally, California and Kentucky provide overtime for workers on their seventh consecutive working day. (Barbara Kate Repa, *Your Rights in the Workplace*, 6th ed., 2002) article, Steven Greenhouse detailed the growing phenomenon of doctoring time cards, which "is far more prevalent than most Americans believe. The practice, commonly called shaving time, is easily done and hard to detect—a simple matter of computer keystrokes—and has spurred a growing number of lawsuits and settlements against a wide range of businesses."

One employee, Drew Pooters, a retired Air Force MP with five children, has witnessed more than his share of payroll theft. Pooters left his job at a Toys "R" Us in Albuquerque after catching his manager shaving time from employee time cards. Then, while managing a Family Dollar store, he was ordered to delete employee hours electronically. Refusing to do so, the district manger shaved the time herself. Pooters again quit in disgust, finding work in Indiana with RentWay, a furniture and electronics chain, where he was forced to work through his lunch breaks without pay. He is now suing Family Dollar, where he says he worked as many as 100 hours a week while being paid for only fifty.

Talk Back/Fight Back

If you suspect you're being cheated, step one is to keep detailed records and save your pay stubs. If you clock into work on a manual time card, make or request a copy. If you clock in on a computer with no paper trail, make your own record. Design a time sheet that spans a pay period and keep track of each time you clock in or out. Get your coworkers to join you; the more proof you have, the better your case will be.

If you find a discrepancy in pay, consult management or the person in charge of payroll. This is not the time to be confrontational; if it was an accounting error, they may resolve it by paying you back wages. If management doesn't respond, however, you have ways to claim the money you earned. For small amounts of money the quickest and easiest solution is to take your case to small claims court. You won't need a lawyer, but you'll need to be prepared. (See "How to Win in Small Claims Court," in "The Rights of Clients" chapter.)

If you prefer, or if you've been cheated for more than the small claims court maximum, you can file a confidential complaint with your local office of the Department of Labor, Wage and Hour Division, which can be found in the

U.S. Government pages of your phone book, or by calling their toll-free information line at (866) 4US-WAGE. Or look it up online at www.dol.gov. In addition to being confidential, the FLSA protects workers who file a complaint, as well as those who assist the investigation, from retaliation by their employers. If investigators find that your employer purposefully broke the law to deny your rights, they can get Justice Department lawyers to bring criminal actions against your employer. In addition, the Department of Labor can award you back wages for up to three years, and in some cases an equal amount in damages. Additionally, some states can pursue back wages for longer than the federal limit of three years. You are also permitted to file your own lawsuit under the *FLSA*. However, if the Labor Department has already resolved the dispute by awarding back wages, or has filed suit to do so, you in effect delegate your right to sue to the Labor Department.

HEALTH IS WEALTH

OSHA covers nearly every worker in the country regardless of the size of the business. In addition, many states have their own OSHA-approved offices (sometimes with different names such as Cal-OSHA, in California, and NYOSH, in New York) that must at least meet, and often go beyond, federal OSHA guidelines. The law requires employers to follow OSHA standards regarding workplace safety and health and to set policies and satisfactorily explain them to their employees. Employers must also keep records of workplace illness and injuries and, in cases of serious injuries or death, must immediately report them to the nearest OSHA office.

OSHA also requires employers to provide training for employees who work with hazardous materials. Employers must develop a written hazard communication program that lists the dangers in each work area and must educate employees on how they can protect themselves. In some cases, employers must provide safety equipment, vaccinations for diseases that can be contracted on the job, and medical evaluations to monitor employee health.

Employees are entitled to request information regarding workplace safety and health including: "details of any hazardous chemicals or other materials on site; the results of tests to evaluate chemical, noise or radiation levels; necessary precautions to avoid exposure and procedures for employees who may be involved in an incident involving hazardous chemicals or other toxic materials." In addition, employers should have copies available of all appropriate standards, rules, regulations, and requirements that apply to your workplace. OSHA also gives employees the right to review injury and illness logs and grants access to exposure and medical records within fifteen days of a request.

OSHA requires your employer to correct all workplace hazards, *even when they are not specific violations of OSHA standards.* If there is a safety or health hazard in your working environment, report it to your manager or the person in charge of occupational safety. Get your coworkers to join you, because the more people reporting the danger, the more likely management will take it seriously. Keep track of your conversations with management and have others do the same. Make your requests in writing to ensure you have documentation of your request. If the hazard persists and management does nothing to address the problem, you can report it to the nearest OSHA or state health and safety office.

Since President Nixon signed the *OSH Act* into law in 1970, workplace injuries have been in steady decline and deaths have been reduced by half. Because of OSHA and OSHA-approved state regulators, workers now have a place to turn to report workplace hazards and improve working conditions. OSHA also has the continuing duty to issue new standards on health and safety, protecting workers from ever-emerging dangers.

But while OSHA is designed to prevent problems, it has very little power to enforce the standards it sets. Many companies continue to subject their employees to nineteenth-century working conditions in the hope of saving money and not getting caught.

CASE STUDY

On October 29, 2002, for example, Guadalupe Garcia Jr., an employee at Tyler Pipe in East Texas, was crushed and nearly torn in half by a foundry factory truck driven by another employee; coincidentally, OSHA was investigating Tyler Pipe for other violations when the incident occurred. Doctors amputated both of Garcia's legs and pumped over 200 pints of blood back into his body to save his life. While recovering, Garcia and the driver of the truck told reporters in separate interviews that the accident was a result of safety hazards constantly overlooked and ignored by the factory's managers, including "poor lighting, inadequate safety training and shoddy maintenance on the truck itself."

Ultimately, OSHA fined Tyler Pipe $196,000 for violations discovered in the October 2002 investigation, the most serious stemming from the accident involving Garcia. The violations included "Thirteen serious violations, four repeat violations and one minor infraction," according to *New York Times* reporters David Barstow and Lowell Bergman. Between 1995 and 2003, the parent company, McWane, Inc., had over 400 safety violations (more than their six closest industry rivals put together), and, while employing 5,000 workers, recorded 4,600 workplace injuries, including many serious burnings and maimings. Nine workers were killed on the job at McWane plants during that span; of those, three were due to deliberate violations of OSHA standards and, in five others, OSHA found that safety lapses played a role. And, because of constant fear of retribution, many other workers continued to work with injuries they never reported. During the same time period, the corporation was cited with another 450 environmental violations affecting the health of workers and neighboring communities.

Among the reasons for McWane's serial violations is that OSHA is a comb without teeth. The nine workplace deaths during that timeframe resulted in just one referral for criminal prosecution and a single misdemeanor involving no company executives. Nor do

OSHA investigators have a way of tracking violations of complex corporate entities like McWane. Federal law makes it extremely difficult to prove an employer's guilt when willful violation of safety rules causes an employee's death. Moreover, the crime is only a misdemeanor, carrying a maximum punishment of just six months in prison, half the penalty of harassing a wild burro on federal property, as Barstow and Bergman point out. The highest civil penalty OSHA can levy for causing the death of a worker is $500,000, less than what the FCC fined CBS for televising Janet Jackson's infamous Super Bowl "wardrobe malfunction."

Despite these paltry penalties, or perhaps because of them, OSHA rarely refers a case of workplace death to federal prosecutors. Barstow found that in the two decades between 1982 and 2002, OSHA investigated 1,242 cases of workplace death due to "willful" violations. OSHA did not seek prosecution in 93 percent of those cases. Seventy of these employers were found to willfully violate safety regulations a second time, and were seldom prosecuted even after multiple violations and multiple deaths.

Talk Back/Fight Back

The lesson from the McWane example is to take a more active role in protecting your health at work. Don't sit back and wait for federal regulators to investigate—make sure your workplace is safe by filing a complaint for any safety violations and staying involved with the OSHA investigation. You can file an OSHA complaint online at www.osha.gov/pls/osha7/eComplaintForm.html, or by telephone, fax, or mail (look up your nearest OSHA office in the U.S. Government pages of your phone book or by visiting www.osha.gov). The best way to get an inspector to visit your workplace is to submit your complaint in writing. Include copies of pertinent documents and be specific with names and dates. If you want OSHA to keep your name confidential, and that of anyone else involved, you must ask in your written complaint. The law protects employees who initiate or participate in inspections from retaliation by their employers.

If OSHA investigates your complaint, be a participant and not a spectator! OSHA allows an authorized employee or union representative to accompany the inspector during an inspection; management is strictly forbidden to choose the representative. In cases where there is no union or employee representative, the inspector must speak "confidentially with a reasonable number of workers during the course of the investigation." Even if there is an employee representative, you have the right to speak confidentially with the OSHA investigator. This is your opportunity to tell OSHA about the hazards in your workplace and management's response to your requests for action. Be specific. Tell the inspector about any injuries, illnesses, or incidents that may have occurred. Be sure to tell the inspector if your employer has altered working conditions for the inspection, including turning machines on or off, recent ventilating of the premises, or any other change from normal working conditions.

Follow up on the result of your workplace investigation by requesting a review if OSHA doesn't issue a citation. Find out if there are any meetings or hearings to discuss your investigation, and get involved. If OSHA issues a citation or an abatement plan to correct the hazard that you don't agree with, you have the right to appeal. Write your local OSHA area director that the abatement plan is unacceptable. If OSHA grants your appeal, all sides will be heard by the independent Health Review Commission.

In extreme cases, OSHA will protect workers who walk off the job because of an imminent workplace danger, but only when all of the following criteria are met:

- Where possible, you have asked the employer to eliminate the danger, and the employer failed to do so; and
- You refused to work in "good faith." This means that you must genuinely believe that an imminent danger exists. Your refusal cannot be a disguised attempt to harass your employer or disrupt business; and
- A reasonable person would agree that there is a real danger of death or serious injury; and
- There isn't enough time, due to the urgency of the hazard, to get it corrected through regular enforcement channels, such as requesting an OSHA inspection

When all of these conditions are met, you take the following steps:

- Ask your employer to correct the hazard;
- Ask your employer for other work;

- Tell your employer that you won't perform the work unless and until the hazard is corrected; and
- Remain at the worksite until ordered to leave by your employer.

  [source: U.S. Department of Labor, Occupational Safety & Health Administration]

File a discrimination claim with OSHA within thirty days if you've been retaliated against for reporting a safety hazard or for refusing to work under an imminent danger. You may have further protections against imminent dangers and other safety hazards through your union or state regulator.

WORKERS COMP

Every state has a workers compensation program designed to cover employees who are injured on the job while also protecting employers from lawsuits. Details on the amount of compensation and what treatments are covered vary greatly from state to state, but these programs generally cover most part-time and full-time employees, with a few industry exclusions.

Workers compensation insurance covers both sudden injuries and chronic or slowly developing workplace injuries or illnesses. If you have a sudden injury make sure you tell the emergency room physician that you were injured on the job and provide the hospital with the information about your workers comp insurance carrier as soon as you can. For chronic or slowly developing workplace injuries and illnesses, you should seek medical care from an occupational illness specialist. This category includes repetitive stress injuries and repeated motion injuries, such as carpal tunnel syndrome, as well as illnesses that develop due to workplace conditions, or from special occupational demands such as hypertension in high-stress fields like law enforcement. When consulting your physician, be specific about how your injury or illness developed and what types of tasks you are required to perform at work in order to get the best possible treatment and rehabilitation plan, including time off work and other accommodations. While the law may not require your employer to cooperate with everything that your doctor recommends, it's important to get the best possible analysis of your condition and share it with your employer.

As soon as you become injured or ill, notify your employer, verbally if necessary and in writing as soon as possible. A written notice should also include the details and cause of your injury or illness. Be sure to check the deadline for filing a workers comp claim in your state, which can vary from just a few days to more than a year. Save copies of all your documents including receipts for any expenses you incur and your medical records, since you will need them if your employer disputes your claim.

If you are denied a workers comp claim, consider consulting a lawyer. Appealing a workers comp decision can be complex, but fortunately compensation specialists usually only charge a fee when an award is won. If you are told you cannot file for workers comp because your employer has classified you as an independent contractor, you may be able to file anyway. Many employers fraudulently classify workers as independent contractors to avoid workers comp insurance and unemployment insurance taxes. If you believe you are falsely classified as an independent contractor, file your workers comp claim anyway; it is your employers' responsibility to prove you are not an employee.

In the case of a workplace injury, see a professional health care provider and watch out for scams. If you want to see a doctor of your choice, you should include that stipulation in your written notification. If you do not, your employer or the insurance company may be able to dictate your health care provider for the first month after the injury. Some stingy companies hire con-men as health providers who are more concerned with lowering company costs than caring for injured employees. Consider another example from Tyler Pipe.

CASE STUDY

The company referred its employees to the occupational health provider Occu-Safe—a company with no history and few clients. It was founded by Mike Adams, who had previously presided over the bankruptcy of a failed air-conditioning business. Despite his lack of experience, Adams assured Tyler Pipe of a reduction in workers comp claims, and, after getting the contract, went out of his way to follow through on his promise. Occu-Safe rarely took workers off the job and even changed doctors' prescriptions to make sure employees could return to work.

Marcos Lopez, who had worked at Tyler Pipe for nearly three decades, slipped on the job and injured his back in 2002. Instead of going to the emergency room, Lopez sat and waited in pain and shock to be taken to Occu-Safe. There he was diagnosed with a strained back, given a few days off, and sent home with some painkillers. When Lopez returned to the Occu-Safe clinic for his third exam, he requested an x-ray, which showed a "bad compression fracture." Even then, Occu-Safe did not notify Lopez of his broken back. Instead, they began looking into the possibility that his bones had been weakened by cancer, which might relieve the company of responsibility. More than three weeks after the injury, Lopez finally saw a surgeon, who told him his condition had deteriorated since the accident and that he was "one hair" from being paralyzed for life. Lopez is suing Occu-Safe for malpractice. Adams countered with a libel suit against the *New York Times* for reporting the incident.

"NO BLACKS OR WOMEN NEED APPLY": DISCRIMINATION AT WORK

After so many civil rights legal victories, it's common for those who don't face discrimination to believe that it's a problem of the past. In a 2003 Gallup poll, a majority of whites (55 percent) believed that "racial minorities have equal job opportunities as whites" (only 17 percent of blacks agreed). However, a groundbreaking study released in 2002 by Alfred and Ruth Blumrosen—key architects of the EEOC from its inception in 1965—found that over one third of 200,000 mid-sized and large businesses engaged in "intentional discrimination" affecting two million women and minorities in 1999 alone. Another study from the same year, by MIT researchers, showed that job-seekers with "white-sounding" names were 50 percent more likely to be called for an interview than those with "African American-sounding" names with the same credentials.

After the terrorist attacks on the World Trade Center and the Pentagon on September 11, 2001, all Americans felt pain and loss along with a new sense of vulnerability. Perhaps none more than Arab and Muslim Americans, who instantly became victims of discrimination and harassment in the workplace. The EEOC (which lost its New York office in the attacks on the WTC) reported 944 charges of "backlash discrimination" in the first three years after 9/11 and a 100 percent increase in charges of discrimination against Muslims in that period.

CASE STUDY

The first "9/11 backlash" case was filed by the EEOC on September 27, 2002, on behalf of Bilan Nur against Alamo Rent A Car. Nur, a Somalian refugee who worked the front desk of Alamo Rent A Car in Phoenix, was disciplined and subsequently fired for wearing a head scarf in observance of the Muslim Holy month of Ramadan a year earlier. Alamo representatives claim that Nur had violated the company's "Dress Smart" policy, despite the fact that the policy states "hair pins or rubber bands should never be visible and can be concealed by using the Alamo scarf." Nur says she offered to wear the company scarf, but Alamo management decided that, while a scarf could be used to conceal hair pins and rubber bands, it could not be used to accommodate an employee's deeply held religious beliefs.

The EEOC filed another 9/11 backlash case that month on behalf of Zia Ayub, an Afghan American refugee and Muslim who had found asylum in the United States from the Soviet invasion of Afghanistan as a child, and became a U.S. citizen in 1992. Ayub had been ostracized by his coworkers at the Worcester Art Museum in Worcester, Massachusetts, after the 9/11 attacks, and was falsely reported by one of them to authorities as a terrorist. Despite seven years of service to the museum, Ayub was fired on January 4, 2002, without the museum's customary oral and written warnings and less than a month after receiving a raise. The museum claimed the firing was because he had taken too long to complete his security rounds, but the EEOC report cites at least four other security guards who had taken as long or longer to complete their rounds without consequence. In 2004, the museum agreed to pay $30,000 in lost wages and another $30,000 in damages.

Many of the post-9/11 backlash cases filed by the EEOC report incidents of harassment wherein managers or other employees use racial or religious epithets referring to the victims as "terrorists," "bin Laden," "al Qaeda," "Taliban," "dumb Muslim," and "sand niggers," along with other derogatory comments and threats of violence. In one EEOC case, filed in July 2003 on behalf of Karim El Raheb, an Egyptian general manager of the Houston-based seafood restaurant Pesce, the restaurant's coowner, Damian C. Mandola, went so far as to suggest that El Raheb could "pass for Hispanic," and should change his name to "something Latin," and later fired him on speculation that his Egyptian name and appearance were responsible for the restaurant's decline in profits in the months after 9/11 according to the suit. The restaurant settled for $150,000 in 2005.

You can defend yourself if faced with such discrimination in the workplace. Title VII of the *Civil Rights Act* of 1964 made it illegal for employers to discriminate on the basis of race, skin color, national origin, sex, and religion in regard to hiring, firing, promotions, pay rates, training programs, or any other aspect of employment, and created the Equal Employment Opportunity Commission to enforce the law. This protection covers all businesses with at least fifteen employees, including federal, state, and local governments, employment agencies, and unions. The *Equal Pay Act* of 1963, as previously noted, requires men and women to be paid equally for equal work. Workers are further protected by the *Pregnancy Discrimination Act*, which extends protections to pregnant women; the *Age Discrimination in Employment Act* of 1967, which extends protection to workers over forty; the *Americans with Disabilities Act* of 1990, which protects persons with physical or mental impairments and requires employers to provide reasonable accommodations in cases where it would not impose an "undue hardship" to the employer— in addition to laws protecting veterans and current members of the National Guard and military reservists returning home from service.

Sexual harassment, a type of sex discrimination in violation of Title VII of the *Civil Rights Act* of 1964, includes "unwelcome sexual advances, requests for sexual favors, and other verbal or physical conduct of a sexual nature when this conduct implicitly affects an individual's employment, unreasonably interferes with an individual's work performance, or creates an intimidating, hostile, or offensive work environment." Often, the harasser is a person in a position of power, such as a manager or supervisor, but the act can be committed by anyone in the workplace, even non-employees. An employer who permits or fails to correct offensive behavior from his workers, customers, or clients may be held accountable for sexual harassment.

Sex discrimination in the United States remains all too common and underreported. Women continue to take home less pay than men and are still subjected to a glass ceiling preventing them from reaching the highest managerial positions. A July 2004 study by the National Partnership for Women and Families found that sex discrimination charges filed with the EEOC rose over 10 percent in the proceeding decade, largely due to significant increases in charges filed by women of color, who face a double dose of discrimination. The report found a 20 percent increase in discrimination charges filed by African American women and a 68 percent increase by Hispanic women. While these numbers are nothing to celebrate, at least part of the reason for the rising rates of charges filed with the EEOC is that more women are aware of their rights and are choosing to defend themselves in the workplace.

Recent lawsuits show that sex discrimination can strike anywhere, from Wall Street to Main Street. In July 2004, Morgan Stanley settled the second biggest sex discrimination lawsuit in EEOC history, worth $54 million to as many as 340 women in top positions at the brokerage firm. The deal was struck just moments before the beginning of the trial, which was expected to reveal incriminating details of workplace stripteases, lewd behavior (including a breast-shaped cake at a company party), charges of sexual harassment, and a culture of discrimination keeping women out of the highest paying executive positions and in fear of retribution. The Morgan Stanley settlement is just one of many recent payouts for sex discrimination by Wall Street firms; Merrill Lynch and Smith Barney have each paid millions to settle lawsuits over the disparity in pay and promotions between men and women in executive positions. A survey by the Securities and Exchange Commission in 2004 revealed that only 19 percent of managing directors are women.

While these few women are well-paid Wall Street power-players, there are many more women in the low-paying service and retail sectors that are also vulnerable to sex discrimination. EEOC spokesperson James Ryan explained that women in low-paying fields "don't know any better and put up with abuse because they don't understand their rights and can't afford to lose their jobs if they complain." Fortunately, at least one high-profile case filed without the EEOC is seeking to even the score for employees of America's largest low-wage, private-sector employer: Wal-Mart.

A pending class action lawsuit, covering 1.6 million current and former Wal-Mart employees, could change the landscape of sex discrimination law. While the retail sector averaged a 56 percent female management rate generally, Wal-Mart's management was only 34 percent female, with mounting evidence of women being passed over for promotions and pay raises. The Wal-Mart case will likely take years to litigate, but the pressure it puts on employers to treat their employees fairly can already be felt. And as with every high-profile discrimination case, the more that workers become aware of their rights, the more willing they become to fight for them.

Still, many women in the workplace find themselves discriminated against without the benefit of a group of lawyers working on their behalf. Victims of sexual harassment often face the terrifying choice between putting up with demeaning, illegal abuse to pay the bills, and taking the often lonely and difficult road of reporting the crime. Many victims of sexual harassment never report it. One recent survey by Louis Harris and Associates found that 31 percent of women and 7 percent of men have claimed to be sexually harassed in their place of work, but 62 percent of them took no action against their harasser.

CASE STUDY

One reason is that a hostile work environment breeds a culture of discrimination, making it difficult to find someone to turn to for help. Take the example of a woman we'll call Jane Doe to protect her privacy. According to the lawsuit filed by the EEOC, the management trainee at an Applebee's Neighborhood Grill and Bar in Pennsylvania was subjected to sexual harassment by management and staff immediately upon being hired in October 2001. The restaurant's manager asked her to participate in a "threesome with his wife and explicitly described to Ms. [Doe] how good he was at 'oral sex.'" Another manager, according to the lawsuit, "made frequent comments regarding her breasts, and made frequent attempts to feel her breasts by placing his hand down her cleavage to remove her name tag."

The woman's nightmare was further compounded a month later when she complained to upper management. The assistant general manager told her to "deal with it," while the general manager laughed and questioned her sexual orientation. That month, Doe transferred to a new location, filed an internal complaint, and complained to the HR department, which informed her that "this was not the first complaint they heard about [that] facility." Then, at a company Christmas party, the manager again commented on her appearance, made repeated "inappropriate sexual comments," and aggressively fondled and grabbed her. She reported his behavior the next day to the Training Coordinator Manager, who told her that that manager was "doing it to everyone—not just you." A few hours later he fired her, saying she didn't "fit in."

Doe took her charges to the EEOC, which filed suit. Just before the trial was to begin, Applebee's agreed to settle, paying $137,500 to her and agreeing to conduct training on sexual harassment and retaliation at both locations. An EEOC spokesman said that this case highlights common discrimination problems in restaurants and bars, which are especially prone to harassment due to the presence of alcohol, along with the combination of young workers and older managers.

Talk Back/Fight Back

If you have been the victim of discrimination in the workplace, you can file a complaint with the EEOC. Also, a person or an organization can file on behalf of another person to protect their identity, though the EEOC protects employees who file charges from retaliation by their employer. Keep in mind, the EEOC gives you only 180 days from the date of the offense to file a complaint, so keep a close eye on the calendar. (Because some states have human rights departments or Fair Employment Practices Agencies [FEPA] that allow up to 300 days to file a discrimination charge, you may still be able to file through your state even if your 180 days have passed.)

Many companies have discrimination and sexual harassment policies and procedures to protect their employees. Ideally, you would use these options to try to resolve the issue before filing with the EEOC. In the case of harassment, confront the person committing the offensive behavior and make clear that it's unwanted and that he or she must stop. If your employer has a procedure for responding to discrimination and harassment, file an internal complaint. Keep a detailed record of these exchanges. Write down all the offending comments, the names of those involved, including the harasser(s), other victims, and any witnesses, and the dates

If your employer fails to resolve the issue to your satisfaction, your next step is to take it to the EEOC or your state's FEPA. You can file a complaint by mail or at the nearest EEOC or FEPA office; to find it go to www.eeoc.gov or call (800) 669-4000 to be connected to the nearest regional office. It doesn't matter which department you take your complaint to—your state FEPA will cross-file to see that you're protected under federal law, and EEOC will do the same for state law.

When the EEOC receives your complaint, it will decide whether to proceed with an investigation or to dismiss your charge if there is not enough evidence. If EEOC investigators proceed with your charge, they will likely request interviews, documents, a visit to your workplace, or any other information pertinent to the case. EEOC may seek to reach a settlement at any time during the investigation; if no settlement can be reached, the investigation will continue. The EEOC may dismiss a charge at any time if it decides that further investigation won't produce enough evidence to prove the discrimination charge.

If both parties agree to participate in its confidential, voluntary program, EEOC will set up a mediation meeting to find a suitable solution for everyone. No attorneys are necessary for the mediation, but either party may have one on hand. Mediation is not for everybody. If you feel deeply wronged by your employer, you may want to continue with your charge—a settlement usually precludes a party from acknowledging wrongdoing. Still, in 2003, the program settled 69 percent of cases that went to mediation in about half the time as the investigative process. If a settlement cannot be reached through mediation, the investigation will continue.

If the EEOC finds that the evidence proves your discrimination charge, it will seek a remedy from your employer. This may include payment of back wages, retroactive promotions, reinstatements, or various other actions to correct the discriminatory practices and may also include reimbursement of lawyers' fees, expert witness fees, and other legal expenses. Punitive

damages may be sought for employers who engaged in intentional discrimination or acted with malice or reckless indifference.

If the EEOC cannot successfully reach a deal with your employer, it may
decide to file a federal lawsuit. If it doesn't, or if a charge is dismissed outright, you will be issued a "right to sue" notice and the responsibility for holding your employer accountable falls back to you. While the process of filing a
federal discrimination lawsuit is time-consuming and expensive, there are fortunately a number of organizations that will help you with a discrimination
case. Additionally many law schools provide legal aid for discrimination and
employment law and in some cases will even represent you in court. Call the
law schools in your area to see what assistance they can offer.

Losing Work: Unemployment Benefits

The "employment at will" doctrine makes it difficult for non-
union employees of private companies to protect their jobs. Unless
an employee has a contract stipulating under what circumstances
employment may be terminated, in most cases you may be fired or
laid off at your boss's will or whim, providing of course the firing
is nondiscriminatory. You may have some claim to wrongful termination if your employer does not follow its own stated policy. So
keep copies of your employer's written policies or employee handbook.

If you are fired without cause, you are most likely eligible for
unemployment compensation benefits. The unemployment compensation program is a complex web of insurance policies run jointly by the states and the federal government and paid for by payroll
taxes on employers. Qualifications and details vary from state to state,
but unemployment insurance generally covers all full- and part-time
workers who lost their jobs without good cause. (For your state's
details, contact your nearest Unemployment Insurance Office or
Employment Security Division.)

Generally, states require that you are a U.S. citizen, or documented worker, who has worked a substantial amount of time (commonly around six months out of the year before becoming unemployed) for a stated minimum in total wages. If you don't meet the standards for your state's minimum earnings in total wages, see if your state is one of the eighteen that offers an alternative base rate to help you qualify for benefits if your earnings were more recent than the standard qualifying base period. States generally require that you are currently available and physically able to perform your previous or an equivalent job.

You cannot claim benefits if you have broken reasonable workplace rules or have been fired for deliberate and repeated misconduct including missing work or showing up late without a valid excuse. If you turn down an equivalent position or similar work without explanation, you might also be exempted from unemployment compensation. Workers on a union strike do not qualify for compensation, but some states do offer benefits to union workers who have been locked out by management. Finally, if you quit without good cause, you cannot qualify for unemployment benefits.

In some cases, you can quit your job and still receive unemployment compensation, such as if you were a victim of abuse or your working conditions were significantly dangerous; if your duties are unreasonably and dramatically altered or your wages or benefits drastically reduced without consent; or if your company moves far enough that it is unreasonable to commute. Usually, however, you need to appeal to management before you quit.

To claim your unemployment compensation, find your nearest unemployment office. Many states will allow you to file over the phone and in some states phone filing is virtually your only option. When you call, or go in person, be prepared. You should have your Social Security number, a state-issued ID, your documentation papers (for legal aliens), as well as your address and phone number.

Have on hand a list of names and addresses of all the employers you've worked for in the past couple of years. In addition, it's a good idea to keep your pay stubs and W-2 forms, because they have the pertinent IRS employer identification numbers. If there is any documentation proving your unemployment, such as a letter of dismissal, have it and your employer's unemployment insurance account number with you.

You may start receiving your benefits right away, but some states may wait to hear your employer's side of the story before they send out checks. You will be notified when your unemployment compensation is approved or denied. Generally you will have to continue to claim each week to confirm that you continue to meet the conditions for receiving unemployment compensation. Unemployment generally covers you for twenty-six weeks, but can be extended by Congress in an economic downturn.

So you can be covered, *if* you're not defrauded by employers. The National Employment Law Project reported that workers were cheated out of $1.3 billion in unemployment compensation benefits in 2002. The most common employers' scheme is misclassifying employees as independent contractors (a classification of worker that doesn't qualify for unemployment and other company benefits). The Department of Labor found that at least 80,000 workers a year lose unemployment benefits to this ruse.

If you are turned down for unemployment benefits, request a hearing to reverse the decision. Your denial letter should inform you of the process and time limits for filing an appeal, generally a week to a month. While you are going through the appeal process, continue to claim your benefits in order to receive payment once your decision is reversed. You have the option of getting a lawyer for the hearing, but this process is generally informal, and you can represent yourself if you prepare carefully.

Join a Union! By far the best way to protect your rights in your workplace is to join a union with your fellow workers. Union members take home 28 percent more in pay than non-union members; are more likely to have health coverage (86 percent compared with 59 percent); and are far more likely to have an employer-sponsored, guaranteed pension plan (70 percent to 16 percent).

The *National Labor Relations Act* preserves your right to join a union and bargain collectively, and that includes freely discussing unions in non-union workplaces; expressing your support for a union; wearing pro-union buttons; and distributing union materials (though this should be done in nonwork areas, like a break room, and while you're off the clock.) These are the rights of nearly every worker in the country, though some management employees and other classifications of employees may be exempt.

In this Bush era, however, businesses are increasingly hostile to employees who want to unionize—so be diligent *and* careful when starting a union. More than half of employers threaten to close up shop if a union is formed—though only 1 percent actually does so. Twenty-five percent of employers fire at least one worker, illegally, for activity during a union drive. And because 75 percent of employers hire consultants to help them fight the union, you shouldn't go it alone either. Find out which unions are strong in your area and profession and ask for their help. Know your rights and get in touch with a professional organizer. For more help, you can look up nearby unions in the phone book, or go to www.aflcio.org/aboutus/unioncities/index.cfm to find a local union council.

Non-union disputes Most workers don't have the luxury of union representation. When a problem arises at work we are often on our own. The best way to get a problem fixed, according to employment law professor Federick T. Golder, is to negotiate with management.

When management is unreasonable, however, there are federal and state laws in place to protect you (as detailed throughout this chapter). Remember, though, when you take your cause to a government agency or to court, an employer may interpret it as warfare. Most of the time, you're protected from retaliation, but if you lose your job, you'll have to prove why you were fired. The legal battle may take years and become very expensive. For a good discussion on the risks involved and other strategies for confronting your employer, see Golder's, *Uncivil Rights: The Better Way of Resolving Conflicts at Work*. To find a lawyer who specializes in employment law, see the National Employment Lawyers Association at www.nela.org.

Fix It: Protecting Workers' Rights

Wages and Hours   We need to reform the Bush administration's misguided changes to overtime rules and set some reasonable standards that protect workers' rights to be paid fairly for their time. In addition, it's time to raise the federal minimum wage. At the current rate of $5.15 per hour, established in the fiscal year of 1996, a full-time worker would make $10,712 a year—not enough to sustain a family. Democratic lawmakers attempted to raise it to a modest $7.00 per hour with the *Fair Wage Act of 2004*, but couldn't get it enacted by a Republican Congress. There is also a growing movement to enhance employee income through local "living wage" laws; scores of local governments are establishing higher minimum pay and benefits as a condition of awarding government contracts.

Health and Safety   David Barstow and Lowell Bergman's investigative series on McWane, Inc., led to a Justice Department investigation of the company's factories across the country, but it also exposed OSHA's weak enforcement record. The Bush administration responded in 2003 by announcing that OSHA would be given new powers to go after sprawling corporate entities, like McWane, who repeatedly ignore workplace safety standards. As a result, OSHA has pledged to conduct more follow-up inspections of businesses with violations of "the highest severity."

Margaret Seminario, director of safety and health for the AFL-

CIO, doesn't think this policy goes far enough. "The idea of trying to focus on employers who are failing to abate and are repeat violators is not a bad idea…. [W]hat seems to be missing in this policy is enhanced enforcement." Seminario's analysis of OSHA's performance during the Bush administration showed that the average fines had decreased 26 percent for willful violations and 68 percent for repeat offenders. Indeed, at the same time that the Bush White House announced the policy changes, it proposed a cut in OSHA's budget. OSHA has raised its maximum fine levels once in its entire history—from $10,000 to $70,000 for a willful violation in 1990—yet it currently has a smaller staff than it did in 1980.

The penalty for the negligent death of an employee should be increased, and enforcement of the crime strengthened. In the words of Reagan administration OSHA official Patrick Tyson, "six months is nuts!" In response, then Senator (now Governor) Jon Corzine of New Jersey proposed legislation to make the crime a felony and raise the six-month maximum penalty to ten years in prison. To help, contact your representatives and tell them to support the lives of workers by supporting the proposed *Wrongful Death Accountability Act*. Even then, the OSHA bureaucracy must be restructured to work with the Justice Department in pursuit of employers who cause the deaths of their employees or repeatedly put lives in danger.

OSHA also needs to regain its role of developing and setting industry regulations. This process has always been slow, but under the Bush administration it has been nonexistent—or in reverse. Not only have no significant new health and safety regulations been promulgated, but the White House and Congress have killed or drastically slowed important new rules on tuberculosis, protective equipment, and record-keeping. The withdrawal of ergonomic regulation was an especially damaging blow to hundreds of thousands of American workers.

Ergonomic injuries are by far the most common type of workplace injury. Some 500,000 to 1 million workers miss work each year due to ergonomic-related problems such as: musculoskeletal disorders, repetitive motion injuries, carpal tunnel syndrome, and back injuries. After a decade of work, and much partisan battling, OSHA finally presented a set of ergonomic regulations that passed a divided Congress. The ergonomic standards were completed in November 2000. But shortly after Bush took office, he became the first president to invoke the power of the *Regulatory Review Act* and overturned the regulations. OSHA's rules would have required employers to evaluate their workplaces and take steps to reduce risks when they're found. Advocates say that the new regulations could have prevented up to half of all cases of ergonomic injuries, protecting employees and saving employers workers comp costs and lost production time due to rehabilitation leave. The Clinton administration's ergonomic regulations would save money—and workers—and should be reinstated.

Continuing the Fight Against Discrimination   The EEOC is an important resource for employees who face discrimination, but only about 20 percent of charges are actually resolved successfully. (The rest are dropped either because of lack of evidence or for administrative reasons.) While it's possible to file a discrimination suit independently of the EEOC, that process is particularly difficult for those in low-income fields, who are most vulnerable to discrimination.

The first step in fighting discrimination is to properly fund the EEOC. Under President Bush, the EEOC faced considerable budget cuts creating an $18 million shortfall in 2003 that threatened to temporarily shut down the agency (the total budget hovers around $325 million). The EEOC is badly in need of additional funding just to keep up with its investigation and litigation efforts.

Additionally, the EEOC should expand its research and track developments in discrimination of various classes of minorities, such as women of color, who have endured an increase in discrimination charges in recent years. One valuable approach was proposed by Alfred and Ruth Blumrosen, who developed a methodology that could allow the government to look at hiring trends in specific companies and by industry based on data already submitted to the EEOC.

To expand worker protections and update the *Civil Rights Act* of 1964, Senator Edward Kennedy sponsored *FAIRNESS: The Civil Rights Act* of 2004. Recent Supreme Court rulings have weakened employee protections for women and minorities. This bill will help counteract those rulings and reinforce equality in the American workplace by allowing victims of wage discrimination to seek punitive damages; giving employees the right to share wage information without the threat of employer retribution; removing the arbitrary cap on awards for victims of sex discrimination; and ending mandatory arbitration clauses that force workers to sign away their right to sue.

CHAPTER 4

THE RIGHTS OF CONSUMERS OF PRODUCTS

[Consumers] are the largest economic group in the economy, affecting and affected by almost every public and private economic decision. Two-thirds of all spending in the economy is by consumers. But they are the only important group in the economy who are not effectively organized, whose views are often not heard.

—President John F. Kennedy

Consumers face a daunting task in the marketplace. Millions of products vie for our attention every day. Advertisements flood our homes and cars on television and radio, our communities on signs and billboards, even public restrooms and taxis are not immune from such invasions—they're so ubiquitous that *Consumer Reports* estimated that the twenty-first-century American is exposed to 247 of them every day!

But how can we tell if the claims ads make are true and what can we do if they're not? The old adage of caveat emptor—buyer beware—is still the best advice. Smart consumers do their research before making a purchase. The Internet has made comparison shopping far easier and less time-consuming. But even the best-prepared consumers still face fraudulent merchants and manufacturers, product and food safety breaches, and countless other problems. With corporations claiming so much power over our lives, it's time to realize that power comes from consumers. When you get ripped off — hold the companies accountable. When you discover a dangerous product—report it. The key to taking back your power is knowing your rights and defending yourself in the marketplace.

KEY CONSUMER LAWS

Contract Law   Consumer contract laws have been developed from centuries of common law rulings in the United States and England which establish that the contract between the buyer and seller is a binding and enforceable agreement. Contracts do not have to be long legal documents full of small print and complicated clauses; they don't even have to be written to be legitimate. In fact, most of our contracts are oral or implied. Whenever the seller agrees to deliver a product or service and the buyer agrees to pay a price, they enter into a contractual agreement. Because oral contracts can be difficult to enforce in a dispute, it's always best to have a written document, especially for high-priced or potentially troublesome purchases. There is no law that the contracts you agree to have to be a good deal, but unconscionable and unfair contracts may not be enforceable.

Uniform Commercial Code (UCC)   In an effort to standardize the various common law rulings, forty-nine states adopted the *UCC* in the 1960s, with Louisiana adopting portions of it later. Among the basic consumer rights ensured by the *UCC* is the "implied warranty of merchantability," your guarantee that the product purchased will do what it's supposed to do. Likewise, the "implied warranty of fitness for a particular purpose" ensures that if a merchant advises you to purchase a product for a specific purpose or under particular conditions, the product must perform for such purposes and conditions.

Magnuson-Moss Warranty Act   Congress enacted this law in 1975, to give consumers more warranty information before they buy and more rights afterward. The law requires warrantors to disclose in the title whether it is a full or limited warranty; to provide a readable document explaining the coverage; and to make that information available to consumers before they make a purchase. The law prohibits tie-in requirements in warranties that would force you to buy the same brand replacement parts when other brands would work just as well and bans deceptive warranty terms that mislead the buyer into believing they have protection when they don't.

Lemon Laws Each state has expanded the UCC and Magnuson-Moss Act by passing legislation that specifically protects auto buyers from the sour experience of purchasing a lemon. Every state covers new cars, and "certified used cars" bought from dealerships, while about half cover leased cars. Only nine states cover used cars. The details of the lemon laws vary from state to state, but they generally require the manufacturer to provide a replacement or a refund if a car repeatedly breaks down.

The Mail or Telephone Order Merchandise Rule The FTC instituted this rule in 1975 to ensure that consumers could rely on a standard level of service for mail-order purchases. The rule also applies now to Internet purchases. It establishes that a business must ship an order within the time stated or within thirty days if no time-frame has been declared. If the merchant cannot meet the deadline, it must notify you of a new shipping date and allow you the option of accepting or canceling with a full refund. Absent your consent, the company must cancel the order and issue you a full refund within seven business days, or one billing cycle for credit card charges.

Cooling Off Rule When you change your mind about something you bought at a store, the company's return policy will usually determine whether or not you can return it, and whether you'll get cash or credit. But for items worth $25 or more that are sold at your home or in another place that is not the seller's usual place of business—as is the case with a door-to-door salesperson or a booth at the county fair—the FTC has instituted a three-day cooling off period. The rule was written to protect consumers from the high-pressure and often misleading sales practices of traveling sales artists that leave people in awe of the product—and the sales performance—until they realize they've just spent $2,000 on a vacuum cleaner they could have had for $200. Salespeople are required by law to inform you of your cancellation rights and provide you with copies of the cancellation forms.

Product Safety Laws During the "consumer decade," from 1965 to 1975, advocates led by Ralph Nader had great success in persuading Congress to enact stricter safety laws for consumers. 1966 saw the passage of the *National Traffic and Motor Vehicle Safety Act* and the *Highway Safety Act*, which created the National Highway Safety Bureau. In 1970, the Bureau became the National Highway Traffic Safety Administration (NHTSA), which conducts research on automobile safety, sets industry standards, and oversees recalls. In 1972, Congress passed the *Consumer Product Safety Act*, which created the Consumer Product Safety Commission (CPSC) to "protect the public against unreasonable risks of injuries and deaths associated with consumer products." The CPSC sets safety standards and oversees recalls for about 15,000 consumer products. The Food and Drug Administration (FDA) has been in existence since the *Food and Drug Act* of 1906. It was expanded to include cosmetics in 1938—and its powers were expanded to test drugs for "safety and efficacy" in 1962 after the thalidomide tragedy. Today the agency is responsible for overseeing about a quarter of all consumer goods.

SHOPPING BASICS

The first line of defense for all consumers is to know what you're looking for before you go to the store or the website. *Consumer Reports* is unsurpassed in its product evaluation and is available online at www.consumerreports.org. But even simple comparison shopping for prices and warranty terms will get you a leg up when it's time to buy, and the Internet has helped level the playing field between sellers and buyers.

It's important to learn about the seller. Take into account word of mouth experiences from friends, family, and coworkers. Good retailers know that it's the best advertising money can't buy and will go out of their way to make customers happy. If you're approached by a seller you don't know, at home or online, always check them out before you buy anything or give them any personal or financial information. To do a background check on a merchant or a manufacturer, you can contact the Better Business Bureau, your state Attorney General's office, or a local consumer authority to see if any complaints have been made against them.

Getting a Good Deal　If you've done your research, you should feel comfortable negotiating. Many stores have price-matching policies to meet or beat their competitors' best prices. Watch out for retailers that stock virtually identical items with different model numbers than their competitors. Whether or not the store advertises price-matching, it's a good idea to bring in advertisements from competitors or Internet ads to see if you can score a deal. While haggling isn't as prominent in the United States as in many other countries, salespeople often have the leeway to negotiate—especially on big-ticket items.

It never hurts to ask for a discount. Many retailers offer discounts to seniors and students, for example. Club memberships, like AARP and AAA, can also save you money, and businesses don't always publicize them.

There Is Power in How You Pay　Remember, you often have the most power before you buy because you have something the seller wants—cash. Once you make a purchase, however, there are still ways to excercise control over the transaction. Paying by credit card gives you the most power. If there's a problem with the merchandise that you can't resolve with the merchant, you can dispute the bill through your credit card company and get a chargeback. (See "Billing Disputes" in the next chapter for more details.) Some credit cards also have perks that extend your warranty on merchandise bought with your card. With a personal check, you can cancel payment if something goes awry before the check clears, and there's a verifiable record of the transaction. Debit cards also have a built-in transaction record, but you have little recourse if there's a problem with the merchant, since the money is electronically transferred almost instantly. Obviously, paying with cash gives you little leeway once you hand it over. Regardless of how you pay, always save your transaction receipt in case a dispute arises—a credit card statement or canceled check doesn't have the same legal clout as your itemized sales receipt.

Know Your Rights   Usually, when there is a problem with a product, the solution is simple: return the item for a replacement or a refund. Knowing the return policy before you make a purchase will save you cash. A lenient policy may be your only resort if you change your mind about a product (if the product is defective, however, the law is on your side). Many states and municipalities have regulations regarding how merchants can issue receipts and return policies. In New York City, for example, consumers should get a receipt automatically for any transaction over $20 and are able to request one for transactions over $5. Merchants can establish their own return policies, but they must make them clear by prominently displaying them on signs or on the receipt. If there is no policy displayed, consumers have twenty days to get a refund in the manner that they paid.

CASE STUDY

When Priscilla Broomell went shopping for a laptop at Best Buy, she ended up buying a less powerful computer than she intended based on a salesperson's recommendation and assurance that she could return it within fourteen days if she was dissatisfied. When Broomell returned it just days later, she found that the store intended to keep 15 percent of her refund, worth over $200, as a "restocking fee." After Broomell told her story to the *Philadelphia Inquirer*'s consumer columnist, Jeff Gelles, Best Buy refunded the remaining 15 percent "in an effort to build customer loyalty." They have a point; policies like Best Buy's "restocking fee" are a disloyal way to punish the majority of honest consumers for the deeds of the few who abuse return policies.

Contracts   Every time you make a purchase, you enter into a contract. One of the basic tenets of the free-market system is that, for better or worse, everybody is free to negotiate the terms of their contracts, which must then be honored. While there are some exceptions for fraudulent, unreasonable, or unconscionable contract terms, there is generally little you can do if you agree to a bad deal.

Everyone has learned how to draft a contract, whether they realize it or not. For most of us, it's just second nature. A contract is completed when an offer is made for a product or service and you accept it by exchanging money or some other consideration, such as a product or service of equal value. You also have the option of making a counteroffer. Once you make a counteroffer, the other party can choose to accept, make another counteroffer, or decline. Until the offer is accepted, the party that made the offer can withdraw it. In the case of most consumer goods, the offer is made in writing via a price tag or advertisement, and the seller must honor the advertised terms.

Oral contracts and written contracts are both binding and legal. When you go to the fruit stand and pay fifty cents for an apple, you probably wouldn't ask for a receipt. However, when you buy household goods and other items, you want a receipt as proof of the contract, so you can return it if there is a problem. The receipt usually says how much you paid for an item and tells you under what conditions you can return it. When you make large purchases, like a car or a house, a written contract is drawn up to better define the responsibilities of the parties involved. If a dispute arises, oral contracts can be difficult to prove, so get something in writing whenever there is a potential for problems.

Implied Warranties   For consumer transactions, the seller is obliged to provide a warranty for the products you buy, whether or not they're acknowledged by your contract. Under the *UCC*, all transactions are covered by an implied warranty of "merchantability," as well as an implied warranty of "fitness for a particular purpose." These warranties go into effect automatically every time a sale is made. The laws apply to people who are in business to sell a product, not necessarily private individuals—in case you needed another reason to buy from reputable merchants.

As mentioned, the implied warranty of merchantability is the seller's promise to you that everything you buy is in working order and will do what it's supposed to do at the time it's sold. In other words, if you buy a watch, the implied warranty of merchantability is a guarantee that the watch will keep time. If the merchant tells you that the watch is waterproof, the implied warrantee of fitness guarantees that it will work underwater. Or to paraphrase a song in *The Fantasticks*, "Buy a carrot, get a carrot, not a brussels sprout!"

Unlike most express warranties, implied warranties are not promises that the product will last a certain amount of time. Nor do they cover problems that arise from misuse or ordinary wear and tear. The *UCC* does not provide a timetable for claims regarding implied warranties, but the statute of limitations generally gives you as much as four years from the date of purchase.

Implied warranties apply to used products as well as new ones. Merchants have the option of disclaiming the implied warranties of fitness and merchantability by marking them "as is." The law requires merchants to inform consumers in a "conspicuous manner" and in writing if they disclaim an implied warranty. The specific requirements vary from state to state, but stores may have a sign at the checkout counter informing customers that all items are sold "as is," or "with all faults," or the goods may be thus labeled individually. A number of states do not allow merchants to disclaim implied warranties at all.* Furthermore, a merchant cannot disclaim an implied warranty if it has offered any kind of written warranty. If you buy an item "as is" that is dangerous or causes a personal injury, the seller is still liable for selling a dangerous product. Disclaiming an implied warranty does not disclaim the seller's product liability.

---

*They are Alabama, Connecticut, Kansas, Maine, Maryland, Massachusetts, Minnesota, Mississippi, New Hampshire, Vermont, Washington, West Virginia, and the District of Columbia.

Express Warranties   Express warranties differ from implied warranties because they are explicit statements that the seller or manufacturer makes about a particular product. Any claim about a product, from an advertisement to a salesperson's promise, is an express warranty. It can cover any number of issues including the durability of a product or the remedy available for defective items, or even personal satisfaction—such as when an advertisement offers "satisfaction guaranteed or your money back."

Express warranties must designate whether they are "full" or "limited." To be considered "full" under the *Magnuson-Moss Act*, a warranty must meet the following terms:

- It must not have any limitations on the duration of implied warranties;
- It must cover anyone who owns the product during the warranty period and not limit coverage to the original purchaser;
- Services offered under the warranty must be of no cost to the purchaser;
- The purchaser must be given a choice between a refund or replacement if the product could not be repaired after reasonable attempts;
- It must not obligate the purchaser to any duty—such as returning a registration card—as a condition of service, unless the seller demonstrates that the duty is reasonable.

Any warranty that does not meet all of these requirements is a "limited" warranty. Additionally, a "multiple" warranty offers full terms for some parts and limited terms for others, or, full terms for a duration and then limited terms for the rest of the warranty.

A written warranty cannot void or change your basic protections under the *UCC*'s implied warrantees. The only exceptions are that a limited warranty can limit the duration of an implied warranty to the length of the written warranty; and, when a manufacturer provides a written warranty for a product, the seller can disclaim the implied warranties, in effect transferring the warranty responsibility to the manufacturer.

Extended Warranty/Service Contract When you go to buy a major appliance chances are you'll be asked if you'd like to spend even more money on an extended warranty. This is becoming increasingly common even for less expensive items. An editor for *Consumer Reports* told of his experience when a cashier pushed a service contract for a $37 DVD player "that would probably cost more to fix than replace."

These extra "warranties" are not actually warranties at all, but service contracts. The idea behind them is that you pay extra in advance to have a product fixed *if and when it breaks down*. You may want to ask a merchant why they sell a product that is so prone to malfunction, but you probably won't get the real answer. Retailers make as much as 40 to 80 percent in profits from money spent on service contracts—for some electronics stores and appliance dealers, milking these cash cows keeps them in business.

In fact, few people who buy these contracts ever need to use them. Most defects appear early (when the manufacturer's warranty is still in effect), or later (after the service contract has ended). Service contracts, in short, are expensive insurance policies to protect your goods against defects precisely at the moment they are least likely to occur.

For most products, you can just say no to service contracts. The experts at *Consumer Reports* advise getting them only for the biggest and most repair-prone purchases. Expensive and fragile laptop computers and new technology like liquid-crystal display (LCD) TVs make their list.

If you do consider a service contract, ask the following questions: Does the service contract begin after the manufacturer's warranty expires? (There's no reason to pay extra to duplicate coverage offered under your manufacturers warranty.) Who backs the contract? (It could be the store, the manufacturer, or an independent administrator.) What happens if the company that backs your contract goes out of business? Will your policy go belly-up with the company that backs it, or is there an insurance policy in place that would guarantee your benefits?

Talk Back/Fight Back

When you have a problem with a product, your first step is to go back to the place of purchase. Most of the time your solution is simple: claim your refund or replacement in accordance with the store's return policy. In many cases merchants will extend their policies to keep your business; so if you're past the deadline, give it a try anyway. If the item is defective, you can use the *UCC*'s implied warranties to back you up.

Clearly articulate your problem. A merchant is less likely to be helpful if demands are made without explanation. Go through all the events and show your sales receipts and credit card statements to back you up. If you're a regular customer, highlight your loyalty by bringing in past sales receipts or credit card transaction records.

Decide how you want the problem resolved and express it clearly. Let the merchant know what will make you a happy customer. Whether it's a refund or exchange, a repair or warranty extension, or a gift certificate, don't make them guess.

If you can, try to go back to the store when it's least likely to be busy. Some stores train clerks to make no exceptions to return policies but allow managers and supervisors to bend the rules; instead of venting your frustration on a sales clerk, politely ask if a manager can help you. Managers and owners are more likely to be around during a weekday and they're your best bet for a satisfactory solution. There may be plenty of reasons to get upset when you're being denied good service, but the best results come from a calm and confidant manner when making your request.

Whether on the phone or in the store, you're usually not dealing with the person responsible for your problem. There are two old adages to keep in mind (not to mix oil and vinegar metaphors). It's true that the squeaky wheel always gets the oil, but you catch more flies with honey than you do with vinegar. While you're not likely to get satisfaction unless you complain, abusive language or behavior will get you nowhere. One consumer representative for a major toy manufacturer told the *Miami Herald* that her company, which offers generous vouchers and refunds to dissatisfied consumers, is likely to forward callers who are impolite or abusive to a "restricted area," where a special manager deals with them.

If returning to the place of purchase doesn't solve your problem, contact the manufacturer. The address and/or phone number for customer service should be included on the product packaging. If you've lost the packaging, or can't find the parent company that owns your product's brand, the *Thomas Register of American Manufacturers* is available at most libraries and has a searchable database at www.thomasnet.com.

There's nothing wrong with complaining to both ends at once. You can return an unsatisfactory product to the store where you bought it, and simultaneously complain to the manufacturer about your dissatisfaction with the product. The merchant wants to keep your business as a customer, regardless of what product caused the problem. The manufacturer's main concern is its brand reputation, and may meet your demands to keep your loyalty.

Don't be afraid to escalate. If the store manager doesn't help you, write a letter to the corporate office. Politely mention your other options to let them know you mean business. They can include going to the media, a consumer group, a government agency—or court.

If the seller or manufacturer doesn't resolve your complaint to your satisfaction, take it to the next level. Contact your state's Attorney General or a local consumer protection office. For criminal fraud, contact your district attorney's office. Your state's Weights and Measures Office is responsible for overseeing the proper measurement of consumer goods. This includes the butcher's and grocer's scales, the meters at the gas pump, odometers on cars, taxi meters, and claims made on packages about the weight or count of the products inside.

The Council of Better Business Bureaus is a network of organizations sponsored by businesses to oversee disputes and complaints. These non-profit organizations do not take sides in disputes and they have no enforcement power, but they do wield a good deal of influence by keeping track of complaints against businesses and by mediating disputes.

According to Sheila Adkins, a spokesperson for the Council of Better Business Bureaus, "most consumer complaints get resolved without entering into a dispute resolution program." That's because the BBB has a relationship with companies. The consumer may get stuck complaining to the bottom rung, but "the BBB goes right to the top." According to Adkins, the BBB letterhead may make all the difference. "Businesses know that consumers trust the BBB and, if the consumer has a complaint, it will go on the record. No business wants those blemishes on the record."

Finally, both the *UCC* and the *Magnuson-Moss Warranty Act* allow you to sue for breach of contract when you have a problem with a merchant. A written, express warranty may require you to enter into an alternative dispute resolution program before filing in federal court (the warranty must disclose this clause), but you may have further protections under state law. You can also recover smaller amounts by taking the merchants or manufacturers to small claims court. (See "The Rights of Clients" chapter for more on this option.)

INTERNET SHOPPING

Knowing who you're dealing with is always important, but *especially* when you're shopping online. The Internet provides the perfect anonymity for scam artists looking for cover.

Most legitimate websites have an "about us" or "contact us" page that gives you information about the company. You should get an address and phone number of the home office that you can contact for more information. Be wary of companies that use only a P.O. box or have foreign home offices. If you're unsure, you can look up online businesses at the Better Business Bureau's online resource, www.BBBOnline.com, and for ratings of online companies by other consumers, check out www.bizrate.com. The BBB also offers a "Safe" seal of approval for sites that meet their safety requirements. If you're still not confidant, don't make the purchase.

Also, take a look at the "privacy policy" and "legal terms" pages to find out what the company will do with your information and how secure the site is. Only make online purchases through secured sites. If you're uneasy about giving out your credit card information, reputable online businesses usually provide a phone number you can call to make the purchase. Write down all of the pertinent information (the time, date, amount of sale, the name of the person you spoke to, and all the product details) and keep it for your records. Never give out your credit card information over e-mail. E-mail is not secure and your financial information can be captured by identity thieves.

Make sure that you understand all the terms of sale, including refund and return policies, shipping costs, and warranty terms, before you make a purchase online. Many mail-order businesses charge a fee for returns or require you to take on the shipping costs—*even when the item is defective*. So check out these policies beforehand, and get it in writing.

Additionally, when you make a purchase, print and save the product description. You'll need it if the merchandise doesn't match the description. Do the same with any email correspondence from the seller, especially if the correspondence includes any claims about the item's suitability for a particular use—it will reinforce your claim to a warranty of fitness and will help you get a chargeback through your credit card company or through alternative dispute resolution.

Be especially careful when you're shopping on auction sites. Many laws that protect consumers don't apply to sales between private individuals. Know all the rules and policies of the site. Does the product come with a warranty? Can you get a refund or cancel your bid? Does the auction site offer a guarantee for items that aren't delivered? Don't get caught up in the action. Establish what you're willing to pay for an item and stick to it. And as with all shopping, but particularly when you can't see the product in person, when something looks too good to be true…it usually is.

SHOPPING FOR CARS

Cars are just like any other consumer product—except they're more expensive, more dangerous, and those who sell them can be notoriously difficult to deal with. Needless to say, when shopping for a car, research is at a premium. There are a number of guides on shopping for a car (my guide, *The Consumer Bible,* is one of them). Jack Gillis puts out *The Car Book* and *The Used Car Book* each year, which rates hundreds of cars from the consumers' perspective, and the Center for Auto Safety tracks safety and durability performances, which you can view at their website, www.autosafety.com. *Consumer Reports* rates cars as well and has an added resource that, for $12, allows you to get a full report on a car—*including what a dealer pays.* That can put you in the driver's seat the next time you go to the dealership. There are a multitude of car guides that can help you figure out what a used car is worth. One of the most widely used is *Kelley Blue Book* (www.kbb.com), and www.edmunds.com is a valuable online guide. The website www.carfax.com allows you to view a free report on the history of a used car—so you can see if that beauty is really just a clunker with cosmetic surgery. But no matter how closely you research your vehicle, the fact is that you may still end up with a lemon.

Lemon Laws   Generally, a vehicle is considered a lemon when a major defect impairs its use, value, or safety, and can't be repaired after multiple attempts. One percent of new cars sold in the United States each year, roughly 150,000, have significant, irreparable defects. Each state has passed its own lemon laws to protect consumers from this bitter experience, but protections vary.

CASE STUDY

Take the experience of Angie Gallant of Broken Arrow, Oklahoma. She and her husband, Jeff Gallant, an Army reservist, bought a 2004 Chevrolet Malibu just before he was mobilized away from home. The thirty-four-year-old had problems starting the car just three weeks later, and she spent ten months battling GM to get it resolved. She enrolled in the BBB's Auto Line program and GM finally offered to repurchase the car, but deducted a $1,530 "user fee" for the miles that she had put on it while she was trying to get it replaced.

"When you're a woman and you've got a small child and you go to the dealership, it's horrible," said Gallant. "It's pretty intimidating. I was in tears."

Gallant eventually paid the fees, but took her cause to the state capital to reform the state's weak lemon law. "I have a problem with having to pay them money to take a lemon off my hands," she said. Oklahoma's lemon law ranked forty-second out of fifty, according to the Center for Auto Safety, prompting one state representative to call it a "dumping ground" for lemons from other states. When the changes to the law passed the state House, 92–0, Gallant celebrated what she called "a small victory in this bigger battle for consumers."

Find out what qualifies as a lemon in your state. Generally, the defect must appear within one or two years or within 12,000 or 24,000 miles, depending on where you live. For serious safety defects, states will allow the manufacturer either one or two attempts to correct the problem. For problems that aren't as dangerous but nevertheless make the car unusable or that significantly lower its value, a state will allow the manufacturer either three or four chances to get it right. The defect must be substantial and each repair must be for the same defect for the vehicle to qualify. Most states will consider a car a lemon if it requires more than a month in the shop, cumulatively, during the first year. States may have other definitions as well. Ohio, for instance, considers any car a lemon which requires eight or more substantial repairs in the first year, even if they are successful. Most states only cover new cars, but "certified used cars" from a dealer also qualify. Additionally, Arizona, Connecticut, Hawaii, Maine, Massachusetts, Minnesota, New Jersey, New York, and Rhode Island all have lemon laws for used vehicles.

Talk Back/Fight Back

If you determine that your car qualifies as a lemon under your state's law, first off, protect yourself—if your car is dangerous, don't drive it. Even if it doesn't present a risk of injury, continuing to drive a lemon can hurt your case by giving the appearance of usability and value.

When you purchase a car it's always important to keep detailed files; when you purchase a lemon, it's even more so. Because you're going to need to prove that you've taken your car in for the needed repair attempts, make sure you have all of your records. Never let a mechanic tell you that you don't need a service record since the car is under warranty—you always need a record when someone's been under your hood. A service record usually includes a repair order (what you asked them to do), a service invoice (what they actually did), and an odometer reading. It's important to get an order and an invoice, because you may bring a car in for the same problem three times, which would be recorded in the repair order, but the mechanic attempts to repair a different part of the engine each time, which might be reported separately on the service invoice.

Keep a notebook of conversations you've had with the mechanic, the dealer, and the manufacturer and note the names and the dates on which they occurred. The Center for Auto Safety (www.autosafety.com) and the National Highway Transit Safety Administration (www.NHTSA.org) both publish safety and recall information, as well as technical service bulletins (notices and recommendations from the manufacturers' mechanics).

If your state requires notice, send a letter to the manufacturer preceding the intended repair that will qualify your car under the lemon law and give a copy to the dealer when you arrive for your repair. Include your name, address, and contact information, the make, model number, and Vehicle Identification Number, along with the dealer's name and address. Describe the problems you've had, the repair attempts that have been made, and clearly note that you know the requirements of your state's lemon laws and that you are prepared to use them if their response is not satisfactory. Include copies of your records—always keep originals—and any records of related expenses you might have incurred, such as out-of-pocket repairs and replacement rentals.

Finally, specify whether you will want a refund or a replacement. You may not be able to choose what kind of solution you receive, but it helps to have your preference on record.

The manufacturer may require you to go to arbitration. If you have a choice, pick one run by your state or your Better Business Bureau. Arbitration is usually cheaper and you won't need to hire a lawyer. However, you won't always be better off, especially if the manufacturer gets to pick the arbitrator. The *Cleveland Plain Dealer* ran a series in 2000 revealing that Ohio's arbitration system often tipped the state's strong lemon law in favor of manufacturers by allowing arbitrators to award "offset" fees based on the mileage of the vehicle, against state law. That rule has since been reversed.

Finally, if you don't get a positive response, or if you get no response at all, you can file a complaint at www.lemonlaw.bbb.org. The BBB might have better luck getting a settlement, or provide a mediation or arbitration service. If none of that works, you can take the manufacturer to civil court to recover your losses. (See "The Rights of Clients" chapter for more on hiring a lawyer.)

Secret Warranties Sometimes manufacturers respond to widespread defects in their vehicles with a "secret warranty." The industry doesn't like to talk about them, but manufacturers will sometimes extend warranties offering ongoing, free repairs for owners of problem vehicles—but not all of them. Occasionally, manufacturers will send a letter notifying the owners of a "warranty adjustment" or "policy adjustment" program, but often they just notify the regional managers of their availability, and customers who complain loud enough will get a warranty extension. California, Connecticut, Virginia, and Wisconsin have passed laws requiring disclosure, but that doesn't guarantee that the manufacturer will disclose them.

If you have continuing problems with your vehicle but don't qualify under your state's lemon laws, make sure you keep good records and complain to the top. Watch the technical bulletins at the Center for Auto Safety and NHTSA to follow service recommendations for your make and model. If you see something that looks like a defect correction, take notice. Send detailed letters about your problems to your dealer, regional management, and corporate management asking them to make the necessary repairs, free of charge.

Product Safety and Recalls

CASE STUDY

In 1998, a Boston couple named Linda and Boaz (last name withheld to protect privacy) faced what all parents dread. Their seventeen-month-old son, Danny, was suffocated to death by a collapsed Playskool Travel-Lite crib. At first, they thought of their tragedy as a "freak accident." But when they discovered that Danny was one of four children killed by that model crib—deemed so dangerous by the U.S. Consumer Products Safety Commission (CPSC) that it had been recalled five years prior—they were horrified.

A family friend, E. Marla Felcher, looked into the tragedy in her book *It's No Accident: How Corporations Sell Dangerous Baby Products.* The crib hit the market in 1991, and by 1993 had already killed three children. The CPSC launched an investigation, and the crib's manufacturer, Kolcraft, announced a voluntary recall, without acknowledging the safety defect. But according to CPSC officials, the recall was "a very disappointing effort." The company didn't keep information on the owners of the crib and refused to launch a "Class A" recall (the most severe) to ensure that stores and the media took it seriously. Kolkraft made a video news release, but fought the CPSC when they tried to distribute it widely. Because of the weak recall effort, more children continued to be victimized by the faulty crib. All told, according to Felcher, 1 out of every 2,000 Playskool, Travel-Lite cribs has led to the death of a child—and there's still no way of knowing how many remain in use.

Protecting Consumers Ralph Nader jump-started the consumer movement by chronicling the deadly rollovers of GM's Chevrolet Corvair in his 1966 book *Unsafe at Any Speed.* It resulted in Congressional action that created the National Highway Traffic Safety Administration (NHTSA). The agency flexed its muscle in the 1970s by recalling 1.5 million Ford Pintos with gas tanks that exploded in collisions. That "consumer decade" also saw Congress extend oversight of consumer products to the already existing Food and Drug Administration (FDA), which regulates food products, prescription drugs, and medical devices and cosmetics; the U.S. Department of Agriculture (USDA), which regulates the meat and poultry industries; and the newly created Consumer Product Safety Commission (CPSC), which regulates some 15,000 household goods. In the decade following the establishment of the CPSC, accidental household injuries and deaths decreased 28 percent and 27 percent, respectively—more than doubling the rates of improvement from the previous decade. And since then, the rates of product-related household injuries have continued to decline.

These agencies are responsible for setting safety standards for the industries they oversee and have the power to launch recalls. Companies must report to the government information they receive about a product that doesn't meet safety standards or regulations, if a product has a defect or could create a substantial risk of injury, or if a product has caused substantial injuries or death.

The agencies rarely use their enforcement powers fully. When a recall is implemented, it's usually a voluntary arrangement negotiated with the manufacturer. Often, consumers are left in the dark while the agencies conduct secret reviews of dangerous products. The CPSC can't even notify the public when a product is under review until it announces a recall. When a company fights a recall— a relatively rare occurrence—it can delay enforcement action for months or even years, during which time millions of consumers continue to be exposed to risky products that the government knows are not safe. The lesson: take responsibility for your own family's safety.

Playing It Safe   Don't take for granted that a product is safe. Research products before you buy and stay vigilant afterward. *Consumer Reports* publishes evaluations on a wide range of products, available at www.consumerreports.org, and has a free section for recalls. The CPSC has information on recalls and prevention at their website at www.CPSC.gov. The NHTSA has a site that provides not only vehicle recall and safety information, but also consumer complaints, vehicle test results, defect investigations, service bulletins, and other safety studies. The FDA has health safety information at www.fda.gov (see the "Rights of Patients" chapter for more on drug safety). Visit the National Library of Medicine's site to find out more about household chemicals. The household products database at http://hpd.nlm.nih.gov allows you to see what's in—and how to handle—your cleaning products, auto supplies, cosmetics, and many more chemicals likely to be hanging around in your closet or under your sink.

When a recall is issued, the manufacturer is usually required to contact all of the known owners of the product by first-class mail. Press releases are then sent to the media and posters are put up in stores. These actions alert many consumers, but hardly enough. Additionally, many retailers and manufacturers provide recall information on their websites, but some lists are incomplete and many companies don't provide any information at all.

Various federal agencies have cooperated to create a single clearinghouse for recall information at www.recalls.gov. Check in to see if something you own has been recalled. Because the site allows a variety of methods to search, if you've lost the packaging or model number on a product, you may be able to find it by description. And remember—safety recalls never expire.

Be especially diligent when buying toys and nursery equipment for children. In 2003, 11 children under 15 were killed by unsafe toys and over 200,000 more were injured. Nursery products kill about 50 children under 5 each year and caused over 60,000 injuries in 2003 alone. Unintentional injury is the leading cause of death among children under fourteen, according to the National Safe Kids Campaign. Go to their site at www.safekids.org for safety tips, product reviews, and up-to-date recall information.

Members of the Toy Industry Association put their toys through stringent pre-testing. For more information on the tests and a list of companies that conduct them, go to www.toy-tia.org. One test you can do yourself to prevent choking hazards in children under three is to see if any parts of the toy can pass through a roll of bathroom tissue—if they do, keep it away from your young ones.

Increase your chances of recall notification by filling out the registration card that comes with many household products. Unfortunately, most of these cards have intrusive questions about your family income and buying habits to help the companies' advertising departments (currently, only manufacturers of car seats are required to provide hassle-free registration forms for recall purposes), but you can just fill in the information you feel comfortable providing. Additionally, some companies provide online registration forms.

Be careful when buying used products at secondhand stores and at garage sales. Used goods and hand-me-downs may have safety defects. It's a good idea to check them out at www.recalls.org. Likewise, dollar stores and other discounters are often clearinghouses for dangerous or defective imports. Watch out for consumer electronics from discount stores. Cheap electrical products like extension cords can cause fires. These dangerous imports often don't have brand names or have incomplete product labeling and company information. So if the package looks fishy, let it off the hook and throw it back.

Talk Back/Fight Back

We're all watchdogs whether we want to be or not. Government regulators rely on consumers to report hazardous products. By reporting dangers, you could save lives. To report a food or product safety issue, immediately contact the appropriate government agency. Be ready to give a detailed description of the product and any incident that led you to believe it is unsafe. You should report how you got the product and any information you have about the product's retailer, manufacturer, distributor, and importer. Provide your name and contact information so the agency can verify your report.

- •To report a problem with food (excluding meat and poultry), prescription or over-the-counter drugs, or cosmetics, contact the Food and Drug Administration. For emergencies such as food poisoning or drug tampering, call the twenty-four-hour hotline at (301) 443-1240. To report a non-emergency involving food, look up your FDA district office in the government pages of your phone book, or online at www.fda.org. To report a non-emergency involving drugs or medical devices, call (800) FDA-1088, or report online at www.medwatch.gov. To report a non-emergency involving cosmetics, call the FDA at (301) 436-2405, or email CAERS@cfsan.fda.gov.
- To a report a problem with meat, poultry, or eggs, or to ask questions about food safety or food-borne illnesses, call the U.S. Department of Agriculture's hotline at (800) 535-4555.
- To report a problem with motor vehicles, tires, or other automotive accessories, such as children's car seats or seat belts, call the National Highway Traffic Safety Administration's hotline at (888) 327-4236.
- CPSC: For nearly every other consumer product, report to the Consumer Products Safety Commission by filing an incident report at www.cpsc.gov/incident.html, or calling their hotline at (800) 638-CPSC.

If you or a loved one is injured by a dangerous product, report the incident to law enforcement and speak to a personal injury attorney (see "The Rights of Clients" chapter for more on this). The manufacturer, retailer, distributor, and importer are all legally liable for products that don't meet safety standards. If the companies refuse to take responsibility for putting consumers in danger, you can consider taking the case to a judge and jury.

Fix It: Protecting Consumer Rights

Ralph Nader, who essentially created the NHTSA, more recently called the agency a "meek consulting firm for the auto industry."

The *Detroit News* reported in 2002 that just four employees at the NHTSA evaluate the 34,000 safety complaints every year. Automobiles account for approximately 3 million injuries each year and over 40,000 deaths. The all-too-late recalls of Firestone tires on the Ford Explorer in 2000 and 2001—which led to the deaths of at least 271 motorists and injured hundreds more—highlighted the problems of oversight in the NHTSA recall system, in which corporations practically police themselves.

After the Ford/Firestone fiasco, Congress passed the *Transportation Recall Enhancement, Accountability and Documentation Act (TREAD)* to create stricter safety standards and to identify safety lapses more quickly. The law also makes it a criminal offense to knowingly withhold information about hazardous defects and raises the penalty for manufacturers from under $1 million to $15 million. These improvements were much needed and should be extended to other consumer agencies.

The CPSC's penalty limit is just $1.65 million per defect, a sum Consumer Union's David Pittle described as a "blemish on their image but not even a blip on their bottom line." Even the agency's record $4 million settlement with Graco Children's Products, levied in 2005 after the company failed to report defects in 12 million of the company's products from 1994 to 2001, hardly instills faith in product safety protections that are based on the voluntary reporting of defects. Nothing can be done to correct the fact that from 1994 to 2001 Graco products, including children's beds and strollers, "posed a danger to young children nationwide," according to the CPSC.

Furthermore, since 1975, according to a *Consumer Reports* investigation, the CPSC staff has been cut by half (down to 470 employees) and so has its budget—in inflation-adjusted dollars. The agency's 2005 budget report indicated that it is "struggling to simply maintain" its information systems.

Meanwhile, Americans continue to buy more and more import-ed consumer products, increasing the likelihood that our household goods are made outside the purview of CPSC oversight and U.S. industry standards. The agency only conducted half of the inspec-tions in 2004 that they carried out in 1999. The U.S. Public Interest Research Group (US PIRG), which conducts an annual toy-safety survey, found an increase in toys that appear to violate CPSC stan-dards. From 1998 to 2003, the average was 43 dangerous products a year—up from the previous decade's average of 21.

There's no doubt that consumer regulatory agencies make us safer, but there is still plenty of room for improvement. For one thing, recall notices never reach millions of consumers who have unsafe products in their homes, leaving them and their families at risk long after the dangerous product was sold. Nearly a third of all vehicles, over half of household products like toys and appliances, and three quarters of child car seats remain in use after a recall.

The consumer movement that began in the 1960s provided the infrastructure to ensure safe products in our marketplace. Unfortunately, over several administrations, but especially during Bush's, consumer regulatory agencies have been defanged—as demonstrated by discussions in this book about the CPSC, NHTSA, and FDA. With so many dangerous products on the market, it is once again time to fund consumer regulatory agencies adequately and to staff them with career professionals dedicated to consumer safety, not with industry cronies obsessed with profit margins.

CHAPTER 5

THE RIGHTS OF CONSUMERS OF FINANCIAL SERVICES

When people ask how much credit card debt is okay, it's a little like asking how much TNT can you keep in your basement. You probably could keep some and get along okay. But the smartest move is to not keep any.

—Elizabeth Warren, Harvard law professor and author of
*The Two-Income Trap: Why Middle-Class Mothers and Fathers
Are Going Broke*

The way we use our money is constantly changing. In 2003, Americans chose plastic cards over paper checks at the till for the first time ever (by about 10 percent according to the Federal Reserve). The rising popularity of plastic payment is largely due to the exploding popularity of the debit card, its use growing at a rate of over 20 percent per year. But did you know that even if your debit card has a VISA or MasterCard logo on it, it doesn't necessarily have the same consumer protections as a credit card?

About 144 million Americans have one or more credit cards, and the average household's consumer debt has been estimated to be as high as $12,000—up from $2,500 in 1990. All told, Americans owed $804 billion to credit card companies in 2005. In the same period, banks and credit card companies have become more ruthless about collecting debts and levying higher fees and interest rates. *Consumer Reports* estimated that we pay over $216 billion in fees for financial services every year.

Your experiences with credit can carry over to other parts of your life. Your credit report, for example, not only affects your ability to get credit and the interest you pay for loans, it could also be the deciding factor in renting an apartment or getting a job. As important as credit reports are, a survey by US PIRG found that 79 percent contain mistakes. And the free flow of personal financial information has made identity theft the fastest-growing crime, affecting millions of Americans each year. Your financial rights and risks depend on how you handle your money. The best route to financial freedom is to know how to defend yourself and your money.

KEY FINANCIAL SERVICES LAWS

Truth in Lending Act   In 1968, Congress passed the first of a series of important credit reforms. The *Truth in Lending Act* requires creditors to clearly state all applicable charges and fees, such as monthly finance charges, yearly interest rates, grace periods, annual and monthly fees, late fees, and any other charges that could be levied against the borrower. Any changes must be reported in periodic statements.

Fair Credit Reporting Act (FCRA)   Before this landmark consumer protection law was passed in 1972, credit reporting agencies kept secret histories on millions of consumers that reported to interested companies not only bad debts but also other private information, such as sexual orientation, alcohol consumption, and personal hygiene habits. The *FCRA* ushered in a system of credit reporting that promotes privacy and accuracy. While discrimination has declined in credit appraisals, women and minorities are still more likely to be denied credit, and financers get around the spirit of the law by sharing internal credit reports with their affiliates, but not with consumers.

Fair Credit Billing Act (FCBA)   The *FCBA*, passed in 1974, gives consumers the right to contest and correct their bills within a reasonable time frame. It also allows you to withhold payment for damaged goods and for fraudulent or unauthorized charges. The

FCBA provides a dispute resolution procedure for creditors and limits your liability for fraud to $50—a charge most creditors waive.

Equal Credit Opportunity Act (ECOA)   This important 1974 law prohibits discrimination against credit applicants on the basis of race, religion, national origin, age, sex, or marital status.

Electronic Funds Transfer Act (EFTA)   In 1978, as technology began to transform the way we pay for goods and services, Congress enacted the *EFTA* to protect consumers from errors in electronic payments. This law covers all electronic transactions not covered under the *Fair Credit Billing Act*. It covers your ATM and debit cards as well as preauthorized transfers from your account, electronic telephone payments, and direct deposit transactions. The *EFTA* requires financial institutions to adhere to a dispute resolution procedure, and limits your liability for lost and stolen ATM and debit cards.

Expedited Funds Availability Act   This law was passed by Congress in 1987 to determine how long a bank may take to deposit funds to your account. While your state may have more comprehensive laws regarding the deposit of funds, this federal law lays out a minimum timeline for banks to make your funds available. With the passage of *Check 21*, this law should be revisited so that consumers can expect their funds to be available every bit as fast as banks can withdraw it.

Truth in Savings   Congress enacted this 1991 law requiring banks to adhere to the same basic tenets that creditors must follow according to the *Truth in Lending Act*. Banks are required to clearly disclose all the relevant information regarding interest rates and yields, transaction and penalty fees, and any other terms for deposit accounts such as checking and savings. Again, any changes to the terms must be announced in periodic statements.

Fair Debt Collection Practices Act   This 1996 law protects consumers from harassment and unfair practices by debt collectors. Debt collectors cannot threaten your person or property, repeatedly call debtors or third parties such as employers or family members, or make false statements about your debt. While this law applies to all professional debt collectors, some of the protections may not apply to the entity from which you directly borrowed the debt.

Fair and Accurate Credit Transactions Act (FACTA)   Consumer rights under the *FCRA* have been expanded recently by *FACTA* in 2003. This law gives you the right to free annual credit reports from each of the three major credit reporting agencies and the right to see your credit score at a "fair and reasonable" price. Because mistakes on credit reports are widespread and costly, use your right to verify your credit report and correct any mistakes. In addition, the law provides some needed protections against identity theft. These new rights come at a heavy cost, however; industry lobbyists ensured that *FACTA* permanently preempts states from passing more far-reaching consumer protections.

Check Clearing for the 21st Century   Commonly known as *Check 21*, this 2004 law streamlines the process for clearing checks by allowing banks to transfer the original check to an electronic image and transmit funds from your account more quickly. The law's primary effect will be to speed up check processing, eliminating the float consumers used to enjoy when paying by check. Unfortunately, *Check 21* has no equal requirement for banks to process consumer deposits more rapidly, so consumers will likely be hit with more bounced check fees and reduced access to their funds.

CREDIT CARDS

CASE STUDY

People who get into trouble with credit cards aren't usually deadbeats or con artists. Take the example of Steve Strachan, a Pennsylvania resident whose flower business thrived throughout the 1990s. Like many businesspeople, he relied on credit cards to help manage his finances and to obtain benefits. He used his US

Bank WorldPerks Visa for the travel bonuses, rarely tapping the $54,000 credit line and low APR of 5.25 percent. Strachan told the *New York Times* that he "never paid a penny of interest," by paying his monthly bill by the due date.

As the economy weakened in the early 2000s, Strachan's business suffered. Suddenly the credit cards he had used for convenience had to be called on to keep him in business. After he began revolving his balances, the banks cashed in by bumping up his interest rates. Despite a good credit score of 730 and a history of paying on time, in 2003 US Bank raised his APR to 20.21 percent, nearly four times the previous rate. "I wasn't late, and I didn't go over the credit limit, and I didn't write bad checks," Strachan said. US Bank blamed the hike on the fact that he was using too much of the balance they had extended to him. So they charged a low rate when it had no effect…but a near-usurious rate when he actually paid interest. Over the course of one summer, his finance charges jumped from $209 to $808, on a balance of around $50,000.

At the same time, Bank One was busy raising his APR to 24.99 percent on another credit card with a $70,000 balance. Strachan's monthly finance charge on that account jumped to around $1,500. Bank One then began reducing his credit limit to just above his balance so that even paying the minimum could trigger an over-limit fee. In doing so, he says, creditors "create their own little monster."

"It was like they almost had a little meeting in the back room and said 'Let's get Strachan.' How does it serve them to treat people like that? Are they trying to force them into bankruptcy?"

Despite his growing credit debt, Strachan chose to refuse the advice from his attorneys to claim bankruptcy and continued to pay off his debts "because I have principles and ethics." That's more than we can say for his creditors. Although Strachan was able to persuade US Bank to restore his original APR of 5.25 percent, they closed his account and cut that line of credit.

To avoid credit trouble, it's important to understand how credit cards work. For starters, you should know the difference between credit cards and charge cards. Credit cards, most often sponsored by banks, provide a line of credit to borrow from when you don't pay off your entire balance within a monthly grace period. These cards charge interest on your monthly balance. Charge cards, like American Express Card and Diner's Club, don't charge interest and must be paid off at the end of each month. Charge cards also generally charge an annual fee for their services, which many credit card providers have eliminated—the most common exceptions are credit cards offering cash rebates or benefits such as airline tickets.

Read the Fine Print   Some cards promise "no annual fee," but sneak in other charges such as a costly one-time membership fee. In 2000, Providian agreed to a $300 million settlement for deceptive practices such as, among other schemes, offering a card with "no-annual fee," while charging a nonnegotiable annual $156 fee for "credit protection."

Credit card companies are compelled by the *Truth in Lending Act* to disclose the terms of your contract, including your interest rate, grace period, fees, and other terms. The interest rate is expressed as an annual percentage rate or APR, but the APR you're quoted is often misleading. That's because, for most credit cards, outstanding balances accrue a finance charge for each month, so you end up paying interest on your interest as well as on your balance.

Creditors use different methods to compute your finance charge, which must be explained in your application:

- The most common "average daily balance method" occurs when a creditor adds your balances from each day of your billing cycle, subtracting payments to your account, then divides that number by the total number of days to compute your finance charge.
- Under the "two-cycle average daily balance method," the creditor applies that formula over two billing cycles to compute your finance charge.

- The "adjusted balance method" is when a creditor uses the balance from the start of your billing cycle, deducts credits and payments from that cycle, and does not add new purchases to compute your finance charge.
- The "previous balance method" is when creditors use the total amount of debt on your account from the beginning of the billing cycle to compute your finance charge.

Credit cards have either a variable interest rate or a fixed interest rate. Variable interest rates change in accordance to an index, adjusted periodically, and may offer lower APRs than fixed-rate cards because *you* assume the risk of a sharp increase in interest rates rather than the creditor. Fixed-rate cards are supposed to maintain a steady APR, but because most contracts have a clause allowing creditors to change the terms whenever they want (usually with a fifteen-day advance notice), even a fixed-rate credit card offers no guarantee that the rate will stay fixed at the rate you begin with. Many creditors have also implemented policies of "universal default" that allow them to raise your APR if you miss a payment—*even if it's to another company.* Confused? That's probably intentional. Every variation can save or cost you money.

Further adding to this confusion, credit cards can have multiple APRs for different types of debt. Some cards may have a separate APR for balance transfers, another for new charges, still another for cash advances, and an introductory APR that only lasts a few months before a regular rate kicks in. Some cards have different APRs depending on what your balance is.

Credit cards generally give you a grace period, allowing you time to pay off a purchase before you start paying interest. The grace period usually lasts the length of the billing cycle, around twenty-five days. If you don't pay off the entire balance before the end of the grace period, you will begin to accrue finance charges. Beware—some sneaky creditors have taken to changing the terms of the grace period to lure you into paying more late fees, so try to pay off your balance early to avoid extra charges and know that some services may not have a grace period; most creditors start charging interest immediately on cash advances.

Watch Out for Penalty Fees! In 1996, the Supreme Court lifted caps on fees creditors can charge, and, ever since, credit card issuers have been steadily raising late fees and over-limit fees from the $5 to $10 range to $35 and above. Some experts predict it won't be long before we're charged $50 for a payment as little as five minutes late. In 2003, penalty fees accounted for over half of all fees collected by creditors, raking in $11.7 billion in profits. Late payments are also a major factor in interest rate hikes, as even one late payment may be enough for your creditor to double your interest rate. Direct Merchants Bank's iAdvantages Platinum MasterCard, for example, offered a 0 percent APR on new purchases for five months, but one late payment would result in a $39 fee and trigger an APR between 13.49 and 23.49 percent. With a second late payment would come another $39 late fee and cause the APR to shoot up to 29.49 percent!

Talk Back/Fight Back

If you believe your creditor misrepresented or failed to disclose information regarding the terms of your credit in violation of the *Truth in Lending Act*, you are entitled to sue for damages and for any money you lose as a result up to twice the finance charge, but limited to between $100 and $1,000. This may include fees or rates that are misapplied according to the terms of your contract, or any other misleading or improper practices. If you win, the creditor can be ordered to pay your court fees and lawyer costs, so you might be able to find a lawyer who agrees to be paid only if you win a settlement. However, many banks slip arbitration clauses into your contract that can take away your right to sue and leave you bound to any decision made by a kangaroo court of credit cronies. You can also contact your state Attorney General's Office of Consumer Affairs, the state banking agency, or the federal regulator in charge of your bank. (See list on page 131.)

Choosing a Card   Banks and other creditors send out over 5 billion applications for credit cards to consumers each year. These "pre-approved" offers flood our mailboxes with promises of 0 percent introductory APRs, no annual fees, cash rebates, free airline tickets, and other perks. Don't be fooled. Credit card issuers are masters of the confidence trick. Zero percent introductory APRs can become 20 to 25 percent overnight. "No annual fee" offers can be replaced by monthly fees and other charges. And once you get into a little credit trouble, creditors can hike up interest rates and nail you with late fees and over-limit fees. When shopping for a credit card, don't just pick any card that prints a lot of platinum promises on the cover of an envelope—research your best option and know the tricks of the trade.

First, consider your needs. If you pay your balance in full each month, the APR is less important than getting a card with no annual fee and a lenient grace period. If you're one of the 55 to 60 percent of credit card users who keeps a revolving balance, then keeping your APR low is more important. You can often get a lower interest rate by choosing a card with no grace period. If you usually pay on time but occasionally need to charge a high-priced item, consider getting a charge card for monthly expenses that you intend to pay off right away, and a low APR credit card for larger purchases. Rebate cards and frequent-flyer cards can offer valuable perks, but make sure the interest rates and annual fees don't cost more than the benefits you earn.

Generally, there are no limits on interest rates for credit cards. Usury laws, which limited interest rates for most of our nation's history, were largely abandoned for credit card purposes in the 1980s when large banks moved their operations to states like South Dakota and Delaware that promised the freedom to charge whatever interest they wanted. Other states began following suit, easing restrictions on credit card interest. One exception is Arkansas-based banks. Arkansas still has unusually strong usury laws, so banks there, like the Pulaski Bank & Trust Co., offer some of the nation's lowest interest rates.

With few limits on the credit card industry, it's up to you to find the best offer. One good resource is www.bankrate.com, which provides up-to-date information on credit card offers and even lets you customize a card search to focus on your needs. They also have helpful calculators that figure out how long it will take to pay off a debt and what you should be prepared to pay monthly to meet your time frame. Make sure to take into consideration every possible charge, including membership fees, annual fees, over-limit fees, late fees, and any other fee a creditor can think up when choosing a card. Some shameless creditors even have fees to charge you if you cancel your account because they raised your interest rates.

Managing Your Debt   To avoid the credit debt pitfalls, watch out for minimum payments. While creditors are required to tell you the terms of your contract, they're under no such obligation to tell you how long it will take to pay off a debt. Thirty-five million Americans pay only the monthly minimum of their credit card payment, which can be as low as 2 percent of the principal debt. This type of debt payment is like fighting a fire with kerosene. Paying a minimum payment of 2 percent on an average debt of $10,000 at a modest APR of 13 percent would take about 33 years to pay off, while accruing an additional $11,450 in interest. For higher APRs, these figures become truly staggering. A late payment or two at any time in those three decades could double or triple your interest rate and make your debt that much more unmanageable. No wonder the industry estimates that 60 percent of cardholders will never pay off their debt.

Try not to borrow more than you can afford to pay back within a reasonable time frame. A good rule of thumb is to borrow only what you can pay back at around 10 percent a month—though it's always best to pay it off in full. Use the minimum payment option only when necessary to avoid late payments, and pay extra whenever you can. If you find yourself losing control of your payments, don't ignore them. Any debt that goes to a collections department will hurt your credit score. Instead call the consumer service department and see if you can negotiate a payment schedule that you can afford until you get back on your feet. If your debt is really out of control, you can go to a nonprofit debt counselor for help (see "Debt Counseling" on page 145), but watch out for *their* tricks.

It's possible—and often very easy—to negotiate with credit card companies. If you have an account in good standing, you may be able to lower your interest rate and raise your credit limit. Shop around and see what other offers are out there, then call up your company and tell them you'd like a reduction. If you've done your homework, you can counter with offers from other banks. A bank that knows that you're looking around is more likely to meet your demands and keep your business. If you are approaching your credit limit and find yourself in danger of incurring over-limit fees, a quick call could raise your limit to give you some breathing room. Be prepared to follow through on your ultimatum by transferring your debt. Most creditors make it easy to transfer debt from one card to another. The results of these negotiations will most likely depend on the status of your credit report and score; the better your credit report, the better deals you'll be offered.

Know the Score Perhaps nothing has a greater impact on your finances than your credit report and the resulting score. Your credit report can make or break everything from your interest rates on credit cards and loans, to housing, insurance rates, and even employment—though prospective employers are required to get your permission before looking at your credit report. Unfortunately, these documents, more often than not, contain mistakes. A 2004 survey by the US PIRG found that 79 percent of credit reports had mistakes and 25 percent had errors serious enough to cause a credit denial.

Your credit score is computed based on information from your credit report. It's estimated that three quarters of American adults have a credit score. Each lender and credit reporting agency may come up with their own score. The standard is based on a secret formula devised by Fair Isaac Co. (FICO), which is determined by the amount of available credit, accrued debt, and your payment history. A FICO score can range from 300 to 850. 850 is the best possible score, the average score is around 720, and scores below 620 are considered a high risk, bringing on sub-prime rates and credit denials.

To keep your credit score high and your interest low, pay your bills on time. Any bill more than thirty days late will most likely have a negative impact on your credit score. Keep your debt well below the limit. If it looks like you have used up most of your available credit, it will count against you. Keeping cards that you've had for a while will show a history of reliable payments, equaling extra credit points for you. Every time you apply for credit, it shows up on your report, so if you apply for too many cards at once, or are repeatedly denied cards that are out of your range, it will affect your score. One of the best things you can do to improve your score is to make sure your credit report is accurate.

Checking Your Credit Report The *Fair and Accurate Credit Transactions Act* of 2003 (*FACTA*) gives consumers the right to a free annual credit report from each of the three major credit reporting agencies—Equifax, Experian, and Trans Union. Go to www.annualcreditreport.com or call (877) 322-8228 to make sure that yours is correct. Because a mistake on one report might not show up on another, take a look at all three. Once you verify that they're correct, it's important to check them periodically to prevent identity theft, fraud, and additional mistakes. You get a free peak at each of the three every year, so you can check one of them every four months or so to improve your chances of catching mistakes, unauthorized activity, or identity fraud early (see "Identity Theft" below). You may see offers for expensive credit monitoring services, but they don't offer anything that you can't do yourself for free. Any offer that says it can erase bad credit should not be trusted. You can have inaccurate information removed by requesting it yourself, but accurate information, bad or good, must remain for seven years, or ten in the case of bankruptcy. Furthermore, *FACTA* gives you more power individually to dispute information a creditor reports than a credit repair organization has.

Know Your Rights:

- You have the right to know when anyone has denied you credit, insurance, employment, or any other service due to information in your credit report.
- You have the right to view the information in each credit report for free once a year.
- You have the right to dispute inaccurate or incomplete information with credit reporting agencies and with the furnishers of the information.
- You have the right to view your credit score for a fair and reasonable fee.
- You have the right to know everyone that has reviewed your credit report in the previous year, or two years for employment purposes.
- You have the right to add an explanation to any item on your credit report that you have disputed.

What to Look For   Make sure all your personal information is accurate. It's not uncommon for a credit report to include information from someone else with the same or similar name, or to include information about a relative or spouse with whom you've shared accounts.

Review all the negative marks on your report, such as late payments, over-limit or delinquent accounts, and debts sent to collection agencies, and make sure that (1) they are reported correctly and (2) closed accounts are not listed as open and that your total debts and credit limits are listed accurately. A 2003 report by the Federal Reserve found that 46 percent of credit reports had at least one account in which a creditor had withheld the credit limit. This alarming practice lowers your credit score by misrepresenting your available credit, thereby making you less likely to receive better offers from your creditor's competitors, and sticking you with unfavorable credit terms.

Talk Back/Fight Back

If you find an error in your credit report, you have the right to dispute it with both the credit reporting agency and the company that furnishes the information. First, file a dispute with each credit reporting agency that reports the error. The procedure for disputes should be included with your report. Under *FACTA*, credit reporting agencies have forty-five days to investigate your dispute. As always, keep the original copies of your documentation, and send your letter return receipt requested.

If the agency finds in your favor, they must correct the error within the forty-five days and provide you with an updated credit report. If the furnisher of the disputed item fails to defend it to the agency within the forty-five-day limit, the credit reporting agency must remove it from your credit report. Credit reporting agencies are further bound to inform creditors and other furnishers of information when you successfully dispute an item on your credit report. The creditors are then required to update their records and strike the inaccurate items that were corrected on your report.

Before 2004, creditors were only required to investigate their records if a dispute was made through a credit reporting agency. Now *FACTA* also allows you to dispute records with the creditors that furnish the information on your report. (For information on how to file a dispute with a creditor, see "Billing Disputes" below.) The furnisher of the information must investigate and respond within thirty days of receiving your written dispute of information on your credit report. If the investigation finds in your favor, the furnisher is required to send the correct information to each of the credit reporting agencies it originally reported the false information to. The credit reporting agency then must amend their records accordingly and send you an updated credit report. Theoretically, disputing with either a credit reporting agency or a furnisher should clear the error, since they're supposed to report changes to each other. But it's always a good idea to correct inaccurate information wherever it appears to ensure a clean and accurate credit report.

If you have a grievance about a dispute procedure with either a credit reporting agency or the furnisher of information, you can request that the credit reporting agency amend the report by including a summary explanation with your account of the item disputed. You can also file a complaint with the FTC at www.ftc.gov, or by calling (877) FTC-HELP. If a credit reporting agency fails to correct inaccurate information, you have the right to sue for damages.

Billing Disputes The *Fair Credit Billing Act (FCBA)* provides important protections for credit card consumers against billing errors and unauthorized charges. For unauthorized charges, resulting from lost or stolen cards or other types of fraud, your liability is limited to $50. Most creditors waive this charge, but, if your creditor doesn't, don't be afraid to ask. Report a lost or stolen card as soon as possible; most companies have twenty-four-hour hotlines for these emergencies. You can't be held responsible for any unauthorized charges made after you report it. You also cannot be held liable if the fraud involves only the credit card number, and not the actual card.

The law also provides a settlement procedure for billing errors (such as charges for the wrong amount), merchandise or services that were not delivered as agreed, damaged goods, and uncredited refunds. If an error was made by a business from which you purchased goods or services, you are usually required to try to resolve the matter with them first, which often is the simplest way to fix a problem anyway. If that doesn't work, however, you can appeal directly to your creditor. The law isn't written to cover goods that are simply of "poor quality"—for these items *Consumer Reports* recommends making a case that the goods "were not delivered as agreed."

Talk Back/Fight Back

Under the *FCBA*, you have sixty days from the time the bill was sent to file a written letter disputing the charge. To establish proof that you sent the letter of dispute, send it certified and request a return receipt. Be sure to send the letter to the address for "billing inquiries," which is often different than the address you send your payments to.

Defend Yourself!

Your letter should be clear and concise. State the dollar amount contested, the details of your dispute, and reference your supporting documentation. Include copies of all the important receipts and statements as evidence, but keep the originals for your own records.

Also suggest a solution. Your letter could state, for example, that you'd like a credit to your account for the charges and any finance or other fees related to the error. Or, for credit report disputes, demand that your creditor strike the disputed information and send an amended report to the credit reporting agencies. Your creditor may fix the error immediately upon receiving your complaint or begin an investigation.

In the case of an investigation, the creditor must provide a written response within thirty days. While the charge is being disputed, you have the right to withhold payment on the item and any other charges related to the dispute. The creditor can count the charge toward your credit limit, but it can't tack on interest, close your account, attempt to collect, or take legal action for the charge in question. Creditors may report that you are disputing a bill to a credit reporting agency, but they are prohibited from reporting a disputed bill as delinquent. Furthermore, the *Equal Credit Opportunity Act* protects your right to dispute charges by prohibiting creditors from discriminating against applicants who have disputed bills. Your creditor must present the results of its investigation in writing within two billing cycles or ninety days from receiving your letter, whichever comes first.

If your creditor doesn't follow any of the procedures under the rules of the *FCBA*, it forfeits its ability to collect the disputed charge as well as finance charges, up to $50, even if the disputed charge is correct.

If the investigation finds that the charge was in error, the creditor must provide written documentation that it will credit the disputed charge and related finance charges or fees and correct the information they furnish to credit reporting agencies. If the investigation finds that you owe all or a portion of the disputed bill, your creditor must provide an explanation of the charge in writing and give you an opportunity to see the evidence that proves its case.

If you disagree with the findings of an investigation or remain unconvinced by the evidence, you have ten days to mail a notice refusing to pay the charges. In this case the creditor can legally initiate collections on your account, but it is required to disclose to you where it sends delinquent credit notices and you can add a disclaimer that you believe the charge is in error.

While you can report any creditor violations to the government, unfortunately regulatory duties are dispersed across government agencies depending on what kind of creditor you are dealing with:

- For most nonbank and store-issued cards contact the Federal Trade Commission at www.ftc.com, or call (877) FTC-HELP.
- For state banks in the Federal Reserve System, contact the Federal Reserve Board's Department of Consumer and Community Affairs at www.federalreserve.gov, or call (202) 452-3693.
- For state banks that aren't part of the Federal Reserve System, contact the Federal Deposit Insurance Corporation's Consumer Response Center at www.fdic.gov, or call (877) 275-3342.
- For nationwide banks, contact the Comptroller of the Currency's Office of the Ombudsman at www.occ.treas.gov, or call (800) 613-6743.
- For federal savings and loan institutions, contact the Office of Thrift Supervision's Consumer Programs department at www.ots.treas.gov, or call (800) 842-6929.
- For credit unions, contact the National Credit Union Administration's Office of External Affairs at www.ncua.gov, or call (703) 518-6330.

For more help, you can contact your state's Attorney General office, local consumer authority, or your district attorney if you believe there may be criminal misconduct. If you have difficulty working with your credit card company settling your dispute, try filing a complaint with the Better Business Bureau, which won't take sides but will help mediate a resolution. For the most egregious violations, you can alert your local media. Most newspapers have consumer affairs departments or columnists that can help you or call attention to the bad behavior of the company you're dealing with.

If all else fails, you can sue your creditor for up to twice the amount of finance charges, plus the disputed amount, but damages are limited to amounts between $100 and $1,000. Because the court can also require the creditor to pay your lawyer fees, try to find a lawyer who agrees to be paid only if you win. Otherwise you might owe more debt to a lawyer than you would to the creditor. You can also take your case to small claims court (see "How to Win in Small Claims Court" in "The Rights of Clients" chapter).

BANK ON IT

Once upon a time our personal finances were handled by local banks and many Americans knew their bankers by name. Now ten national banks dominate the market and consumers have become accustomed to long phone waits, impersonal computerized systems, and fewer branches. Instead of dealing with another human being, we're encouraged to use electronic ATM kiosks and our home computers. Technology has revolutionized consumer finances, often making it more convenient, but when problems arise it can be difficult to find a real person to turn to. At the same time, banks have found a new stream of income by raising fees on just about everything, from ATM withdrawals and check processing to bounced checks and stop-payments. Taking the time to navigate personal finances can be frustrating but rewarding.

Choosing a Checking Account There are different checking accounts to choose from. Some banks offer "negotiable order of withdrawal" or NOW accounts that promise interest on deposits. These accounts usually have the highest fees and pay interest at such low rates that most consumers lose more in fees than they earn in interest. And with high minimum account requirements, you're probably better off with more of your money in higher interest-earning savings accounts, keeping just enough money in a regular checking account to qualify you for free checking.

Regular checking accounts don't earn interest, but have smaller fees. Free-checking accounts are now widely available, but they are rarely actually "free." These accounts usually require you to keep a minimum balance to avoid monthly fees and to agree to other terms, such as the direct deposit of your paycheck. If you meet all of the bank's requirements and terms, and use no other services that they charge a fee for, then you might actually be eligible for a free checking account. Some accounts may forego their fees only if you accept copies of checks. Few banks provide the original checks automatically these days, but to preserve your rights when you dispute a check charge, demand a paper "substitute check" to be sent with your monthly statement, or at least made available to you by request.

Look at different offers from a variety of banks, including neighborhood savings banks, credit unions, and big banks. Consider your finances realistically. Look at your recent statements and calculate the total number of checks you wrote and your monthly balances. How often would your balance fall below the different minimum requirements? How much would you accumulate in per-check fees? How long will it take to post your deposits?

For years the conventional wisdom in choosing a bank has been, the smaller, the better. Small banks have more incentive to keep your business, the theory goes, and so will go out of their way to keep their fees down on checking accounts and interest up on savings accounts. But for frequent travelers and regular ATM users, according to *Consumer Reports*, that wisdom may be history. In the '90s, Congress deregulated the industry to allow banks the freedom to branch out all over the country, rather than confining them to one state. At the same time, banks, still recovering from investment disasters of the '80s, began charging fees for ATM use, creating a new revenue stream.

While the Federal Reserve reported in 2002 that small banks can save you $1 to $3 a month in checking fees, big banks have far more ATM locations—so the issue is convenience vs. cost. *Consumer Reports* rated about 400 checking accounts from ten of the biggest banks in the United States and found that Bank of America rated best overall in categories that included multistate convenience, electronic banking, and penalty fees. Chase came in last. According to *Consumer Reports*, big bank fees have gone down considerably over the last few years, and they offer more free-checking accounts than small banks. But if you're among the 37 percent of Americans who don't use ATMs, smaller banks and credit unions are probably still your best bet. And remember, big banks innovated the unconscionable ATM charges and other exorbitant fees, so staying small might protect you from the next wave of big bank "innovations."

When selecting an account, make sure you know what the monthly charge would be if you fall below the minimum balance requirement. Avoid banks that charge for simple customer service necessities; some banks even charge you for the privilege of calling in to see how much of your money they have. Other accounts may charge a fee to access a real person inside a branch rather than relying on an electronic ATM kiosk or a consumer service line. And beware of ATM double-dipping, which is now the norm, with your bank taking $1 and the nonnetwork ATM taking around $1.50. At an average of $2.50 per transaction, this can add up to be the costliest fee in the banking industry. One of these charges a week, and you end up paying $130 a year, *just to get access to your own money.*

Floating on Thin Ice   A law that went into effect in 2004, the *Check Clearing for the 21st Century Act*, commonly called *Check 21*, has dramatically changed the way your checks are processed. A check you write at the store used to go from bank to bank until the original made its way back to your bank and was deducted from your account and then sent back to you for your records. Now, under *Check 21*, any bank along the way can convert the check to an electronic image to expedite the process. For consumers accustomed to floating a check for a day or two before payday, this law may cause an upsurge in bounced check fees, which averaged $21 in 2002.

Unfortunately, *Check 21* does not require banks to speed up your deposits. So while the check you wrote for groceries this morning may have gone through this afternoon, that check from your uncle in Florida that you deposited two days ago may not go through for another three. That's because your deposits are still governed by the *Expedited Funds Availability Act* of 1978, which gives banks a timeline to credit your account. "Low-risk" checks like cashiers checks or government-issued checks should be credited no later than the following business day. (You should ask your bank to guarantee the same treatment for your payroll checks, or arrange for direct deposit to make your paycheck deposit instant.) For local checks, banks can hold the check for two business days, and out-of-state checks can be held for five business days. Unless you have golden overdraft protection, forget about floating checks; only write them for amounts that your current balance can cover.

Check 21 also virtually guarantees that when you write a check, you'll never see it again. Any bank along the line can destroy the original and convert it to an electronic image. Not only does this make it more difficult for consumers to prove forgery or other alterations to the original check, but this law also seriously affects your rights to have disputed charges credited back to your account. When a bank transfers your check to an electronic image, it is also required to create a paper copy called a "substitute check," which must have the legend: "This is a copy of your check. You can use it the same way you would use the original check," as well as a full image of both the front and back of the original check.

Talk Back/Fight Back

If you have a returned substitute check, you can claim a recredit up to $2,500 while you are disputing the charge. The claim must be made within forty days, unless you have extenuating circumstances such as illness or travel, and must be posted to your account within ten days of your request. You can make the claim over the phone, but the bank may request you submit it in writing. If the bank fails to recredit your account or resolve the dispute despite clear evidence, you have the right to sue for damages. Even if you don't have the substitute check, you can request a "provisional credit" for the disputed amount. While banks are not required to recredit your account without a substitute check, many make it their policy to replace the funds during a dispute. Check disputes are generally covered under your state's *Uniform Commercial Code*; so contact your state banking agency or Attorney General's office for more help.

Choosing a Debit Card   When ATM cards were first introduced in the 1980s, they had one use: to withdraw your money from ATM machines. Now banks offer debit cards, which can be used at many businesses to pay for purchases directly out of your account after you punch in a PIN at the point of sale. On top of that, most banks offer debit cards with a VISA and MasterCard logo on it. Like the original debit cards, these can be used as an ATM card or a debit card where you enter your PIN, or anywhere that accepts VISA or MasterCard with just your signature approval.

Don't mistake that VISA or MasterCard logo on your debit card as a promise of the same customer protections that credit cards offer. Credit cards are covered by the *FCBA*, which protects you when the items are not delivered as agreed. A debit card comes with no such promise. Even with a check, if you're dissatisfied with the quality of goods or services, you can cancel payment before it clears. But with debit cards the charges are usually transferred immediately, so you'll more than likely have to negotiate with the store for a refund or exchange.

With lost, stolen, or other types of fraud on VISA and MasterCard debit cards, your protections are virtually the same as with credit cards. Under the *Electronic Fund Transfer Act*, which covers all debit and ATM cards and other electronic payments, you have to act fast to cover yourself in the case of fraud. According to the *EFTA*, you are protected for any losses over $50 if you report the card within two days. If you wait longer, you could be liable for $500, and if you don't report the lost card within sixty days, you could lose your entire account.

Savings   The traditional accounts include passbook accounts and statement savings accounts. Statement savings accounts have the advantage of monthly statements and ATM access, and some banks will allow you to connect them to your checking account to qualify for a minimum deposit requirement or for overdraft purposes. The interest rates for these two options are about the same, though statement savings interest rates have historically been slightly higher.

An important factor in considering an account is the method that the bank uses to compute your interest. The "day of deposit to day of withdrawal" method is the best because you earn interest on your balance every day. Another common method, the "average daily balance," computes your interest earned based on your average for each period. This will penalize you if there is a large withdrawal at the end of a given period because the bank will average it with the higher balances from the rest of the period. Money market rate accounts usually have higher interest rates than traditional accounts and allow you a small number of checks per month, but often carry a higher minimum balance and don't earn as much interest as a real money market fund or Certificate of Deposit (CD) account.

The *Truth in Savings Act* requires banks to fully disclose the terms of all your bank accounts, including savings and checking, money market rate accounts, and CDs. When you open your account, you should receive information on how the bank computes interest, yields, fees, minimum balances, and deposit requirements. Any changes to their policies should be outlined in your statement.

CASE STUDY

Bank errors are unfortunately common and can come in a variety of forms. It's impossible to know how many mistakes go undetected by unwatchful consumers, but anyone who's dealt with them can quantify the trouble of having to correct problems with the bank. That's what Nancy Watrous, a resident of Akron, Ohio, found out when a check she wrote her credit card company for $36.91 was cashed for $3,691.

With only $1,200 in her account at the time, the error caused the account to be severely overdrawn and put her in danger of bouncing other checks. Watrous went to her National City branch to resolve the issue, and twice was told that she would have to wait for the credit card company to return the money. "I've never bounced a check in 48 years," Watrous told the *Akron Beacon Journal*. "This has been a nightmare."

Eventually, the problem was corrected and the money was credited back to Waltrous's account. But not until her account lingered in the red for days, making her own money inaccessible to her. Watrous was right to expect better treatment. Most banks will add a provisional credit to your account while a dispute is being investigated. The specific requirements for check disputes are usually covered by your state's *Uniform Commercial Code*, which commonly requires a bank to decide on a provisional credit within ten days.

Talk Back/Fight Back

Generally speaking, there is no safer place to keep your money than a federally insured bank. But because a bank can lose a deposit, double bill a check, or incorrectly charge a fee, remember to keep good tabs on your money. Keeping a receipt for payments and deposits and a thorough balance book will help you discover errors when you review your statements. And when you find a discrepancy, don't hesitate to defend yourself.

If you have a problem with a bank account, call the customer service line. If your customer service representative can't or won't help you, calmly ask to speak to a supervisor. You can continue to escalate your case any time someone doesn't help you. So if the supervisor won't respond, ask to speak to a manager. No luck? Try the president's office.

Perhaps the best chance for a quick resolution with your bank is to speak in person with your branch manager. If you bring in all of your evidence, it will be difficult for a real person to deny you face to face.

Even if you get a promise of a resolution over the phone or in person, you will often need written verification to trigger legal protections. So always follow up with a letter sent return receipt requested. Your letter should include a thorough description of your dispute and your proposed solution. Include copies of your documentation (always keep the originals in your file) and recount your phone conversations, including names and dates.

If you can't get a resolution to your dispute from your bank, complain to a regulatory agency. For customers of national banks, this will mean appealing to the Office of the Comptroller of the Currency. Recall that the OCC is funded by banking industry fees and has rarely used its power to rein in financial institutions. But the OCC does pride itself on helping thousands of consumers settle small disputes each year. Contact the OCC at www.occ.treas.gov, or call their toll free customer assistance line at (800) 613-6743, or file a formal complaint by writing a letter.

If you don't get anywhere by making an official complaint to a regulating agency, see if your state Attorney General or banking regulator can help. You may want to consider getting a lawyer, or making your case in small claims court (see "The Rights of Clients" chapter).

To further protect consumers, Congress must repeal the mistitled *Bankruptcy Abuse Prevention and Consumer Protection Act of 2005.* That law instituted a strict means test requiring every household above a certain income to repay any remaining debt after bankruptcy on a court-imposed schedule, regardless of circumstance. As Harvard law professor and bankruptcy expert Elizabeth Warren explained in Senate testimony, "A family driven to bankruptcy by the increased costs of caring for an elderly parent with Alzheimer's disease is treated the same as someone who maxed out his credit cards at a casino."

While the new bankruptcy policy makes it harder for low-income and middle-class families to declare bankruptcy, it does little to stem the abuses of wealthy individuals who would still be able to protect their money in asset protection trusts and homestead protections. It doesn't change those bankruptcy rules that allow businesses to protect their assets from employees and consumers. So corporations can be protected from consumer lawsuits and from being compelled to pay wages and benefits, but workers and consumers who've suffered a job loss or a personal injury aren't similarly protected. And, of course, it does nothing to protect consumers from predatory lending practices and bloated hospital bills that hit the uninsured with rates four times higher than those charged to insurance companies. Bankruptcy shouldn't be a means to a free ride for anybody, but it is a necessary tool for a second chance. We need to revisit the law so that families may have the chance to recover when circumstances bury them in debt.

IDENTITY THEFT

CASE STUDY

When Steve Dunn, a consumer specialist with Maine's Public Utilities Commission, began getting letters from collection agencies, he was a little startled. "It was quite a surprise to get a bill in the mail saying, 'Your check was no good,'" he told the *Portland Press Herald.* "I had no account with that bank and no checks with that account number."

The checks, totaling $420, were cashed in his name in South Carolina by identity thieves who had made up phony accounts and IDs with Dunn's correct name and address. Dunn responded immediately to the attack against his good name. "Having a background in law enforcement and regulatory matters made it easier for me," he said, "but it's still very time consuming."

Dunn offered proof that he was not in the places his checks had been cashed at the times the crimes took place. He called Maine's Office of Consumer Credit Regulation to file a formal complaint, and contacted credit reporting agencies to put an alert on his files. He went over his other accounts to verify their security, and then followed up by password protecting them. "All the agencies were very helpful. It was just that the collection agencies seemed not to want to listen."

Dealing with the identity theft took Dunn over a year. "It's extremely frustrating, because you do everything you're supposed to do, but it took a long time to get them to stop contacting me and threatening me with collections."

Preventing ID Theft   Identity theft is the fastest-growing crime of the new millennium. The FTC reported that, between 1998 and 2003, 27.3 million Americans became victims of identity theft, with 9.9 million in 2003 alone. Victims spend, on average, 175 hours clearing their names, at a personal cost of nearly $1,000 each in a process that can last years. *FACTA* provides new rights and resources in the fight against this invasive crime.

An identity thief can strike in a variety of ways. Access to your social security number, credit card, bank account, checks, ATM card, or driver's license can allow a thief to pose as you and open lines of credit in your name or get access to existing accounts. He or she can also prey on preapproved credit card applications. Once an identity thief strikes, he or she can wipe out your savings or run up debts that ruin your credit rating. As always, the first line of defense is prevention:

- Sign all of your credit and ATM cards.
- If a card is lost or stolen, report it immediately. Keep a record of account numbers and emergency phone hotlines to report your card as soon as you can. Make sure you get your card back every time you use it.
- Unneeded copies of receipts with private information should be torn up and disposed of.
- Keep a keen eye on your transaction statements, and account for all of your purchases. It never hurts to check out an item on your statement that you don't remember.
- Promptly notify all of your credit and banking companies of a change in address.
- Keep your account and your social security numbers secret.
- Don't give that information out over the phone or online unless you know the company to be trustworthy and reputable. If you're not sure about a company, check with the Better Business Bureau or a local consumer protection authority first.
- Preapproved credit card applications in your name should be torn up thoroughly before discarding.

- Check your credit reports often to screen for unauthorized activity.

Talk Back/Fight Back

If you've become a victim of identity theft, quickly contact the issuer of any line of credit or bank account associated with the crime and report that the fraud has occurred. They should freeze or cancel any accounts involved in the crime and begin an investigation into the fraudulent charges and debts. Start a file incorporating everything related to your case and keep it; even when a case seems closed, you never know when it might resurface. Include all your statements and receipts, any written correspondence, your dealings with law enforcement, and all your credit reports.

Contact the fraud units of any of the three credit reporting companies and request a fraud alert. The contact information should be included on your free credit report. Theoretically, once you contact one of the credit reporting agencies, it should notify the others to place fraud alerts, and all three will send you a free credit report.

In cases where you *suspect* you are a victim of identity theft but can't yet prove it, you can place a ninety-day initial fraud alert on your credit report, asking creditors and anyone else that reviews your report to contact you directly to verify new applications for credit. Companies that review this alert are required to take steps to prevent identity fraud on your accounts, but they are not required to verify each application with you before approving them. After you file an alert, you are entitled to a free credit report within three days.

If you *have evidence* that you are a victim of identity theft, you can put in place an extended fraud alert, which lasts seven years and has broader protections. The alert will be attached to your credit report and any score during the seven year period, unless you request to end the alert sooner. An extended credit report exempts you from lists the credit reporting agency provides to third party insurance and credit companies, and qualifies you for two free credit reports. With this alert, companies are required to contact you before approving credit or authorizing new accounts. You can "opt-out" of preapproved credit card offers permanently, or for a two year period, by calling (888) 5OPTOUT, which is also a good preventative measure if you won't miss the incoming credit card offers piling up in your mailbox.

Report identity theft to your local law enforcement agency and, if necessary, to the law enforcement agencies where the crimes took place. Share all your documentation and evidence, but keep the originals in your file. Dealing with the police may be frustrating because identity theft is a notoriously difficult crime to solve and many overworked departments don't devote enough resources to each complainant. Many victims find themselves doing all the detective work themselves and still can't get the police to seal the deal. Nevertheless, you may need a police report for your records to prove you're a victim, so get a copy of yours and keep it.

You will also need to contact the companies involved directly. Call the fraud department initially and then follow up with a written letter. If you don't have a police report, you can fill out an FTC identity fraud affidavit at the government's identity theft website, www.consumer.gov/idtheft/. The financial institutions should provide you with their records of fraudulent transactions and receipts free of charge, which you can share with law enforcement.

Have your account numbers changed and get new checks and cards to prevent further abuse. A joint report by CalPIRG and Privacy Rights Clearinghouse advises that your old accounts should be processed as "account closed at consumer's request," rather than "card lost or stolen," because future creditors may read carelessness into the latter. To further protect your new accounts, password protect them whenever you can. Always avoid obvious passwords that can be easily guessed, such as birthdates or your mother's maiden name.

If a debt collector comes knocking to collect fraudulent debts, you may need to complete either the FTC fraud affidavit or one provided by the collector. Take down all the information from the collector, including the company's name, your representative's name and contact information, and all of the information regarding the debt—and get the debt collector's documents as well. While much of the identity theft process will be handled over the phone, always follow up in writing, return receipt requested, to document your correspondence. In your letters, recount your telephone conversations and refer to the representatives you deal with by name and include the date of all of your discussions. Request a letter from the collector stating that you are not responsible for the fraudulent debt and confirming that the account in collection has been closed.

In the case of check-writing fraud, close your checking account and notify the applicable check verification companies. Two of the biggest are TeleCheck ([800] 710-9898), and Certegy, Inc. ([800] 437-5120). If one of your checks is unexpectedly refused at the point of purchase, ask which verification company rejected your check and get their contact information so you can follow up. You can have a stop-payment placed on any checks that may not have cleared.

If someone is fraudulently using your driver's license number to verify bad checks, contact your state's DMV. You should be able to put a fraud alert on your name and get a new driver's license number. You can also file a report with the FTC that will be entered into a nationwide fraud database.

Dealing with Debt

Debt Collection Falling behind in your debt payments can be stressful, but it doesn't have to ruin your life. If a debt collector is harassing you with repeated phone calls to you, your family, or your boss—or threatening liens, wage garnishment, or prison—they may be breaking the law. Debt collectors used to have free rein to use strong-arm tactics to collect for their clients. One debt collector reportedly parked a hearse in front of a home with the inscription, "A deadbeat lives here." The *Fair Debt Collection Act* was enacted to end such abusive behavior.

The law applies specifically to debt collectors (such as agencies and attorneys that collect debts for others), which take the responsibility of collecting a debt for a fee. It does not generally apply to the original lender such as banks collecting credit card bills.

Under the law, collectors cannot call you at work if they know your boss disapproves. They also must refrain from contacting you before 8:00 A.M. or after 9:00 P.M., without your consent. A debt collector can contact you in a variety of ways, such as telephone, mail, telegram, or in person, but not in such a way that makes it clear to third parties that they are collecting a debt; they can't print phrases like "collection agency" or "delinquent bill" on the outside of an envelope, for instance, or use a postcard. Within five days of when you first contact a debt collector, they must deliver a statement regarding the details of your debt, including the amount, the lender, and a procedure to follow if you don't believe you owe the money.

You can stop a collector from contacting you at all by sending a letter asking them to cease further communication. Once they receive it they'll have to desist, except to say that they won't contact you again or to inform you of a new action. *Don't forget about the debt, though!* You can still be sued if you don't pay off a legitimate debt. Between then, if you get a lawyer, the debt collector can no longer contact you directly.

Debt collectors are strictly forbidden from engaging in any collection practices that constitute harassment (including threats of violence, abusive language, repeated calls, or public disclosure of your debt); false statements (including misrepresenting themselves as law enforcement or government employees, implicating you in criminal activity, misstating the amount of your debt, or misrepresenting the legal status of paperwork they send you). Debt collectors cannot threaten you with arrest. If they threaten to sue, to garnish wages, to seize property, or to put a lien on your house, it must be a legal option that they fully intend to use.

Talk Back/Fight Back

If a debt collector is hounding you for a debt that you don't owe, defend yourself. If you respond to the first notice informing you of the debt, in writing and within thirty days, you cannot be contacted again until the collection agency provides proof that you owe the debt. If you're unsure that the debt is yours, simply ask the collector to provide verification of the debt.

If you know the debt is not yours, send a letter explaining why, along with any documentation you have to prove that it's been paid, such as a credit card bill or returned check. If it's a bill you've disputed with your credit card company or with a retailer, send copies of your documents that prove your case. Demand written confirmation of your settlement.

If you only owe part of the bill, send a letter explaining what you owe and why, along with a "payment in full" check for that amount. You can write on the back of the check that it can only be accepted as payment in full for the disputed amount.

Use your right to get collectors to cease communications as your leverage. You can tell them that if they don't agree to the settlement that you propose, you must insist they not contact you in the future. If you don't owe the
debt, then there's really no reason to go on dealing with a collector anyway.

If you owe the bill but can't afford to pay it, don't evade it or offer excus-
es. No one is less sympathetic to tales of woe than the debt collector. You can
buy some time by asking for a verification of the debt. After that, try to work
out a payment schedule that you can afford. Debt collection notices may have
a due date in big bold letters, but they can still be negotiated. Collection agencies usually would rather get a little at a time than nothing at all. When negotiating a payment plan, never promise to pay more than you can afford, or
refuse to pay when you can afford even a little. If they agree to a proposal,
make sure you get the terms of your payment plan in writing, to avoid future
misunderstandings.

If a collector has violated your rights under the *Fair Debt Collection Act*,
contact the Attorney General's office in your state. Also, file a complaint with
the FTC at www.ftc.gov or call (800) FTC-HELP to report the wrongdoer and
help others. Furthermore, you can sue for damages, and attorney and court
fees.

Debt Counseling   If you are in serious credit trouble, with multiple accounts in the red or with missed payments piling up late fees
and triggering 30 percent penalty APRs, there may be hope yet.
Credit counseling services offer an alternative to bankruptcy that
can help you get out of delinquency and back in the black. But even
if you haven't hit credit trouble quite that bad, you may benefit from
credit counseling. According to a joint report by the National
Consumer Law Center and the Consumer Federation of America,
anybody whose unsecured debt payments (excluding secured loans
like those for your home and car) surpass one fourth of their after-
tax income could be on the edge of financial trouble and in need of
counseling. That is, if they use a service that actually helps them and
doesn't compound the pain instead.

That report, *Credit Counseling in Crisis*, documents the rise of
profiteering in an industry that was a free consumer service just a

decade ago. Not only do most credit counselors now charge fees, many get paybacks from credit card companies to push consumers into certain debt management programs, while others engage in deceptive practices and abuse their nonprofit status to take your cash. The FTC and some state attorneys general have cracked down on a few big violators for such indiscretions as claiming their services were free while charging a "voluntary charitable contribution" involuntarily, and paying consumers' credit bills late, racking up penalty fees, and taking a cut. Credit counseling services are indeed helpful for many consumers, but wade carefully because there are sharks in the waters.

Credit counseling agencies offer a range of services, from help managing a budget to bankruptcy assistance. But their bread-and-butter service is the debt consolidation plan. For people drowning in credit debt, a consolidation plan can be a lifesaver. Basically, an agency consolidates your accounts so that one monthly payment to them is divvied up between your lenders. Through relationships with creditors, a counselor can negotiate new terms for your debt, including reducing interest rates and fees and even "re-aging" them to stop your delinquent accounts from hurting your credit score. Sometimes a plan can even lower the total balance of your debt. In return, you agree to pay the same payment every month until the debt is paid.

Consolidation plans are not a cure-all. In some cases you can manage to negotiate with creditors yourself and may benefit from not paying a credit counseling agency to do it for you. Those with limited resources may need to concentrate on secured debt, like home or car loans, which cannot be included in a consolidation plan. For others, a consolidation plan may not lower their monthly fees enough, leaving bankruptcy as the best option to protect their assets.

Choosing a Credit Counseling Agency   The most reliable agencies belong to the National Foundation of Credit Counselors

(NFCC), the original debt counseling organization. In 2001, NFCC organizations averaged $12 a month for a debt consolidation plan with a $19 enrollment fee and $14 for counseling sessions to rank among the lowest in the business. They have over 1,300 affiliates nationwide. You can search for one at www.nfcc.org, or by calling (800) 388-2227. Most agencies operate as nonprofits, so don't be too impressed by those who broadcast it most loudly. Be wary of agencies with a lot of advertising, which tend to operate more like for-profit companies. You can also call the Better Business Bureau and your state's Attorney General's consumer office to find out which agencies have had multiple complaints filed against them.

Be skeptical of claims for free services. When researchers from the NCLC and CFA surveyed credit counselors, the 20 percent who initially claimed their services were free charged a fee. Make sure you can get a written price quote. Before you sign on to a debt consolidation plan, verify that your creditors have already agreed to the terms. An agency might show you a great proposal before your creditors have signed on. Know your monthly payment, including fees, and how long it will take to pay off, and don't sign up for a plan you can't afford.

Fix It: Preserving Consumer Financial Rights

For far too long financial institutions have been able to write their own rules without concern for the American consumer. It's time to bring predatory lending and other abusive practices to an end and protect consumers from identity theft.

Credit Cards Consumer groups like Consumer Action, the Consumer Federation of America, Credit Card Nation, and U.S. PIRG have united to fix the credit card industry. They promote banning "universal default" and other unfair, indiscriminate, and arbitrary terms in credit card contracts; limiting penalty fees to bear some relationship to what it costs the lender; forcing creditors to acknowledge the true terms of credit, including the cost of making minimum payments; banning deceptive practices; and limiting out-of-control interest rates. (For more information see www.thetruthaboutcredit.com.)

While these reforms are far from the priority of the 109th Congress at the moment, there is hope. Bernie Sanders (I-VT) proposed the *Consumer Credit Card Protection Act* in 2005, along with four co-authors. The law would (1) ban "universal default," (2) require advance notice to precede any rate hike, and (3) require a warning on minimum fees. Further, his *Loan Shark Prevention Act* would set a nationwide cap on interest rates, and cap fees at $15. That bill found eighteen co-authors in the House. In the Senate, Chris Dodd (D-CT) proposed the *Credit Card Accountability Responsibility Disclosure Act*, which calls for similar measures.

ID Theft   *FACTA* provides needed relief to victims of identity theft by giving consumers more access to their credit records and more power to correct them. But Congress has done little to actually protect our private records or even to call on companies to notify us when our financial data is compromised.

Beginning in 2005, we've seen seemingly endless headlines about major corporations admitting to massive security breaches subjecting millions of consumers to potential identity theft. ChoicePoint, a company that compiles consumer data, reported a breach of hundreds of thousands of consumer Social Security numbers and credit reports to thieves posing as legitimate creditors; Bank of America reported that a lost backup tape made the Social Security numbers of over a million customers potentially available to identity thieves; Citigroup lost data for millions of credit card accounts, including Social Security numbers; and CardSystems Solutions lost the data for about 40 million credit card customers. Think this doesn't affect you? Think again. Hospitals, universities, retail establishments all have information about each of us, and they have all had serious security breaches in recent years.

Most of these incidents would never have come to light if not for California's groundbreaking privacy-protection laws enacted in 2003. These laws force companies to notify California consumers when information is lost, stolen, or otherwise compromised. "The California security breach notice law has had a profound effect nationwide," says Beth Givens, of the Privacy Rights Clearinghouse. "The general public now expects to be notified when there is a security breach."

But while California's laws may have implications for consumers nationwide, there is no federal law that requires notification. There should be. Corporations don't own us or our private financial records, and they should be held accountable when they put our personal information—and life savings—at risk.

Senator Dianne Feinstein (D-CA) attempted to make this a legislative priority in the Senate by introducing the *Database Security Breach Notification Act* in 2005. If you take your financial privacy seriously, prod your elected officials at both the federal and state levels to protect you from identity theft and force corporations either to protect your information or to notify you when they fail.

CHAPTER 6

THE RIGHTS OF TAXPAYERS

In its compliance activities, the IRS was like a police department that was giving out lots of traffic tickets while organized crime was running rampant.
—Charles Rossotti, IRS Commissioner, 1997–2002

When the federal income tax was reenacted in 1893, there was concern that the wealthiest and most powerful Americans—like John D. Rockefeller—would simply choose not to pay it. Luckily for the government, Mr. Rockefeller did pay $14,961.39 on a declared income of $1,247,252.65—a figure more than 1,200 times the average annual salary at that time. In later years, Mr. Rockefeller even left instructions that he desired "not so much to reduce the amount of the tax which he pays as to pay what the law requires him to pay, no less and no more. He desires, above all things, for us to have the reports accurate as possible." In that spirit, this chapter is not about the loopholes you can jump through or the tax havens where you can hide. It's about how you can protect yourself and defend yourself while truthfully fulfilling your responsibilities to the IRS and your country.

From the riotous Boston Tea Party in 1773 to Lincoln's imposition of the first income tax, to fund the Civil War, to the 2004 filing season in which more than 125 million Americans filed with the Internal Revenue Service (IRS), taxes have always been close to the center of American life—and of public discourse. Americans are still struggling to understand that "taxes are the price we pay for civilized society," in the immortal words of Supreme Court Justice Oliver Wendell Holmes Jr.

Contemporary tax debates reflect deep-seated ideologies on

what an equitable, effective system should look like. But whether you believe in a progressive income tax (a tax schedule based on each taxpayer's ability to pay), a flat sales tax, or something in between, we can all agree that whatever the system, it ought to be free of citizen cheating and government fraud. These are still major problems in a system that collected over $2 trillion in revenue in 2004.

That year the National Taxpayer Advocate, an IRS watchdog office, wrote that "more than $300 billion a year goes unreported, under-reported, or simply unpaid," while at the same time 39 percent of Americans thought that many or most people cheated on their taxes. When the policy questions of our day include saving Social Security from possible future bankruptcy, the rising costs of health care, and the ballooning national deficit, this billion-dollar tax gap obviously hurts us all.

The IRS is hardly blameless. In 1988, one IRS report found that about half of all correction notices sent to taxpayers were wrong or incomplete—and more than ten years later, the IRS wasn't even studying these errors to prevent systemic problems. So how many errors might there be in the more than 100 million notices sent out in 2004? Nor are the numbers better for taxpayers actually calling the IRS for tax information; a recent government report found that 38 percent of taxpayers who called the IRS were given erroneous information. If the IRS receives 16 million calls about tax laws, as they did in 2004, then over 6 million diligent people received bad information from the IRS—meaning many of them paid the wrong amount of tax. These contemporary tax grievances may not be as consequential as those that confronted the colonists, but they are certainly significant. As one humorist put it, "Taxation with representation ain't so hot either."

KEY TAXPAYER LAWS

The Sixteenth Amendment to the U.S. Constitution Various excise taxes were imposed throughout colonial and early-American history—most often in order to finance wars at home and abroad—but it took an amendment to the Constitution to solidify the individual American's direct relationship with federal taxes. The first income taxes, imposed as noted to pay for the Civil War, were repealed after the war ended and Congress didn't pass them again until 1893, when there was a growing consciousness that sales taxes alone let rich people get off without paying their fair share to the government. But when the Supreme Court ruled such a progressive income tax unconstitutional (because it didn't tax the states according to their population), Congress countered with the Sixteenth Amendment, which reads: "The Congress shall have power to lay and collect taxes on incomes, from whatever source derived, without apportionment among the several states, and without regard to any census or enumeration." The amendment was finally ratified in 1913 and the ubiquitous Form 1040, the U.S. Individual Income Tax Return, was born. At the time, the federal income tax only applied to annual incomes over $3,000 and at rates under 7 percent. Less than 1 percent of Americans filed then.

Taxpayer Bills of Rights of 1988 and 1996 Of course, over the next century, tax rates rose and the IRS became a behemoth government agency—easily intimidating the average taxpayer. But it wasn't until 1988 that Americans finally got their first *Taxpayer Bill of Rights* when Congress put certain restrictions on the behavior of the IRS—particularly in regard to taxpayer audits—and required the IRS to publish taxpayer rights in clear, nontechnical terms. Key provisions of this bill include: (1) the IRS must return any erroneous fine or tax to an individual upon a written determination from the IRS; (2) the IRS must immediately end an audit interview if the taxpayer expresses interest in speaking with a tax lawyer; and (3) the

IRS must extend the required notice of a levy from ten days to thirty in most situations.

When Congress revisited and expanded these rights with a second bill of rights in 1996, they replaced the Taxpayer Ombudsman with the Taxpayer Advocate, an expanded office of the IRS charged with assisting taxpayers in disputes. The Office of the Taxpayer Advocate is entirely independent of the rest of the IRS and reports directly to Congress. This law also requires an annual report from the Taxpayer Advocate on the twenty most serious problems facing the taxpaying public each year. Other expanded or clarified rights—there were about forty—include a guarantee that the IRS will return money to you if your files don't warrant the payment and that the IRS will abate any interest on unpaid balances accrued due to IRS delays. The law also multiplied the amount that a taxpayer can recover from the IRS for reckless assessment by ten times to up to $1 million. The *Taxpayer Bill of Rights* is today outlined in the IRS's *Publication 1*, which is available at the IRS website and at your local library.

IRS Restructuring and Reform Act of 1998   In the 1950s and '60s, the IRS was a leading government agency in efficiency and computer technology, but then failed to maintain and update its system as the years passed and as the economy and tax laws changed. So by 1985, overwhelmed workers in one IRS processing center were hiding and disposing of unprocessed returns in restroom trashcans. A little over a decade later, the Senate Finance Committee held explosive hearings into the failures and infractions of the IRS, with witnesses testifying behind screens to protect themselves from retaliation.

The media fallout from the hearings pushed Congress to pass the *Internal Revenue Service Restructuring and Reform Act of 1998*—a law that literally shook up the IRS from top to bottom. The IRS is no longer organized around a national hierarchy and instead categorizes its work by the type of taxpayer, so that one division handles a return from start to finish instead of its being passed ever upward through the bureaucracy. The four main divisions are: (1) small business; (2) mid-size and large business; (3) tax-exempt; and (4) the wage and investment division (the one we'll focus on in this chapter). In addition to reshaping the IRS, the *Reform Act* also included the *Taxpayer Bill of Rights* III. Among its sixty or so provisions, this third law shifted the burden of proof from the taxpayer to the IRS in tax disputes as long as the taxpayer has provided the backup information for his or her claim. The bill also sanctified the relationship between a taxpayer and tax professional as one like that between attorneys and clients.

The State of Local Taxes   Obviously, federal taxes are only part of the tax experience. Most of us also pay state and municipal taxes. While we can't cover them here, you can get more information about your state revenue agency from the Federation of Tax Administrators, a national group representing the tax services of all fifty states (www.taxadmin.org). Also, your state's website will likely have links to help put you in touch with your state revenue agency and taxpayer advocate.

FILING: THE IDES OF APRIL

CASE STUDY

On March 15, 1938, President Franklin Delano Roosevelt sent his incomplete tax return and a check for $15,000 to the Commissioner of the IRS with a cover letter that began, "My dear Commissioner...I am wholly unable to figure out the amount of the tax" owed on his 1937 income. After explaining his confusion, the president continued: "As this is a problem in higher mathematics, may I ask that the Bureau let me know the amount of the balance due? The payment of $15,000 doubtless represents a good deal more than half what the eventual tax will prove to be." Obviously, few of us have such a powerful ally at the IRS. But if you know your rights and the resources offered by the IRS, you just might feel as if you're getting FDR's special treatment. For example, there are several national volunteer-driven filing programs where well-trained volunteers will file your taxes for free if you are a senior or a low-income taxpayer.

Jane Smith, a Michigan taxpayer, wife, and mother of a middle-aged disabled son, had always filled out her own taxes until the year her husband became ill and was laid off. She was afraid they owed money—money that they couldn't afford to pay. She took her tax information to an AARP Tax-Aide location in a nearby community center, where a volunteer tax preparer found that Ms. Smith hadn't claimed all her credits—particularly for her dependent son—and actually was due a substantial refund. "They were in a really bad way," said the volunteer. "That money meant a lot to them." Realizing that Mrs. Smith was likely due money from other returns, two volunteers offered to amend as many prior returns as the IRS allowed. In the end, Mrs. Smith's total refund was over $5,000.

It is practically impossible to say anything new about filing taxes—every joke has been made, every complaint voiced, and every opinion stated. Perhaps the only aspect of taxation that isn't overplayed is the truth—that is, the actual details of paying your taxes and defending yourself against mistaken or illegal IRS rulings. Americans who are afraid of finding an IRS agent at their front door don't realize that there are things they can do to avoid that knock from the very start of our filing process.

While the first rule of filing is remembering that you are legally responsible for the truth and accuracy of your filing no matter who penciled in the numbers, you can protect yourself by carefully weighing all of your filing options from the start—particularly when deciding whether to pay Uncle Sam on your own or with the help of a tax preparer. Typically, self-prepared returns are more likely to contain errors; in 2002, about 9 percent of self-prepared forms had errors compared to about 3 percent of paid-preparer returns.

Going It Alone   Despite the headache IRS forms can cause, millions of Americans still break out the proverbial shoebox of receipts each year and start penciling in their taxes. Every year, the Wages & Investment Division processes the returns of over 100 million individual and joint filings—and more than half of those are prepared by the filers themselves. You can confidently join these self-sufficient ranks if your tax situation hasn't changed much since the previous year or if you have only a few pieces of information to be filed. With only a couple of W-2s, a few deductions, and maybe some investment income, you should be able to get through it with a pencil and some patience. In 2004, the IRS thought the average taxpayer would spend 13 ½ hours on their 1040 form—that's an increase of four hours over ten years. It may sound like a long time but that number takes into account everything from gathering materials to dropping the return in the mail, certified with a return receipt request, of course.

If you need assistance at any time while slogging through, there are several places to look for help. Obviously, there is the IRS website, www.irs.gov, which has most of the forms or publications you might need. For tax questions, you can call the IRS helpline, (800) 829-1040, but given the notorious inaccuracy rate (38 percent) of that resource, you may be better off going to a local storefront IRS Service Center. (It will be listed in the "Government" section of your phone book.) These service centers will also have information on other local nongovernmental tax resources—a local library, school system, or other social service organization will probably have a tax clinic. If you are a low-income filer, ask about IRS-sanctioned tax clinics—like Volunteer Income Tax Assistance (VITA), Tax Counseling for the Elderly (TCE), and Low-Income Taxpayer Clinics (LITCs)—which can provide you with free face-to-face help. AARP also runs a topnotch program called Tax-Aide that offers help to low- and middle-income filers of all ages. You can get more information on Tax-Aide at www.aarp.org or by calling (888) 227-7669. Of course, you can also find numerous tax resources on the Internet, but be extra cautious of the sources of any information you find. This is not an area where you should rely on the knowledge of strangers.

Electronic Filing (e-filing)   In recent years, the biggest change in personal filing has been the movement to electronic filing—nearly 67 million returns in 2005 were e-filed and Congress outlined in the *IRS Reform and Restructuring Act* that it hopes that electronic filing will be up to 80 percent by 2007. In general, e-filing allows you to fill out your return using computer software and file it via the Internet. You can quickly pay owed taxes with a credit card or have returns direct deposited into your bank account. E-filers often get any refunds within two weeks of filing and can track their returns on the IRS's website. Software programs will lead you through your return step-by-step with a series of questions that tailors the return to you. So, if you're relatively comfortable using a computer and have a basic understanding of your tax situation, purchasing software can be a great investment that can save you the cost of hiring a professional.

One of the most popular programs is TurboTax, which runs about $30 each year. You'll have to buy separate software to complete your state taxes, but if you watch your local advertisements, you'll probably find a deal that will offer a substantial rebate if you buy federal and state software at once—which is considerably cheaper than the several hundred dollars you may pay to a storefront preparer like H&R Block or other tax professional. Of course, software can miss deductions and may be less aggressive in strategy than some taxpayers might want—however, several companies offer to pay the difference if there are any inaccuracies caused by the programming and not by the taxpayer. (If you have a computer but do not have access to the Internet, any software will allow you to print out your taxes to mail them.)

Online Tax Preparation   The only difference between e-filing and online filing is that, with the latter, you'll fill out your return on a website instead of a software program. Proponents see online tax preparation as a mixture of the best parts of filing yourself—affordability—and hiring a professional—experience. Most of the software companies and storefront preparers offer a package deal where you fill out your tax forms online and then a professional will review them for accuracy. If you choose to file online, just be sure to double-check the provider's security protocols and to carefully read the service agreement before giving them your credit card number. For low-income filers, the IRS has a "Free File" program that provides free filing services through commercial companies. To find out if you qualify, visit the IRS's Free File website.

CASE STUDY

Imagine you went to a tax seminar where Chad Prater, head of Tax Informer Entities and the TaxInformer.com website, is talking about how you can get refunds of taxes from previous years. He's carefully explaining how Section 861 of the Internal Revenue Code exempts incomes earned from American-owned companies from federal income taxes. You can buy Chad's tapes, newsletters, and books to learn how to fight the IRS on your own. His materials look professional and mention that he has held seminars like this one across the country. You see that you can hire Chad himself to file the papers necessary to get back all that money you have been paying into government coffers. Sure, you're skeptical, but Chad is talking about actual parts of the code, he has a great-looking website, and look at all the people at the seminar. This just can't be a con.

Or so believed almost 1,000 Americans who paid Chad Prater over $3.5 million for his tax "expertise." Prater would file affidavits on behalf of his clients that claimed the IRS didn't have jurisdiction to tax his client and, when the IRS didn't respond, Prater would file default notices. Unfortunately for his clients—some of whom paid up to $20,000—these mock-ups of legal actions did not relieve them of their tax liabilities. And when the government caught up with Prater in 2002, it estimated that his scams cost the government $18 million in unpaid taxes.

According to Texas Attorney General Greg Abbott, "Outright tax evasion—as this was—will bring the tax man calling. In this case, [Prater] falsely stated to prospective clients that his companies could provide a permanent shield from obligations that most taxpayers willingly meet. Consumer beware—if it sounds too good to be true, it's usually bogus. There's no legal argument that can be made to excuse you from paying income taxes."

Hiring a Tax Preparer Like so many government agencies, the IRS has created a huge private industry—in this case, of tax preparers. From storefront firms like H&R Block to CPAs to tax lawyers, the IRS estimates that individual filers paid $15 billion for preparation in 2000, that more than half of filers used a service in 2001, and in 2002, 83 percent of taxpayers would use a preparer again. The Government Accountability Office, the research arm of Congress, found that 77 percent of taxpayers believed that they did not pay more than they legally owed in 2002 and taxpayers who used preparers that year accounted for half of the $945 million that American taxpayers overpaid. To avoid shelling out too much to the IRS or to a "preparer" like Chad Prater, be prudent in choosing a preparer:

- make sure it is someone with lots of experience with financials like yours and ask what percentage of their clients have been audited;
- get started as soon as you receive all your W-2s and 1099s— the longer you wait the busier your professional is going to be;
- never pick a professional because she promises a big return; if you get one it was because you paid too much in taxes throughout the year and should claim more exemptions;
- never sign any blank forms;
- never accept a Refund Anticipation Loan because the interest

and fees can be as high as 900 percent and you will be giving up even more of the interest-free loan you have already given the government;

- no matter how much you trust or how much you paid your preparation professional, double-check the math and the accuracy of the return; and

- reach a fee agreement *before* you start the return.

Remember, whether you pay a storefront preparer $200 for your entire return or a tax attorney $200 an hour, you are responsible for the return—and if there's a problem, the IRS will come after you, not your CPA.

Talk Back/ Fight Back

Because the IRS has focused less on enforcement in the years since the 1998 Reform Act, your chances of being audited are slim. In 2003, about 1 in 94 filers who made more than $100,000 were audited, and only 1 in 164 who made less than $100,000 were. Still, since 80 percent of audits result in the taxpayer paying more money, you should do what you can to "audit-proof" your return from the start.

Unfortunately, many Americans think that if they don't take all the deductions they are legally allowed, they won't be audited. This expensive theory is rooted in the IRS' Discriminate Function System (DIF)—a computer program that compares filers' deductions to national averages for similarly situated people. DIF flags people with higher than average deductions and produces almost a third of IRS audits. This means that more than two-thirds of audits commence because of other criteria. So, yes, while not taking all your deductions might keep you from being flagged by DIF, you still might be selected as part of a random sampling or as part of any number of IRS audit programs that target specific sectors of the economy and taxpaying public. Not taking all of your legally owed deductions only means you are giving up hard-earned money that an audit would only prove to be yours. Understand that an audit is not a conviction of tax fraud.

You can audit-proof your return in a better way. According to Daniel Pilla, executive director of the Tax Freedom Institute, "The key here is to provide sufficient information with the return at the time of filing." Instead of trying to trick DIF—and pay more taxes than you owe in the process—Pilla suggests preemptively addressing the next link in the chain to an audit: the human reviewer who analyzes the DIF (or otherwise) flagged filers. Send as much hard evidence of your deductions as you can with your return at the time of filing. This means two things: including disclosure statements (Form 8275) and affidavits if you have a large deduction that does not have a significant paper trail. Form 8275 gives you the opportunity to provide a detailed explanation of the deduction so that an IRS reviewer who receives an audit recommendation can make an informed decision at first glance that you do not need to be audited.

Affidavits are another strong part of audit-proofing and though they sound like a lawyers' tool too complex for the layman, you will see shortly how easy they are to obtain. Plus, on top of audit-proofing your return, affidavits can "penalty-proof" it as well. Why? Because the IRS is required to operate on a sort of "A for effort" principle: it's prohibited from fining filers who fully disclose their deductions—even if those deductions turn out to be improper.

When the IRS Is at Your Door   While much of the IRS's power comes from taxpayers' fear of the unknown, a little patience and some research will go a long way to alleviating these fears. Here's another fact that should make you feel better: the IRS will not dramatically come banging on your door like an FBI SWAT team with a warrant for your arrest. Though that image really belongs only in movies, congressional demands for a kinder, friendlier IRS have met some success. Only five years after the passage of the *Reform Act*, former IRS lawyer Eliot Kaplan said that IRS employees "used to be like pit bulls, but now they're like lap dogs," and that "the run-of-the-mill IRS guy is more scared than the clients."

If you are selected for an audit, you will most likely find out from your mailbox. The agency is charged with processing millions of returns and has turned to an automatic notice system that will notify you if the IRS has any questions about your returns. If you receive one of these letters, remember that it is not an indictment. An IRS notice generally only requests information or indicates that a simple mistake was made. It might simply mean that you forgot to sign your returns or that a social security number was entered incorrectly. Of course, you will be responsible for any fines or fees due to mistakes, but unless you did something very wrong—and you would know it if you did—you are not going to jail and probably are not even going to tax court. So, if you receive a corrections letter that accurately demonstrates an error you made, pay the assessment and check your work more carefully the next time around. But if you believe the corrections notice is wrong, read on.

Talk Back/Fight Back

If you receive an erroneous corrections notice, immediately send the IRS a letter expressing your strong disagreement and demanding an abatement of any fines or new taxes. As long as you send this letter within sixty days of the date on the flawed notice, the IRS must cancel any new charges. After you do that, there is a very good chance that you will never hear about the matter again, because the IRS does not try to reassess half of all abated taxes. IRS publications recommend calling an IRS service center or sending an informal letter explaining your disagreement if you believe your notice is wrong, but it is better to send a strong abatement letter. Why? Because Section 6213(b)(2) of the Internal Revenue Code (IRC) reads, "a taxpayer may file with the [IRS] within 60 days after notice is sent...a request for an abatement of any assessment specified in such notice, and upon receipt of such request, the [IRS] shall abate the assessment." Simply, that means if you ask for it, you get an abatement. To give you an idea of what your firm letter should sound like, here is some language from an example letter written by Daniel Pilla. After sternly reiterating the facts under contention and your disagreement, Pilla suggests the following language:

> This is notice under the provisions of IRS code section 6213(b) that you are to abate the tax liability shown in your notice immediately.

> Under the terms of that statute, the IRS has no alternative but to abate the assessment. Before collection action is

taken, I demand that a notice of deficiency be mailed in accordance with code section 6213(a) so that I may exercise my right of appeal.

Under the law, I have sixty days in which to protest this assessment. My protest is timely. Therefore, the tax must be abated."

You probably noticed that the language requests a "notice of deficiency." This is a precautionary measure so that if the IRS does reassess the abated taxes, you will have already set the wheels in motion for an appeal by asking for the proper notification of collection. It's important to get this notice because it has the information necessary for you to begin an official appeal or to set up a payment plan—both of which we'll cover shortly.

AUDITS, AGENTS, AND APPEALS

CASE STUDY

Al Risch's thought was "Why me?" when he received notice that the IRS was auditing his 1997 tax return. As careful people in their sixties, Al and his wife, Alison, did not know why they had been selected for this dubious honor. "We keep track of our accounts with a computer accounting program, so we had documentation of everything," Mr. Risch told *Kiplinger's* magazine. "We could just punch a key and get printouts of everything that took place during that year." Armed with the printouts and the accompanying receipts to their accounts and those of their landscaping business, the Risches went to meet with the auditors at the appointed place—a motel not too far from their home. There the auditor reviewed their information and pronounced, "It looks good. I don't know why the computer picked [your return]."

Of course, not all audits go so smoothly, even when the filing is complete and accurate. One Massachusetts accountant, Jeffrey Levine, explained, "a few years ago, one of my clients went through an audit where there was no objectivity at all. The concept was 'Everything here is wrong unless you prove otherwise.'" In the end, Levine's client "had to spend a lot of time and money proving he was right all along" about transactions as small as $2.

Over the years, the IRS has done little to disabuse the American public of far-fetched audit fears. And they won't anytime soon, because that fear is one of its best policing tools. How else could they try to keep more than 125 million taxpayers in line each year? If you are selected for an audit, chances are it will start with a letter that gives you a time and place for you to meet with the audit agent assigned to you. The purpose of that first meeting is for you to bring all the materials you used to file your return to show the IRS agent that it is all correct. This means bringing all your W-2s, proof of your mortgage deduction, and/or proof of your dependents.

If you used a tax professional to prepare your taxes, you might want to review your return and your backup information with your preparer in order to make sure that you can easily and confidently answer the questions. It is not uncommon for this process to require more than one meeting and for the IRS agent to ask for more information from third parties—like employers or banks. When the agent has completed the audit, he or she will issue what is called an "examination report," a document that outlines what the agent found and that will assess more taxes. Taxpayers can still protest the new taxes at this point, because the agent does not have the right to personally impose new taxes. Once you have the examination report in hand, you have thirty days to decide between two options: (1) you can sign the report, agree to the findings, and pay the stated taxes, fines, and interest, or (2) you can appeal the findings.

If you decide to appeal, you will likely have to provide further information to your auditor or her supervisor, and then a second examination report will be issued. At this point, you can again decide to sign the report and pay up or you can write a letter of protest to the IRS Appeals Office. To find out more about the appeals process, get a copy of IRS Publication 5, *Your Appeal Rights and How to Prepare a Protest If You Don't Agree,* and Publication 556, *Examination of Returns, Appeal Rights, and Claims for Refund.*

Talk Back/Fight Back

There are many things to remember when slogging through an audit, and several strategies will ensure your success in proving your truthfulness or easing the consequences of any errors.

First, according to Daniel Pilla, you must assume that you are right. Remember that when you filed, you did it with honest intentions like John D. Rockefeller, to pay no more and no less than you owe. While the IRS may have instigated this audit, you have no reason to believe that it is because you are guilty. Remember that the audit agent does not have the power to seize your bank account, put a lien against your house, or put you in jail.

The second right afforded to taxpayers as outlined in IRS Publication 1 reads: "You have the right to know why we are asking you for information, how we will use it and what happens if you do not provide requested information." That's awfully clear language even though many of the 400 IRS letters, audit or otherwise, are notoriously vague. Chances are that any letter you receive will not carefully outline the reasons the IRS wants information nor specifically outline what information they want from you. So you need to write them back immediately, stating your right to specific information, your request for specific information, and your willingness to undergo the audit as soon as you have all the information. Not only is it your right to have this information, but you are more likely to be successful if you know what they are looking for and can prepare to answer their questions ahead of time.

There are three other important considerations to think about:

Tax counsel. If you don't want to meet with the IRS agent yourself, you don't have to. You can send authorized tax professionals—lawyers, CPAs, or other enrolled professionals—in your stead. This can seriously diminish the IRS's power of intimidation and prevent you from making any naive mistakes. Jeff Schnepper, author of *Inside the IRS: How It Works (You Over),* writes, "Never represent yourself at your own audit. You may know what to say, but you don't know what not to say." However, depending on the situation and how you deal with confrontation, you may find that just consulting a professional beforehand will give you the confidence to go it alone. It is important to remember that you, as a taxpayer, never give up your right to counsel and if—at any time, in any meeting—you express desire to consult with counsel, the IRS agent must end the meeting immediately.

Affidavits. As mentioned previously, affidavits are a key tool to fighting back, whether you are demanding an abatement for an incorrect notice or proving a deduction in an audit. Sometimes there legitimately is no paper trail to "prove" an event or an income. In these cases, the IRS has to accept an affidavit—a written declaration of facts or events made before a notary public under the penalty of perjury. Since any claims the IRS makes against you are merely one agent's assertions, an affidavit easily ends the "he said–she said" standoff.

Control. Stay in control of the situation. For example, if any meeting, including the first one, is at a time or place inconvenient to you due to personal, medical, or professional commitments, write a letter expressing this and asking for it to be moved to a different time or location. You can even delay a meeting in order to have time to collect materials and consult with any professionals. Also, since you are at worst guilty of a few errors, you don't ever have to let the IRS agent into your home or office. (At this level, your auditor has no reason or authority to get a search warrant.) Another option you have is to complete the audit by mail. While the IRS may feign that it can demand you appear, you don't have to. If you respond with good faith that you are willing to complete the audit with all due speed by mail, the IRS will have to allow it. If you chose to go ahead and meet with an agent, know that you can audio record the entire meeting. This is a great idea because it establishes that you are no pushover and decreases the chances that the IRS agent will say anything even mildly intimidating or deceptive.

Paying the Taxman

CASE STUDY

When Betty and Gerard Wesley, a Maryland couple, couldn't pay the tax associated with a withdrawal from Gerard's retirement account one year, they set up an installment plan with the IRS. Making monthly $175 payments, the Wesleys were paying off their balance until Gerard fell ill and they missed a payment. Since a standard condition of IRS installment plans is strict adherence to the payment schedule, the Wesleys soon received a notice demanding the missed payment within thirty days in order to prevent cancellation of the agreement—and a demand for the full balance owed. With the help of a loan, the Wesleys were able to pay up within the time frame and make the next payment as well. Thinking that they were now in the clear, the Wesleys were astonished when a month later the IRS seized everything in their checking account except 23 cents—especially when the IRS seemed as stumped as they were. "Nobody at the IRS can explain why this happened. They honestly don't know," Mrs. Wesley told the *Washington Post*.

Whether it's writing a check on April 15 or one for the tax balance resulting from an audit, collection is the most danger-ridden part of the IRS process for taxpayers. This is the area in which the IRS has the most tools to use against you to produce what you owe. 2004 was a record year for collection, with the IRS bringing in over $40 billion in enforcement revenue. So know the options that can help you protect yourself and your financial health.

Can't Pay Your Return?   Aside from private sector alternatives such as taking out a loan, in this situation you have two options. First, you can apply for a six-month extension to pay your bill. You need to file Form 1127, the *Application for Extension of Time for Payment of Tax*, and prove a few conditions: (1) that you did plan properly to pay your taxes; (2) that you can't immediately pay them due to circumstances outside your control; and (3) that paying immediately will cause economic hardship. (This is separate from filing Form 4868, which grants a filer an automatic four-month extension in time to file the returns.) Of course, with an extension, you will still have to pay the interest that accrues on the bill over the six months and provide security against the extension. Essentially, you must offer assets on which the IRS can place a lien—a legal state in which the IRS has claim on your assets so that you can't sell them or borrow against them. Liens ensure that the assets will still exist later if the IRS should have to seize them due to lack of payment. Obviously, a lien isn't a good thing, but if you can realistically pay within six months, then this is the best option.

If you cannot pay on April 15th—or if your application for an extension is denied—your second option is to apply for an installment plan. While Congress specifically provided for this option, there are steep requirements in order to qualify. You must file Form 9465 to start the application. You will be guaranteed an installment plan only if:

1. You owe less than $10,000.
2. You have paid all taxes on time over the past five years without the aid of an installment plan.
3. The IRS agrees that you cannot pay in full when the payment is due and you provide all related financial information. (You'll have to fill out Form 433-A, which details your financial state.)
4. You can pay the full amount within three years.

Assuming you meet these requirements, the IRS will use Form 433-A to figure out what your disposable income is each month (and it will likely be a higher figure than your actual disposable income) and then charge you that amount each month. If your financial situation is so bad that you cannot pay anything at all now or for the foreseeable future, you need to apply for "uncollectible status" and start working hard to improve your situation, because even in this uncollectible status you will still be accruing interest and penalties.

Talk Back/Fight Back

While both the extension of time and the installment plan can be applied for before you miss your payment, only the installment plan application may be used after you have received notice of owed payments. At first, you will receive notices that say you must pay within a certain number of days. This does not mean the IRS can repossess your house after the waiting period, but it does mean they will add more interest and penalties after that date. You will eventually receive a "Final Notice," which gives you thirty days to pursue one of the two following options before the IRS can lay a lien or levy against your assets.

First, you can immediately write to the listed address asking for an installment agreement and, by itemizing your expenses, you should show how much you can pay each month. Send a copy of this letter to your local Taxpayer Advocate, whose office can stop enforcement actions before they happen or release them after the fact. With such a letter, you are trying to avoid a lien or levy, because either of those will not only make it difficult to cover living expenses but may make it impossible to pay taxes owed, since you will not be able to take out a loan.

Your other option upon receiving a collections notice is to file a request for a Collections Due Process Hearing. Just filing the request Form 12153 will put a hold on the collection action threatened. If your appeal is accepted, your hearing will be an informal meeting between you, or your counsel, and an Appeals officer. This is your chance to talk about all the circumstances of your tax situation—from the causes behind your delinquency to any problems with the IRS's behavior—and to offer alternative solutions like an installment plan. The key to this meeting is to show why the threatened action is worse for the IRS than your alternative plan. Be specific, bring any backup information, and be professional. You will be better served by a serious discussion than by a tearful story. And, if you disagree with the officer's ruling, you can appeal further within thirty days. This time you will be appealing to the U.S. Tax Court or U.S. District Court. You may have obtained counsel at some point along the way but, if not, you should seek a professional's advice about how to proceed at this point.

Liens. If you do not respond to the "Final Notice" within thirty days, you may be subject to a lien against your assets. The problem with liens is that once you have one you will not be able to take out a loan to pay the taxes you owe. Liens do not actually transfer the title of an asset to the IRS, but they do give the agency the right to control if and when you sell or borrow against it and to determine where any proceeds go. But if the lien was not properly processed or if it will hurt your ability to pay the taxes, you can apply for a "lien withdrawal" through your local IRS office. To do so, again you need to write a clear, concise letter. Describe why the lien should be withdrawn and include a copy of the original IRS notice and a description of the property under the lien. Another option is to apply for a lien subordination—meaning that the IRS will make its own legal claim to your asset secondary to a bank's or other lending organization's.

Levies. Since levies can turn your paychecks or bank accounts over to the IRS almost immediately, there is no time to waste once you've received notice of one, or your financial troubles will multiply. First, if the IRS places a levy against your wages, fill out IRS Form 668-W, which allows you to claim exemptions from the levy for you and your dependents. Without this form, the IRS will automatically take half of your check each pay period after your regular withholdings are taken out. Chances are that if you have reached this point, living on only half your take-home pay will compound your problems and make it more difficult, if not impossible, to repay the IRS. Next, whether you have a levy against your wages or against your bank accounts, you can apply to have it removed if it was imposed improperly, if removal will help you pay the taxes, or if it causes economic hardship. Address this letter to your local Taxpayer Advocate outlining the same issues as you would in a lien letter.

Taking Advantage of the Taxpayer Advocate. Given that the Internal Revenue Code is more than a million words long—or more than 130 times the length of this chapter—we obviously could only cover a few of the more common problems taxpayers have with the IRS. If at any time you need additional information about your tax situation or find that you have not been able to solve your problem through the standard IRS channels, contact the National Taxpayer Advocate's office at (877) 777-4778, or you can find your local advocate in the Advocate's brochure, IRS Publication 1546. Generally, the Advocate's services are available to you if you are facing financial hardships or if IRS actions have been unnecessarily delayed. Fittingly, the *Application for Taxpayer Assistance Order* is Form 911.

Fix It: A Taxing Challenge

Referring to the problems of the tax system, former Georgia Senator Sam Nunn reportedly said, "It's hard to tinker with a monster." He was right. The sheer size and mandate of the IRS makes real reform a clumsy if not impossible task—but that size and mandate also underscore the importance of improving the system. We need to start thinking about the IRS more than just in those hectic weeks in April.

The first step toward improving our tax system is an obvious one: crack down on fraudulent and evasive taxpayers. As IRS Commissioner Mark W. Everson argues, "average Americans deserve to feel confident that when they pay their taxes, neighbors and competitors are doing the same." With the tax gap—the difference between taxes actually paid and the amount legally owed—at hundreds of *billions* of dollars every year, it's bewildering that the IRS isn't fully funded. But President Bush is unwilling to put the money where his mouth is—his 2005 proposed budget was the fourth time he had called for hiring more IRS agents but didn't provide the cash to do it. This is not only bad politics, it's bad business; one indicted tax evader did not pay taxes on $450 million over four years. Even though other tax cheats probably are not hiding quite so much money, catching them will be awfully lucrative. And the IRS needs to think more creatively about finding them. Traditionally, the main way the IRS uncovers fraud is through reviewing the computer-generated red flags on individual tax returns, a process that inherently targets the less wealthy. For example, it is easier for computers to detect errors when one's return can simply be checked against the reports of an employer, bank, or investment adviser, but if a taxpayer is a business owner, he or she can control much of what the IRS knows. The IRS has made some advances in this area in the last few years but needs to keep thinking outside the box.

As important as fighting fraud, improved customer service must become a priority at the IRS. Significant advances were made after the passage of the 1998 *Restructuring and Reform Law*, but in 2004—six years later—four of the Taxpayer Advocate's 20 "most serious problems encountered by taxpayers" were customer service issues vis-à-vis the IRS. The report describes problems of access and accuracy in service provided over the phone, face-to-face, and via electronic channels—and yet the IRS doesn't conduct research on these issues. In all four customer service problem areas, the Taxpayer Advocate suggests that the IRS study its performance. How can a behemoth agency even begin to improve on customer service if it has not taken a hard look at its current operations?

Beyond the operational pitfalls of filing, U.S. tax policy itself is backward. As Ralph Nader wrote, "During the past twenty-five years, the trend has been unmistakable. Both relatively and absolutely, corporations pay less income tax. Relative to the middle class and the poor, the super wealthy are paying on the whole a smaller percentage of their income in overall taxes.... The tax burden continues to shift from the wealthy to the working class." Fixing this problem is going to take a real discussion about what an *American* tax policy—and what the 6,000-plus-page Internal Revenue Code—should look like. And it's not the Bush tax cuts of 2001, 2003, and 2005, which used a rhetorical bait-and-switch to hide the fact that the middle-class would lose. According to the Center for American Progress, the majority of taxpayers in 2003 got less than $850 in tax cuts, but Bush's fuzzy math said that the "average taxpayer" got $1,800. The fuzzy factor: the wealthiest 1 percent of the country got about $52,000 apiece in cuts. Another middle-class tax albatross is the Alternative Minimum Tax (AMT). Originally meant to prevent wealthy taxpayers from paying too little tax, the AMT is not indexed for inflation and will trap a third of taxpayers in the next few years. Unfortunately, the need for reform is not limited to individual returns; Congress must close the loopholes that allow major corporations to hold their monies in tax-free offshore accounts or to win government contracts while owing millions in back taxes.

As two smart progressives wrote in *The American Prospect*, "It's time to make the argument for public investment in education and the economy, and to link it to a campaign against the loopholes and tax dodges that allow corporations and the well-heeled to avoid paying their fair share of taxes."

CHAPTER 7

THE RIGHTS OF SHAREHOLDERS

Shareholders don't stand up for their rights for reasons that are hard to explain. What is a CEO? Too many of them are just guys who buy private jets without using their own money. They're using our money, the shareholders' money, and they don't even let you ride on the plane.

—Carl Icahn, financier

"Those of us who know nothing about the stock market will never understand it. That puts us right in the same class with economists and brokers who know all about the stock market," wrote journalist James Kilpatrick in 1987. And while he may have been right that no one has the answers when it comes to getting-rich-quick, he was wrong when it comes to the rules of the game: corporations and stockbrokers know the laws and regulations of the securities markets while most investors—often to their financial detriment—do not. We all want that rags-to-riches stock tip, but shrewd investors will learn about and protect their rights as shareholders. After all, what good is that golden tip, or long-term financial plan, if you are defrauded by your stockbroker or the very company in which you invest?

In the last few years, we've seen high-profile corporate scandals in which investors lost billions—and their livelihoods. And, beyond Enron, WorldCom, and Tyco, we've heard over and over from World Trade Organization protesters and Wal-Mart detractors that the companies in which we buy stock are engaging in amoral or immoral behavior that's bad for labor, for society, and for the economy. And every year, we hear about those investment phone scams in which the naive and the elderly lose everything because someone promises thousands from pennies. Whether dreams of getting rich or of enjoying a secure retirement draw us into the markets, the securities industry can appear to be a foreign world of risks, traps, and—especially lately—fraud.

If investor rights seem like an issue for slick Wall Street types and the super-rich, think again. Sheer numbers tell otherwise: 49.5 percent of American households own stocks and the number of individual investors has nearly doubled to 84.3 million in the last twenty years. By 1998, nearly half (49.9 percent) of middle-class households owned stock—directly or through a pension—and nearly one-third of them held more than $10,000 in stock. In fact, middle-class stock ownership tripled in fifteen years. And consider the now infamous Enron collapse: 15,000 ordinary workers lost $1.3 billion of a $2.1 billion 401(k) retirement plan, which invested heavily in Enron's own stock. While Enron is the poster child for corporate malfeasance, many big companies—like General Electric, Coca-Cola, and McDonald's—have "held their collective breaths" as their stock prices fell by more than 20 percent in recent years. Why the anxiety? Because their employee 401(k) plans are self-invested Enron-style, too.

For more than half of America's workforce, employer-sponsored pension plans represent their entire savings. To paraphrase that old General Motors cliché, if these stocks catch a cold—whether because of fraud or legitimate cycles in the economy—average workers get pneumonia even while their executive counterparts get company-funded pension plans or golden parachutes. Thus, with such increased market participation by the middle class and such risky pension investment by big corporations, the shareholder movement is a cause that should unite forward-thinking people of all economic classes. Indeed, as Senator Joe Lieberman said after Enron's collapse, investor protection "affects the quality of life of those firefighters [I met] in Florida and millions of other middle-class investors who want to participate in the larger American dream of growth and prosperity—without fear of being swindled out of their hard-earned savings and investments." Logically, investor rights should be an integral part of Wall Street—because when investors feel they've been had and lose confidence, the corporate poobahs feel the effects in divestiture and falling value.

KEY LAWS FOR SHAREHOLDERS

Securities Acts of 1933 and 1934 Before the U.S. stock market crashed on what became known as Black Tuesday in October 1929, investors gave little thought to the dangers of the largely unregulated stocks and markets. But the market fell by $14 billion in one day, and the country spun into the Great Depression in which 5,000 banks failed and unemployment rates reached more than 20 percent. Aiming to prevent another crash, empower shareholders, and create more secure markets, Congress passed the *Securities Acts of 1933 and 1934* to start holding both the companies offering the securities, called issuers, and the brokers trading those securities, accountable. In a sense, with the passage of these laws, shareholder activism was born.

The *Securities Act of 1933* had two objectives: first, to assure that investors receive all significant information about securities available for sale and, second, to ban misrepresentation in the sale of all securities. Basically, this means that brokers and issuers can't lie to or withhold significant information from investors. This might sound like a clear-cut, commonsense standard, but it's actually difficult to achieve in the unpredictable and complex investment world. So Congress set up a registration process that applies to nearly all securities traded in the United States, requiring the disclosure of basic and accurate information about the issuing company, its management, its finances, and about the security itself.

Institutionalizing the goals of the '33 law, the *Securities Exchange*

Act of 1934 established the federal Securities and Exchange Commission (SEC)—the most important government ally of and advocate for today's investors. By consolidating broad, regulatory power in one constant government body, Congress hoped to finally restore the public confidence in the markets that Black Tuesday destroyed. Specifically, the '34 Act empowered—and charged the SEC with oversight of—market self-regulatory organizations called SROs (e.g., the stock exchanges, the National Association of Securities Dealers). In addition to expanding the registration process to include stockbrokers and dealers, the Act outlined the manner in which corporations must prepare shareholder votes and banned specific types of investor fraud like insider trading and market manipulation. Today, defrauded investors can sue for recovery under both the 1933 and 1934 Acts.

Also, one of today's best tools in the effort to create a culture of transparency is the SEC's Electronic Data Gathering, Analysis and Retrieval System (EDGAR). Though at first a bit overwhelming to laymen, EDGAR is a fully searchable, online, free-of-charge database of the financial documents that companies and other securities actors are required to file, including corporate annual reports (10-Ks), quarterly reports (10-Qs), mutual fund prospectuses, and so on. Available to anyone who can use the Internet, EDGAR represents a major step in empowering investors as it provides relatively efficient and immediate transparency. (EDGAR is available at www.sec.gov/edgar.shtml.)

Investment Company and Investment Advisers Acts of 1940

These two laws were natural follow-ups to the transparency-focused 1930s laws. The *Investment Company Act* extends registration and disclosure requirements to companies that specialize in investing in the securities of other companies, that is, mutual funds. Specifically, it was meant to identify and prevent any conflicts of interest in these companies that produce their own securities to sell to the investing public. Similarly, the *Investment Advisers Act* aimed to regulate those whose primary business is making investment recommendations to clients. Advisers, if not already registered as a broker or other securities agent and if they manage more than $25 million in assets, must also register and disclose pertinent information to the SEC.

The Sarbanes-Oxley Act of 2002   Unfortunately, the recent rash of high-profile broker and corporate scandals clearly demonstrates the patchwork state of securities regulation, particularly at its intersection with corporate responsibility. We watched as Enron declared bankruptcy after overstating their assets by over a billion dollars, as Tyco executives were caught giving themselves tens of millions in interest-free—and later forgiven—loans from the company, and as WorldCom collapsed after an $11 billion accounting scam. The ensuing public outrage led directly to the *Sarbanes-Oxley Securities Act* of 2002. Called "SOX" by industry-types, this securities law targets accounting and executive fraud in large publicly traded corporations. In fact, the first words of the legislation assert that SOX is an act "[t]o protect investors by improving the accuracy and reliability of corporate disclosures made pursuant to the securities laws, and for other purposes." The main provisions of the law:

- Establish the Public Accounting Oversight Board (PAOB) to regulate the auditing of public companies and to register and police public accounting firms that deal with corporations issuing securities;
- Improve auditor independence by prohibiting accounting firms from providing other non-audit services at the exact same time;
- Expand corporate responsibility by requiring that an issuer's CEO and CFO certify financial reports as true and complete;
- And raise the criminal and civil penalties for corporate fraud and white-collar crime—hiking the maximum fines and prison terms for those who knowingly defraud investors through corporate securities, auditing, or mail or wire fraud.

Though certainly moving in the right direction, these advancements raise the accountability bar by inches, not feet or yards.

In her insider expose of the rampant corporate fraud in American companies, *Other People's Money: The Corporate Mugging of America*, Nomi Prins takes SOX to task, calling it, "reform, Washington-style, [that only] consisted of a dramatic series of photo-ops and media sound bites; perp walks for the frequently indicted, yet rarely convicted executives; SEC and other regulatory agency settlements for fractions of the money the culprit corporations lost the public and their own employees; and Senate hearings televised only on C-SPAN." Prins, a fifteen-year Wall Street veteran, points out that even the SOX-regulated corporations probably didn't find the law effective; some 50 percent of executives surveyed by one of the "Big Four" accounting firms said that the "law would have *no* impact on corporate confidence" and only 4 percent thought it would actually create significant changes in their company's compliance practices.

CASE STUDY

Making, at most, $20,000 annually throughout her career, Berhardine Timmerscheidt, a Brooklyn, New York, hairdresser, was lucky enough to receive a "modest inheritance" before her retirement at sixty-two. Seeking enhancement of her retirement income from Social Security, Ms. Timmerscheidt opened a brokerage account with a local stockbroker, telling him, "don't do anything to place my principle at risk."

Her broker proceeded to aggressively trade on her account in order to generate commissions for himself—a fraud called "churning"—and then fudged account statements to hide the losses in her account, a common form of broker misrepresentation. When Ms. Timmerscheidt and her tax preparer discovered the fraud, she found a securities lawyer and entered into the investor arbitration process of the National Association of Securities Dealers (NASD). Ultimately, a three-member panel found that her broker was indeed guilty of churning, misrepresentations, and omissions, and was liable for the damages to Ms. Timmersheidt. The panel awarded her $150,000, plus lawyers fees and other costs.

But Ms. Timmerscheidt's trouble wasn't over, because her broker asserted that "I'm obligated to pay, but I don't have the money. If they're going to go ahead and pursue it, they will never see a dime." Because this situation is common, lawyers usually file complaints against the brokerage firms as well as the individual, but in Ms. Timmerscheidt's case the brokerage firm was out of business and being liquidated for the Securities Investor Protection Corporation (SIPC), a nonprofit corporation that protects investors' assets from theft and failed brokerages.

As a Florida financial columnist wrote, "...this case is one that should unsettle any investor who deals with a brokerage. Is the company not only reputable but financially stable enough to weather a few storms? And have you done all you can to prevent problems from occurring in your account?"

FINDING A BROKER

While you can invest in most stocks and bonds without a broker, two out of every three investors have at least one brokerage account and 49 percent have an account with two or more brokerage firms. So don't let disheartening stories like Ms. Timmerscheidt's scare you off brokers altogether. In 2004, according to the Securities Industry Association, 90 percent of brokerage investors were "very" or "somewhat" satisfied with their service, and 68 percent said their broker did a "good" or "excellent" job at keeping "my best interest at heart in making or suggesting investments." Realistically, Ms. Timmerscheidt's saga should be a warning to choose a broker wisely and then keep our eyes open.

There are two big things you should look for in a broker. First, remember that financial portfolios and investment needs vary from investor to investor, so you'll want to find a professional familiar with situations like yours. In this area, one thing to think about is whether you need a full-service or discount brokerage firm. Generally, full-service firms will buy and sell your securities and offer investment advice and research, while discount firms will only buy and sell on your behalf.

The second thing to carefully consider is pricing. Does the brokerage have a flat fee for transactions? Will your potential broker get special commission for selling certain products—like those produced by his or her firm? Stockbrokers are salespeople trained to sell securities, and many of them have salaries directly tied to what you buy. "That creates a conflict of interest," points out ubiquitous financial journalist Suze Orman. "Do you really think that commission-based financial advisers [and brokers] never have it in the back of their mind exactly how much money they will make if you follow their suggestions?" So, unless you already have a close relationship with a broker, look for one that will charge a flat fee for managing your assets and for one who is independent of any investment banks. You want your advisor to be thinking about what *you* should buy, not what *she/he* wants to buy.

There are lots of resources available to help you find a broker—especially on the web and at your local library, which will certainly subscribe to any number of financial magazines that often make up-to-date recommendations on specific brokerage firms. It's also a good idea to ask trusted friends, family, and coworkers about their brokers. In the long run, a trusted recommendation can be the best reference. Of course, you should be extremely careful if you start your search with the phone book.

When you've found a few potential brokers or firms that you like, you should do a free BrokerCheck with the NASD—a self regulatory organization (SRO) with which virtually every player in the securities market is required to register. The NASD is the largest of the SROs in the United States, with over 65,000 branch offices and half a million securities professionals under its jurisdiction, and its BrokerCheck is a fast way to find out about the professional background, registrations, and any criminal or investor complaints lodged against your broker or firm. Not only will this allow you to spot any red flags, but it will also familiarize you with his or her work and business practices. To request a check, visit www.nasdbrokercheck.com or call their toll-free hotline at (800) 289-9999. And, if this seems like a lot of work just to buy some stock, remember Ms. Timmerscheidt's troubles; though the high-profile cases of securities fraud are on the corporate level, individual investors can and do regularly lose money due to broker mistakes and scams.

Another type of securities professional you might come across or consider hiring is a financial adviser. Often brokers are advisers and will perform both advisory and transaction duties for you. But some investors prefer to hire an adviser independent of the actual dealing—the idea being that the adviser won't receive any fees or commissions on specific securities like a broker might. Unfortunately, this isn't true of all advisers. They, too, can receive special compensation for promoting particular securities, so make sure your adviser is independent as well. To check out the history of an adviser firm, visit the SEC's Investment Adviser Public Disclosure website at www.adviserinfo.sec.gov (the NASD does not regulate professionals who are purely advisers). Currently, the SEC website only offers information on adviser firms, not their individual personnel. To check out an individual adviser, contact your state securities regulatory body. You can find yours at the North American Securities Administrators Association (www.nasaa.org or [202] 737-0900).

FIGHTING BROKER FRAUD

Since securities markets are complex and a fraudulent broker will purposefully obscure things, it's important to have an idea of what broker-orchestrated fraud can look like. Here's a list of four common areas of broker fraud (they are the most frequently reported to the NASD):

- *Simple swindles.* As the saying goes, "a fool and his money are soon parted," so there will always be those con artists—posing as brokers or dealers—who will convince investors of a great opportunity, then take the money and run. There are innumerable variations of this idea—like pyramid schemes and boiler rooms. Be careful of any high-pressure pitches or cold calls that "guarantee" big returns.

- *Misrepresentation.* Like the stereotypical car salesman who sells you a lemon promising a peach, shady brokers make exaggerated claims about the money-making potential of an investment. But brokers have a fiduciary duty to be completely honest with you. Even omitting information is usually a type of misrepresentation, as in Ms. Timmerscheidt's case.

- *Churning.* Crooked brokers often make trades in a customer's account to generate commissions rather than to improve the customer's finances.

- *Unsuitable Recommendations and Unauthorized Trading.* Both of these are just what they sound like—when your broker sells you something incompatible with your financial goals and when your broker acts without your authorization.

CASE STUDY

Gene Murdock, a level-headed nurse-anesthetist from Georgia, wanted to take out some of the $2.8 million he had in Merrill Lynch brokerage accounts in 2000 to pay off his house, his daughter's college education, and to get a new boat. But his broker, a close friend, told him not to bother because markets fluctuate and the recent market dip would turn around. But it didn't. In fact, it kept dipping, and Mr. Murdock watched his one-time $3 million accounts fall to less than $500,000 value in two short years. Over that time, Mr. Murdock's broker had advised him to stay the course, except for suggesting other hot dot-com securities that ultimately tanked.

So Mr. Murdock entered arbitration and was—two years later—awarded $525,000. While brokers aren't generally responsible for a bad tip, what might have made a difference in this case is that industry analysts, according to the *New York Times*, "routinely gave positive recommendations on companies that they disparaged in private." In a similar case, another Merrill analyst publicly supported InfoSpace stock but privately said it was "a piece of junk."

About that same time, Floridians Gary and Lisa Friedman were letting Merrill Lynch's analyst ratings direct their stock choices. They ended up with a mixed portfolio of blue chips and some of those hot stocks riding the bubble. Their portfolio peaked at over $6 million but fell by $4.9 million over three years. Building their case on the fact that Merrill had rated nearly none of their more than 1,400 researched stocks as "sell" or "reduce," the Friedmans filed for arbitration, too—and were ultimately awarded just over $1 million. In their case, the arbitration panel "found 'clear and convincing evidence' that Merrill analysts knew the stocks they recommended to investors were overvalued."

Talk Back/Fight Back

How to Fight Your Broker in 4 Steps. With the successful arbitration stories of Mr. Murdock and the Friedmans as inspiration, if you feel you've been a victim of similar brokerage scams, here are several steps you should take.

Step 1: The first rule of fighting back is "Start now." If you feel your broker has acted illegally, don't put off taking action. Delaying action and, ultimately, the resolution of the issue could be detrimental if for no other reason than in some cases there are legal time limits on certain processes.

Step 2: Take it to your broker, the branch manager, or the firm compliance officer. Knowing that brokerage firms are often hectic environments—and that mistakes aren't uncommon—think about whether you want to give your broker the chance to rectify any errors made. If the answer is yes, then promptly send your concerns to her in writing, providing any related documentation, and perhaps describe what sort of compensation you are seeking.

Be sure to ask for any explanations in writing—even if you have a conversation on the phone or in person. If you strike out with the broker or aren't comfortable taking your initial concerns to her, then go instead to the firm's branch manager. Approach her in the same manner. And if the manager isn't helpful, your next outlet is the firm's compliance officer. Since the SEC requires brokers and firms to catalog and investigate any complaints, firms have a compliance officer who takes such complaints seriously. Generally, you can find that office by calling your firm's headquarters or by visiting their website.

Though speaking with your broker, the branch manager, or the compliance officer may help you comfortably continue to invest with that brokerage, you are unlikely to receive any sort of monetary reimbursement at this level. Brokerage firms are for-profit enterprises and will not likely return any of your money—unless legally compelled to do so or your complaint is so strong that they want to resolve it to avoid regulatory action. Even compliance offices—charged with keeping their brokers in line—will be very reluctant to hand over any cash.

THE BIG QUESTION:
Do I need a lawyer? When should I find one?

Throughout this process, you should continuously gauge whether you should pursue these avenues without a lawyer. According to Larry Soderquist, an attorney and author of the excellent *Investor's Rights Handbook*, "No matter what else you are doing about your problem, I wouldn't wait more than three or four months from the first questionable event that occurred before speaking with a lawyer. Usually, you should talk to a lawyer much sooner than that." A lawyer can help you decide whether you have grounds for a complaint, draft effective documents at every stage of the process, and help determine the best strategy. Use common sense: the more money involved, the higher the stakes, then the faster you should find a lawyer.

If you decide it's time to get counsel, it may be hard to find a lawyer near you that deals with securities issues. But it is more important that your lawyer have the right experience than the right zip code, since legal proceedings can generally be completed remotely. One resource is the Public Investors Arbitration Bar Association, a group of lawyers that specifically represents investors. You can visit their website at www.piaba.org or call them toll-free at (888) 621-7484. Also, both the SEC and the American Bar Association have lawyer search resources at their websites. Another idea is to call a lawyer you already trust and ask for his or her recommendation for a securities lawyer.

One great option that might be available to you is a local law school clinic. Generally, these free clinics serve investors with claims of less than $100,000 who might have trouble finding a practicing lawyer to take their case. Law students, guided by professors, will give you free legal advice, but you will still have to pay any filing and procedural fees should your case come to that. To find a clinic, simply call law schools in your state and ask if they have a clinic.

Step 3: Contacting the Regulators. Whether or not you have a lawyer, once you feel you've exhausted your outlets with your broker, the branch manager, and the compliance officers, the next step is to report to the regulatory agencies available to you—usually the SEC and your state securities administration. Filing these complaints will not only strategically help you as a wronged individual but also help protect your fellow investors by calling attention to fraud that may extend beyond your accounts.

SEC. Filing a complaint with the SEC is easiest through its website, which has electronic filing forms specific to several types of complaints (www.sec.gov/complaint). These forms ask for all the basic information surrounding your concern: the broker and firm name, the type of investment in question, what action you've already taken, etc. In response to your filing, the SEC can advise you on any possible solutions or remedies, and may send a letter to the firm involved asking for an explanation. Upon receiving that letter, the firm may feel pressured to respond to you and appease you financially while they try to avoid a formal SEC investigation. However, the SEC is not your personal lawyer and won't take legal action on your individual behalf, only on behalf of the public at large.

State Securities Administrations or Attorneys General. Every state has a securities administration, though the name and organization of each varies. To find yours, contact the North American Securities Administrators Association (NASAA) at their user-friendly website www.nasaa.org, or at (202) 737-0900. The NASAA website is a great resource; it has a simple complaint form that will be forwarded to the proper regulator as well as other general resources on filing complaints and how to avoid becoming a victim. You can find your state attorney general's office in the government section of the phone book or at your state's website.

Step 4: Enter Mediation or Arbitration through a self-regulatory organization. In an ideal world, you and your broker will have reached a satisfactory resolution by this point. But in the real world, entering into mediation or arbitration may be the only way you'll recoup any of the funds you lost to broker fraud. You might wonder why you can't sue, but if you remember back to when you opened your brokerage account, you were probably required to sign some sort of new account agreement. And that agreement probably included a clause stipulating that you would arbitrate any disputes that arise. This precludes you from individually suing your broker or firm in court and means you'll use the dispute resolution processes of the major SROs—usually the NASD or one of the stock exchanges—like Ms. Timmerscheidt, Mr. Murdock, and the Friedmans all did.

The arbitration system has experienced record participation since the dot-com bubble burst and since New York State Attorney General Eliot Spitzer went after Wall Street corruption. As Christopher Bebel, a securities lawyer, explained, "The vast majority of investors around the country have sustained losses on their accounts and are now more motivated than ever to seek revenge and obtain justice because they feel emboldened and encouraged by the actions Spitzer has taken." Peaking in 2003, the NASD, which handles a majority of all the industry's complaints, received over 8,900 arbitration filings—that's more than double the number of filings from 1990 and an increase of 62 percent since the dot-com burst in 2000.

As with the SEC or your state securities administration, you'll start the arbitrations process by filing a complaint with the appropriate SRO. Their websites, particularly that of the NASD and the New York Stock Exchange (www.nyse.com), have extensive information on how to lodge your complaint and start mediation or arbitration. Generally, mediation is an informal process in which a trained, impartial mediator will facilitate negotiations between you and your broker. Mediators do not have the authority to settle the dispute, only to help both sides come to a resolution together. This may sound like a toothless option but, in recent years, as high as 86 percent of NASD's mediation cases have settled, saving the involved parties the time and costs of the longer and more expensive arbitration process. Still, some prefer arbitration because it gives a panel of trained arbiters the power to decide whether fraud was committed and award any restitution. Over the last four years, investors have won some monetary or nonmonetary relief in about 50 percent of arbitration cases, but it's difficult to discern trends in rulings because arbiters don't usually provide much explanation for their decisions. However, some of the most common frauds investors cite are breach of fiduciary duty, unsuitability, and misrepresentation.

While you're not required to have a lawyer, you should by this point. These procedures may not take place in a court per se, but they are awash with legal procedures and standards, *and* arbitration rulings are final. For more information about arbitration procedures, visit the NASD website or the NYSE website, or call their dispute resolution departments at (301) 590-6500 and (212) 656-2772, respectively.

TAKING ON THE CORPORATION

Everyone recalls Michael Douglas (aka Gordon Gekko) in the movie *Wall Street* saying, "Greed...is good. Greed is right. Greed works." But few remember that his iconic remarks came as he was exercising his rights as a *shareholder*. Speaking at an annual meeting, Gekko stood up and talked back to the board members of the fictional Teldar Paper. A basic tenet of shareholder activism is that if shareholders stand up for their rights as owners who can influence the company's behavior and direction, then the corporation and society are better off. Like a good sports coach that consistently critiques your form, your speed, and your agility in order to make you a better athlete, shareholders can hone their companies into profitable *and* responsible organizations.

Today, the corporate concerns of investors and their fellow Americans focus in two areas. First, we want better governance—whether it is from new legislation or from better enforcement. In 2002, during a time of record-breaking corporate bankruptcies and accounting scandals, some 59 percent of Americans were concerned that regulators would "not go far enough toward" improving accountability and confidence in the markets and U.S. corporations. Moreover, 61 percent thought that the then newsworthy cases of

CEO malfeasance were "a widespread problem"—not the result of a few corrupt individuals. This discontent sustains the shareholders movement. Indeed, according to Carol Bowie of the Investor Responsibility Research Center, "Right now, investors are still stinging from the impact of corporate scandals. The realization that things weren't working as they were supposed to is still promoting healthy skepticism and activism and criticism...."

American investors are also concerned with improving corporate business practices, sometimes called corporate social responsibility (CSR), across all industries. Whether the issue is child labor, pollution emissions, fair trade goods, green buildings, or nondiscriminatory hiring practices, investors want to know what kind of behavior their companies are engaging in. By 2003, around 200 mutual funds and $2.16 trillion in managed portfolios were using some form of "social screening" in choosing investments. Investors are realizing that they can expect more than just dividends from their corporations. As Robert Monk, a longtime and influential shareholder activist, said, "[Investors] have a long-term viewpoint. And they have a spacious viewpoint. They want to retire in a clean, civil and safe world."

This first step in becoming an active, effective shareholder is to know your company. Luckily, as we discussed earlier in the chapter, transparency has been the key goal of the last seven decades of corporate legislation and SEC regulation. There are two main disclosure requirements to which publicly traded companies must adhere: regular financial filings to the SEC and annual reports to all shareholders. Realistically, your corporation's SEC filings—probably 10-Ks and 10-Qs—are not an efficient way for you, as an average shareholder, to glean up-to-date information. 10-Ks are essentially the industry's versions of an annual report (10-Qs are quarterly reports) where the numbers are more likely to speak for themselves. The advantage of these reports is that they provide a lot of financial information without the obfuscation of company propaganda; but they don't provide any context that would help average investors interpret the report's meaning. But if you do have time to tackle these reports, they are available to you free through the SEC's EDGAR system with tutorial resources that explain what you're looking at.

Your company's annual shareholder report will likely yield more information to you than the SEC filings. Also required by the SEC, annual reports will outline the issuer's current finances as well as those of the past year. Ranging from a bare-bones four-page document to a glossy, multicolored brochure, these reports contain valuable information, but—beware—it's often masked under feel-good company publicity. (If your company is involved in any corporate social responsibility efforts, you can count on them being hyped here.) And even so, such reports can be accidentally prescient: "Enron is moving so fast that sometimes others have trouble defining us," said that company's 1999 annual report.

Annual reports must include specific financial information that has been certified by an independent auditor. It comes in two forms: (1) a balance sheet, an overview of assets and liabilities, and (2) an income statement, an overview of company revenues and expenses. Be sure to discuss your annual reports with your broker or analyst. For more help dissecting these reports, pick up a copy of Adolph Lurie's *How to Read Annual Reports...Intelligently*, a slightly dated but investor-focused book.

While SEC filings and annual reports were and are a big part of your investor protections, they aren't enough. For if a corporation is engaging in unethical governance or social behavior, these reports will be carefully constructed to hide or obscure it. These offenses can be difficult to prove—particularly as governance frauds often take place behind closed doors and ethical lapses can be hard to track (for instance, how does a corporate outsider measure pollution levels or discover the use of child labor?). Fortunately, we do have the

SEC, industry-specific regulatory agencies, and independent watchdogs who make careers of investigating these frauds that are too big for the average shareholder to uncover. Yes, this web of monitors is imperfect, but right now, they are your best defense against broad corporate corruption like:

- *Insider Trading and Market Manipulation.* Dishonest corporate insiders can cheat other investors by timing trades with company events—like the release of a new product or a favorable financial report—in order to make more money on the fluctuating stock price. Similarly, insiders might use those company events and announcements to artificially alter the price of stocks—even if it's bad for investors.
- *Accounting Misrepresentation.* Cooking the books is an age-old practice that malicious corporate citizens still engage in. In fact, "All public companies fudge their numbers," is what Richard Scrushy, indicted and acquitted HealthSouth CEO, reportedly said to one of his chief financial officers. Whether the motive is to increase profits, hide failing numbers, or disguise embezzlement, fraudulent corporations and their supposedly independent auditors can manipulate their current and projected finances to fool the industry and investors.

CASE STUDY

In March 2003, New York Attorney General Eliot Spitzer received an anonymous letter signed only "Concerned." That individual's claim would eventually expose million-dollar kickbacks and bid rigging at the world's largest insurance company, the publicly traded Marsh & McLennan. "Concerned" wrote that, "The point is to appear as if Marsh is providing a service to the insurance market rather than the reality which is that Marsh is receiving major income for directing business to preferred providers/insurance markets." Translation: Marsh was taking two payments for commercial insurance sales, one from the buyer and the other from the insurance companies writing the policies. After a two-year investigation that only found more troubling behavior at Marsh and plunged their stock by 43 percent, the company agreed to pay an $850 million civil settlement and apologized for employees that had "unlawfully deceived their customers."

Reporting Possible Fraud While it's likely that thousands of man hours went into Spitzer's Marsh & McLennan investigation, it's a great example of how one person with an inkling of a problem can expose corporate fraud. In this case, "Concerned" probably had access to information that average investors did not, but the lesson stands: if you suspect unethical behavior in your company, report it to the appropriate state and federal regulatory agencies. For example, if it's a pollution problem, look to your state's environmental quality department or, federally, the Environmental Protection Agency. If you need help finding the right agencies, visit your state's website or the official website of the federal government (www.first-gov.gov).

CLASS ACTION LAWSUITS

Filing Class Action Lawsuits A second tactic is a class action lawsuit for restitution. An important consumer tool in any industry, class actions are the closest thing to an equalizer that shareholders have when facing their corporate boards. In the post-Enron world, these suits—which allow similarly situated claimants to pool their stakes in order to make litigation a reasonable and affordable option—have become high-profile, newsmaking events. According to Bruce Carton of Institutional Shareholder Services, "We've never seen the sums of money that are going into this pool before....The settlements in these cases where the damages were enormous are themselves going to be enormous." By June 2005, Enron investors had won a total of $4.7 billion in class action settlements, and while that's only a fraction of the value investors lost, it's an "eye-popping" number to the industry. In total, in 2005, a record-breaking $12 billion in class action settlements were still open for investor claims.

With such huge exposures, companies will often settle without going to court. In the last five years, we've seen J. P. Morgan settle with angry investors for $2.2 billion, Cendant for $2.9 billion, and Citigroup for $2.6 billion. For such Fortune 500 companies, the goal is to get away with paying as little as possible while not admitting guilt. Unfortunately, corporate lawyers finesse the language of the settlement to neither admit nor deny any wrongdoing, thus protecting themselves from further investor lawsuits and the threat of increased accountability.

Talk Back/Fight Back

To start a class action suit, you will need a lawyer (see the "Rights of Clients" chapter and the earlier box in this chapter for help in finding a lawyer). Make sure you choose someone with experience, particularly in the relevant company's industry. Now, the basic theory behind class actions is this: if you're defrauded in bulk, you should be able to sue in bulk—which offers smaller defrauded shareholders a number of advantages:

- *Power in Numbers.* When you and other defrauded shareholders come together, your case gains weight and stature by being able to demonstrate a more substantial and widespread harm—improving your chances for and the size of a recovery.
- *Easy membership.* You can join almost any class action as long as you fit the characteristics of the harmed class—and you usually won't pay any fees upfront to do so. In securities class actions, you must have purchased the offending security during a specific range of dates to be a member of the "class period." In the course of a suit, the plaintiffs' lawyers will be required to "notify" those who may be qualified members of the class. Since it's rarely possible to directly contact all possible claimants, lawyers will usually run announcements in newspapers, magazines, or other media specific to the

class. There are a few reliable Internet databases that continually catalog suits and can also help you find out if you qualify for any suits. In particular, check out the National Consumer Law Center, at www.ConsumerLaw.org, and Stanford University's Securities Class Action Clearinghouse, at http://securities.standford.edu.

- *Easy resolution.* As a member of a group, you likely won't need to do anything except wait and be able to prove ownership. But class actions can take years and awards can vary drastically—so don't spend that award money just yet.

Class action suits have a lead plaintiff, a member of your injured class who has suffered a large financial harm and whose injury is similar to those of the rest of the class. Lead plaintiffs have some control over the direction of the case and receive an extra award if the case is successful. However, if your financial interest is in the hundreds of thousands of dollars, you should think about opting out of the class action, because you may be able to get a better award on your own. Talk to a securities lawyer if you find yourself in this situation—you don't want to be bound to a smaller ruling than you deserve.

One recent detrimental development on class actions was the passage of the *Class Action Fairness Act* of 2005. The law will take many major class actions out of state courts and send them to the clogged federal system. Federal judges regularly dismiss large, complex class actions, arguing that there is no general federal consumer protection law and they prefer not to dabble in the specifics of state laws. Contrary to the supporters' claims that this bill advances justice, it creates a catch-22 situation for investors, who can be denied access to state courts if they come from different states (as they usually do) but can then be bumped from federal courts because resolving claims from several states is "unmanageable."

SHAREHOLDER RESOLUTIONS

Irritating the executives of the corporate world, a good corporate gadfly plays that important role of getting companies to become more transparent, honest, and even efficient through continually "stinging" the company into action. The most powerful mechanism shareholders have at their disposal—aside from their dollars—is their vote. As a shareholder, you have the right to vote on major decisions that affect the direction of the company—such as major sales of stock and changes in the board of directors. (Note that while many companies offer you one vote for each stock, some have more complicated voting systems. Ask your broker or analyst about these systems.) You can vote in person at the annual shareholders' meeting, by phone, through an electronic ballot, or by proxy—the ballot that the SEC requires your company to send to you.

The proxy statement, helpfully, must include several items that boil down the finances and issues of the corporation to the barest minimum. It must include the total compensation of the company's top five executives and the performance of its stock compared with others in the industry and against the S&P 500, a market index that tracks the prices of 500 stocks. It also includes a ballot, complete with recommendations from the board of directors, asking you to elect board members and vote on any number of issues—including shareholder resolutions. A recommendation or requirement for company action that you submit for your fellow shareholders to vote on is a shareholder resolution.

CASE STUDY

"Unless they have access to life-saving medicines, every one of the 42 million people currently infected with HIV/AIDS will die—and soon. When they do, in the most economically productive years of their lives, the capacity of the world's most vibrant emerging markets will die with them." One section of the Interfaith

Center on Corporate Responsibility's 2003–2004 annual report opens with those words. The ICCR, one of the most respected and effective corporate social responsibility organizations working today, files over 100 shareholder resolutions each year and estimates that the combined value of its 275 members' portfolios is $110 billion. Its health care working group has made the global HIV/AIDS pandemic one of its priorities.

In 2002, the Coca-Cola Company, which has 60,000 employees in Africa, committed to ensuring that their fifty-plus African bottlers were providing anti-retroviral treatment for HIV-infected employees. "But bottlers who want to treat their workers must pay 50 percent of the cost," explained Sister Doris Gormley. "All bottlers have agreed to do so in principle but slow implementation of the program has frustrated us." Concern over this slowdown spurred several convents and the labor union SEIU—all ICCR members—to file a resolution in 2004 asking Coca-Cola to "review the economic effects on its operations of the HIV/AIDS pandemic" in Africa.

The shareholder resolution passed with an astounding 98 percent of shareholders' support and, for the first time in Coca-Cola's history, a shareholder resolution had the backing of the board of directors. ICCR representatives met with Coca-Cola's Africa management team and hammered out a plan for (1) "robust" public reporting on the pandemic, (2) a study on the economic effects of HIV/AIDs on the company, and (3) improved treatment and prevention plans. Coca-Cola's statement read, "It is in [a] spirit of collaboration that we welcome this opportunity to work with our share owners in coordinating additional resources and skills in the fight against HIV/AIDS." Coca-Cola has since published their report and made it available to the general public on their website.

As a shareholder, you can put policies up for a vote on the proxy. Similar to the direct democracy initiatives you see on statewide and local ballots, shareholder resolutions provide an opportunity to put your concerns front and center—as long as you meet the SEC's strict requirements. These resolutions can be a great tool to influence the policies of your company, but they are a strategic tool, not a direct weapon. Resolutions rarely pass and, even if they do, they don't become corporate law. The power of shareholder resolutions is in their ability to force company officials to respond to questions and to catalyze internal discussions on new issues.

So, is it worth it? Take, for example, when Ralph Nader's "Campaign GM" filed resolutions in 1970 with General Motors demanding they place public representatives on the board. Of course these efforts didn't pass, but shortly thereafter, GM appointed Rev. Leon Sullivan, an African American community leader, to the board. He then used his position to advance an agenda stating that companies should not implicitly recognize South Africa's racist apartheid polices, which ultimately fell when GM and other businesses began divesting from the country. Or more recently, take the Coca-Cola example above. Shareholders used a request for information to highlight a related issue: the delay in African bottlers' providing HIV/AIDS medicines to their employees. On the surface, the ICCR was asking Coca-Cola to look into the problem, but the real message was "Do something!" And with Coke's promise to improve treatment and prevention programs, the ICCR can claim victory. Coca-Cola has now, in a sense, made a compact with their shareholders to take this issue seriously—a precedent you can be sure the ICCR and other shareholders will leverage at Coca-Cola and other companies in the future.

Part of the reason shareholder resolutions have been relegated to having only strategic value has been the lack of votes—see Step 4 below—but that is turning around. In 2003, a record 161 proposals won majorities of shareholder votes. And 2004 saw some significant victories: 37 percent of the oil company Apache Corp. supported a resolution for a report on the company's greenhouse gas emissions, and 63 percent of Fifth Third Bank's investors supported a nondiscrimination hiring policy for gay and lesbian employees. That's not nothing; if investors have been able to use shareholder resolutions effectively in their current state, who knows what a future with strongly supported, high-profile resolutions might hold?

Talk Back/Fight Back

How to file a shareholder resolution:

Step 1: Eligibility. The first step in filing is making sure you are eligible; you must own at least 1 percent of the company's stock or $2,000 market value of the stock for a year before the shareholder meeting and throughout the entire process. If you're on the cusp of these minimums, it's a good idea to be aware of the markets during this time, as you may have to purchase more stock to stay eligible. Get a copy the SEC rule 14a-8, "Proposals of Security Holders," from the SEC website or your local library. This is the rule that governs shareholder resolutions, and it is extremely important that you adhere to each part of it because your company's management will use any infraction to keep the resolution off the proxy. When you start, also be aware of the filing deadline. You can probably find it on last year's proxy statement or in the annual report.

Step 2: Writing and Filing Your Resolution. When you move on to writing a shareholder resolution, look at other examples, which you can find on the Internet or at your local library. Briefly, proposals cannot be more than 500 words and must be in two parts: (1) the resolution and (2) a supporting statement that contains information on why the resolution is pertinent to the company, and any supportive studies or data. You will submit your resolution to the secretary of the company—sending a draft early can help open the lines of communication on the issue at hand and help to dispel any potential adversarial tension. Within fourteen days of submission, the company must write to you if there are any procedural or eligibility problems you need to fix before the deadline. If the company lets it stand as is, your resolution will appear on the proxy statement with their recommendation to shareholders on how to vote. If the company materially opposes the resolution, as they likely will, move on to Step 3.

Step 3: Sending a Copy to the SEC. When you send your resolution to the corporation's Secretary, also send a copy to the SEC. Companies have to file with the SEC if they want to keep a resolution off the proxy—they often wait until the last minute—and it can help your chances of making the cut if the SEC has already seen your resolution. In addition to filing with the SEC, your company must send you, the resolution sponsor, notice no less than eighty days before the proxy materials are distributed. Officially, you don't have a role to play in the SEC's review of the company's appeal to omit, but you should send a response to them explaining why the resolution should stand. After that, it's up to the SEC as to whether it appears on the proxy or not.

Step 4: Campaigning, Presenting, and Starting Again. If your resolution is to appear on the proxy, you'll probably wonder what you can do to boost support. Unfortunately, the cost of obtaining a list of all shareholders is astronomical and mailing to them could cost hundreds of thousands of dollars. Moreover, the corporation can create legal hoops for you to jump through to get this list. It is much easier to find out who the institutional shareholders are and try to meet with them. The power of institutional investors is a growing area of shareholder rights. They control large blocks of votes and often represent pension funds—the media darling of the securities industry. And, obviously, if you are filing with a large corporation and you can get media attention, that is an excellent way to get the word out about your effort.

At the actual annual meeting, you or your representative has to present the proposal before the vote—again according to the specifications of the company. To be blunt, the goal is to get at least 3 percent of the vote, which is the number that allows you to bring the resolution back next year. In the second year, the goal is 6 percent and in the third, 10. (If your resolution doesn't get the needed number of votes, find another shareholder to sponsor it next year.) Assuming that you get the needed number of votes, use the next year to refile and to reach out to the company and to try to negotiate a solution to your issues—as ICCR was able to meet with Coca-Cola's management on the HIV/AIDS issue. Often, management would rather find a solution than have the resolution on the proxy again next year—after all, you've brought it to the attention of all the shareholders once already.

A New Jersey Supreme Court Justice once wrote, "Reform is not for the short-winded." That is certainly true of shareholder resolutions. If you are interested in starting this process, you should contact ICCR, at www.iccr.org or (212) 870-2295, or Social Investment Forum's Advocacy and Policy program, at www.sriadvocacy.org or (212) 870-5313. They can offer you advice and may be able to put you in touch with other like-minded shareholders—and lawyers who would be invaluable in this process.

Fix It: Ideas to Invest In

In 2005, financial journalist Gretchen Morgenson opened an article with a significant question: "After years of investor activism are shareholders winning or losing the struggle to be treated with the respect that company owners deserve?" It's true that many of the strategies discussed here are just that—strategies and not perfect mechanisms to get the resolution you deserve. But while tackling shareholder issues can be difficult, the outlook is good. The shareholder movement is still in its infancy—investors are figuring out by trial and error what works effectively. But while they do that, we need to keep thinking about the big picture—how to reform the securities industry to protect investors and give them a stronger voice.

First and foremost, investors and regulators must get over our protectionist feelings toward Wall Street and Corporate America. We cannot continue to be afraid of staining their reputations or hurting profit margins if we disclose frauds; for if we don't, then the average investor or pensioner will suffer the consequences and the bigger the next crises are going to be. Take for example how we acted in the booming '90s. As Arianna Huffington wrote, "it was as if denial had replaced baseball as the national pastime. We buried our heads in the sand—unwilling to question the integrity of the bulls rushing down Wall Street for fear it might jeopardize the 30 percent rate of return we had come to see as our birthright."

Specifically, there are a number of important corporate and securities reforms that will make the market safer for the average investor:

- *Make corporate boards independent.* Standards for board independence should—at least—be based on the New York Stock Exchange criteria requiring that a majority of board members be completely independent of the company. "Independent" must mean that the member has no professional relationship with the company and does not provide any services—banking, legal, or otherwise—to the corporation. Then the board will answer to shareholders and act in the best interest of the company itself—not its executives.

- *Make Fraudulent Corporations Admit Guilt.* If we force offending companies to start admitting guilt, more investors will win just restitution from corporations and, eventually, insurers will lose enthusiasm for providing insurance policies that cover those awards. Then entrenched corporate executives will experience a new level of accountability. Certainly, as Massachusetts Secretary of the Commonwealth William Gavin said, "How seriously are [corporations] going to take securities law if it's going to be a game of touch football? The only way you're going to get significant change is when you start treating things seriously—and an admission of guilt is serious."

- *Bring Back the* Glass-Steagall Act. In 1999, Congress repealed key sections of the *Banking Act* of 1933—the banking industry's equivalent to the *Securities Acts* of '33 and '34. These sections—called *Glass-Steagall*—prohibited commercial banks and investment banks from entering each other's business. According to Nomi Prins, "Only the type of clear distinction of roles, instilled in the 1930s with passage of the Glass-Steagall Act, would reduce banks' incentive to speculate with consumer money and use retail customers as fodder for the stock and bonds of favored corporate clients." In other words, if you want analysts and stockbrokers to really act without a conflict of interest, they need to be in separate companies.

- *Create a Grassroots Shareholder Movement.* Robert Monks, the shareholder activist, once said, "A corporation with a million shareholders has no owners." If investors want to improve their individual rights as well as pursue the more difficult problems of industry reform, they have to come together and speak collectively. Individually, our power is only as great as the size of our stock ownership, but a group is a force to be reckoned with.

- *Expand Shareholder Influence.* With an organized movement, investors push the limits of their existing rights—democratizing the markets in a real way. For example, they can then call for thorough explanation of rulings in SRO arbitration cases, lobby for repeal of the anti-consumer *Class Action Fairness Act* of 2005, and demand better access to shareholder rolls so that we can effectively lobby for our resolutions.

Chapter 8

THE RIGHTS OF SPOUSES

[Divorce] laws may mandate equality on paper, but in practice, judges who apply those laws hold mothers to a higher standard, whether it involves sex and dating, moving out of state, going back to school, working, or not working. Not only have women lost their advantage in the courtroom, but the rules of the custody game are often applied against them.

—Gayle Rosenwald Smith and Sally Abrahms, *What Every Woman Should Know About Divorce and Custody*

For better or worse, divorce is part of our culture. We have splashy Hollywood fights—both on screen and off—and annually spend almost $30 billion in legal fees. With over a million divorces each year, most of us have some personal experience with it via a family member, a friend, or ourselves. In spite of—or perhaps because of—this familiarity, society tries to protect the institution of marriage with stiff divorce laws even though we, as individuals, would like divorce to be accessible, efficient, and fair. Given this conflict between the goals of public policy and those of would-be *exes*, divorce and family law is one of the most confusing and corruptible areas in our legal system—and it comes as no surprise that few people know how to protect themselves and their families when running this painful gauntlet.

The divorce industry is fraught with double standards. Take, for example, the fact that government programs promote marriage among the poor but divorce—with an estimated average cost of $15,000 to $30,000—is truly a luxury item. Or the fact that we condemn parents who use their children as weapons but yet force them all through an adversarial legal process that pushes them to *win* rather than play fair. And then there is the most pernicious of inequities: how the system keeps wives from having their proverbial day in court. Women lose out monetarily because they are less likely to handle the family's finances and are more likely to have given up a career (and earning power) to stay at home with the kids. And women, who are conventionally condemned by the courts and society if they don't want or win physical custody, are often penalized for showing emotion when threatened with losing their children. In short, women are set up to end up with a bum deal from the very start.

Conventionally, we dream about our weddings and orchestrate elaborate affairs to fete ourselves upon marriage. Naturally, we don't dream about our divorces but we should at least devote the same care to their execution as we do to our weddings. After all, with the average wedding totaling $20,000, we spend about as much to enter into marriage as to leave it. And with the divorce rate at some 40 percent of newlyweds and with only 5 to 10 percent of couples signing prenuptial agreements, it's time to start taking a closer look at divorce.

KEY LAWS ON DIVORCE

Divorce falls under the purview of state law. In the early twentieth century, when divorce laws were particularly strict on the East Coast, entrepreneurs in Reno took advantage of Nevada's loose divorce laws and opened up "divorce ranches" where wives would stay for a six-week divorce and the bonus of a gambling holiday. We usually think of Nevada as a marriage capital, but it used to be a real-life "Splitsville." Even then, the divorces of the rich and famous—Adlai Stevenson, Rita Hayworth, Gloria Vanderbilt—provided titillating headlines for newspapers across the country. Eventually, a reform movement in the 1970s brought divorce laws across the states into closer alignment. Today the three main areas of divorce law are (1) grounds, (2) property and alimony, and (3) custody. To find out more about your state's divorce laws, visit your local library or contact your state bar association. (The American Bar Association maintains a directory of state and local associations at www.abanet.org/barserv/stlobar.html.)

Fault vs. No-fault Laws   In the time of Moses, a husband just had to gather a couple of friends to witness his telling his wife she was no longer so—and poof! Divorced! But by the time American colonists brought divorce over the Atlantic, public consensus concluded that divorce should require "grounds" of misconduct on the part of one of the spouses—in other words, someone had to be at fault. Today, many states have fault-based divorce laws, some have only no-fault laws, and some have both. Fault-based laws usually list grounds resembling these elements: "cruel and inhuman treatment," abandonment, imprisonment, and adultery. No-fault laws preclude the need for a specific type of offense as grounds for divorce and lump all divorces under "irrevocable differences."

Technically, every state has some form of no-fault divorce, but in practice many of those laws make such a divorce so difficult to negotiate and obtain that it's a fault-based law in practice. For example, in New York, no-fault divorces require a year-long separation and perfect agreement on a settlement. To avoid these hurdles, many would-be divorcees agree that one spouse will claim "constructive abandonment"—the withholding of sex for one year—even when it's not true. So the battle between fault and no-fault laws rages on. Women's groups and churches, strange bedfellows, have traditionally objected to no-fault laws. The former because such laws often leave women without the leverage needed to obtain a fair settlement from guilty husbands, and the latter because they believe that divorce destabilizes the institution of the family.

Division of Property and Alimony   For the most part, a divorcing spouse gets to keep his or her own "nonmarital" assets—the assets one had before the beginning of the marriage and that never became "community" or "marital" property; for instance, if one never deposited an inheritance in a joint account or never added one's spouse to the deed of a summer home. The assets—and sometimes debts—that a judge will divide between the parties are usually limited to those that were earned or acquired during the marriage. When it comes to the specifics of property division laws, there are two general types: (1) the basic fifty-fifty rule (you get half, he gets half), and (2) "equitable distribution" laws wherein judges can use a number of different statutory factors in deciding how assets are separated.

Judges, under both laws, can take into account many factors when tallying up the total value of a marital estate and then parceling it out; common factors are (1) the current and future earning potential of each partner, (2) whether one partner supported the education or work of another, (3) the length of the marriage, and (4) whether one spouse wronged the other. Courts are beginning to recognize with more regularity that less-wealthy and stay-at-home spouses must be compensated for lost earning potential and lost retirement funds. Even if you have a valid pre- or postnuptial agreement, judges will sometimes consider these factors and whether or not the agreement was fair to begin with when executing that contract.

When it comes to alimony, or "maintenance," the general rule is that the wealthier spouse will pay the other a regular allowance for day-to-day costs until the spouse no longer needs it or is no longer entitled. While husbands in the past often had to pay their wives alimony until she remarried or died, today's settlements are more likely to include stipulations on the length of payment—including whether she has a job, will continue caring for any children, needs to return to schooling, or has significant "nonmarital" assets. As the traditional roles of men and women in a marriage change, alimony does too—women occasionally pay their husbands alimony and sometimes no alimony is awarded at all when neither spouse is financially dependent on the other.

Custody   Since the addition of children to any legal confrontation naturally pulls on the public's heartstrings, custody fights are the most vicious of all of divorce's ugly heads. Assuming that the child is not experiencing abuse at the hands of either parent, there are two types of custody to be awarded: physical and legal, both of which can be fully awarded to one parent or jointly to both. Awarding of the former is often based on which parent is already the primary caregiver and what kind of environment the child will live in. Legal custody refers to how major decisions—about education, medical treatment, or religion—will be made for the child. Judges decide custody on "what's in the best interests of the child," but the subjectivity of that statement has created a pattern of bitter parents and hurt children. Many states allow the court to appoint lawyers to protect the interest of the children or appoint *forensics*—often unregulated "expert" evaluators—who analyze families to give judges an "impartial" opinion as to where children belong. The problem with these forensics is that few states have any minimum qualifications, basic standards of analysis, fee caps—parents are required to pay all forensics' bills—or any appeals process should a parent disagree with the findings.

Because child support awards were varying too greatly across the country and across cases, Congress passed the *Family Support Act* in 1998 to establish the guidelines for child support, requiring each state to create a standard formula for determining support levels. Three basic models cover most states: (1) the Income Shares model allots the amount of money that would have been spent on the child were the parents still together and divides that burden between the parents in proportion to their individual incomes; (2) the Percentage of Income Model sets a sliding or flat percentage rate that the non-custodial parent must pay, and (3) the Melson formula determines support payments by considering each parent's self-support needs, the children's basic needs, and everyone's standard of living. This formula also divides the final amount between the parents according to the proportion of their incomes.

Annulment and Legal Separation   With the rise of no-fault laws and divorce's decreasing social and religious stigma, civil annulments and legal separation have generally gone out of favor. While both are still available, many people find that their narrow definitions make them equally or even more difficult to obtain than a divorce. Reasons for an annulment—a legal judgment that voids the entire marriage—generally include fraud, misrepresentation, and misunderstanding. In practice, many annulments are based on issues of age or the ability to have children and usually are pursued to end a marriage of short duration. Legal separation is more than just two couples living under different roofs but is less than a divorce. While definitions vary from state to state, separation is generally when a judge divides assets, alimony, and custody but doesn't grant an actual divorce. (In some states, legal separations are one step of the no-fault divorce process.) The couple is still married and neither can remarry without further court action. Separation was a much more popular option for unhappy couples when religion strongly condemned divorce.

TYPES OF DIVORCE

While *Divorce Court* and legal television dramas portray lengthy, juried divorce cases, there are other types of divorce that are often more productive, less expensive, and less divisive. In ascending order of cost and time and descending order of amicability, the options are self-preparation, mediation, collaborative divorce, and litigation. Realistically, the cheapest form of divorce, self-preparation at about $300, is for *very* few couples. While it may be low-cost and the resources may be readily available, your marriage would have to be bizarrely simple for this to be your best choice. You would need to have clear ownership of any assets as well as absolute agreement on how any custody agreement would work out. If you are *at all* unsure about how equally the divorce is working out or about whether you're making the right choice in preparing the papers yourself, find professional help and seriously consider a different form. In particular, self-preparation is not a good choice if one spouse has drastically less knowledge of the marital finances, as the risk of ruining that spouse is too great.

CASE STUDY

When their eighteen-year marriage came to an end, Warren and Charlene White didn't rush to divorce court. Instead of declaring war over their nearly $2 million in assets, they worked together to create a settlement that everyone could live with—including their two children. As Mr. White told *Kiplinger's* magazine, "We did all the heavy lifting ourselves." So, this Houston couple made budgets and projections and made sure the kids' happiness and security were the main factors in their decisions. For example, the Whites decided that they would keep the house in both their names until the kids were grown. This meant that the kids could stay in their familiar surroundings for the rest of their childhoods and that both parents would split the proceeds—and any resulting tax burdens— from the sale of the house down the road. As for the division of the remaining marital assets, the Whites based their decision on their projected future earning power. Since Mr. White had the potential to earn more, he took 40 percent of the assets and Ms. White 60 percent.

The financial benefits of this good-faith agreement went beyond just a mutually satisfactory division of assets, for the Whites also saved a bundle on lawyers fees. Since they had already worked out the details of the divorce, both only needed to hire a lawyer to look over and approve the documentation. So in a time when divorce costs reach into the tens of thousands, the Whites spent less than $7,000 each on lawyers. Not to mention that their amicable negotiations saved them and their children considerable stress and trauma. It may have been a bad marriage, but it was a good divorce. As Ms. White explained, "What we had going for us was character and trust."

In mediation, a hired mediator will meet with both spouses together several times and try to come up with a resolution that takes into consideration their practical and emotional needs. While an impartial mediator works for both spouses, it is important that you hire professionals to advocate for or at least help you identify what is a reasonable resolution for you. Most people do not have a deep enough understanding of issues like financial planning and custody to defend themselves alone—even in mediation. The next option is collaborative divorce, a good option available to most couples who don't want to go to court but need substantial legal representation. In this process, each spouse can hire a team of divorce specialists including a lawyer, a financial planner, a mental health expert, and a divorce coach. The advantage of going the collaborative way is avoiding the loss of control that both spouses experience in court where the judge has final say—even if both spouses disagree. On the other hand, if you can't come to agreement through collaborative law and need to go to court after all, you've just thrown a lot of money down the drain and your lawyers are legally required to resign from your case. So you'll have to find someone new that you can trust—something that's hard enough to do the first time around.

Finally there's divorce litigation. Here's where the dramatic courtroom scene complete with crying children and a mistress sitting in the gallery comes into play. While movies and television might teach us that the faithful spouse always wins the day in court, the truth is that divorce litigation is expensive and can be surprisingly risky for both spouses—after all, you've both given up all control to the judge and both of you could end up unhappy. As one New York divorce lawyer said of a case, "There was never even a thought that the court would say, 'A pox on you both.' What people should know is that getting a divorce is not a slam dunk."

Talk Back/Fight Back

Remember how the divorce industry moves billions of dollars each year? There are strategies you can pursue—no matter which form of divorce you choose—so that you don't needlessly contribute to those coffers but still get the things you need. First, *before* you talk to your spouse or hire a lawyer, you have to take a level-headed look at your situation to decide how to begin. There are two important questions you need to answer for yourself:

1. *Can I afford a divorce?* For many, this might seem like an irrelevant question to which the only answer is, "If you want out, get out." But the unhappy reality is that the legal professionals you may have to employ—not to mention your bank, your mortgage, and your regular necessary life expenses—don't care how unhappy you are when it comes to paying the bills. So when considering divorce, you need to think about whether you can pay for the divorce proceedings *and* can afford to continue to run an independent household. If you think you can't afford a divorce, you should think about going to counseling with your spouse—a relatively cheaper solution—or finding local low-income divorce or separation resources.

2. *How civil can your divorce be?* This question is important because it will begin to determine which divorce process is the best for you and help you understand how much you are going to spend. According to personal finance journalist Scott Reeves, "Getting nasty is expensive, and it's nastiness—not division of property—that leads to attorney's fees hitting $100,000 or more in what should be simple cases." Think about whether you can be as honest and fair as Warren and Charlene White. If you have trouble gauging this, underestimate your spouse's and your own ability to play fair. Better safe than sorry.

The next key strategy is to become your own best ally and advocate. No one, not even your lawyer, is going to fight for you like you can. So start managing your divorce—think of it as your new and possibly second full-time job. Do your own research, be your own paralegal, and learn everything you can about your rights and your needs. Start at your local library and just keep reading. It might seem overwhelming at first, but you'll develop an invaluable sense of the kinks and biases in your state's divorce proceedings. According to expert divorce lawyer Bradley A. Pistotnik, "Only you have the ability to plan an effective strategy and win the divorce war."

A major corollary is that you must plan ahead for your divorce—even months before talking to your spouse. Divorces are won and lost on the first try, as very few appeals result in substantive changes. You need all the information you can possibly have at your disposal—and you can't risk that he or she will retaliate by hiding and freezing assets or by turning the children against you.

The next best piece of advice for anyone in divorce is to always be professional. This means two things: being calm and being tough. Yes, divorce is a difficult process, but emotions —anger, hurt, revenge, despair—do not mix with the proceedings. Your lawyer will bill you for hours you spend on an emotional tirade in his office and your judge will not be moved by tears. In fact, as with the other areas covered in this book, both lawyers and judges are more likely to respond to calm, collected, and levelheaded appeals. Traditionally, playing tough can be difficult for women. Pistotnik, author of *Divorce War! 50 Strategies Every Woman Needs to Know to Win*, points out that men's "daily practice of winning in the competitive business world gives them a natural edge when fighting a divorce. With this in mind, you must attempt to level the playing field by learning businesslike tactics."

Finally, an obvious but often broken divorce rule: never ever lie to, or withhold information from, the court. This will almost certainly backfire and hurt you more than disclosure would have in the first place.

IF YOU OR YOUR CHILDREN ARE VICTIMS OF DOMESTIC VIOLENCE...

Thirty percent of Americans say that they know a woman who is abused by her husband or boyfriend, and around 4 million American women are victims of major assault by a partner every year. Abuse can come in many forms—physical, verbal, stalking, and more. If your spouse is abusing you or your children, the most important thing to do is to get out of the situation immediately. Call the National Domestic Violence Hotline at 1-800-799-SAFE (7233) or visit the website (www.ndvh.org) for help. Hotline advocates will help you deal with crisis situations and help you create a safety plan. They have information about shelters and other resources in every state. Through the Hotline advocate or the local shelter you are directed to, you will be able to find a local organization like New York's Safe Horizon that provides expert legal assistance to victimized women seeking restraining orders, custody, and divorces. You can contact Safe Horizon at 800-621-HOPE (4673) or www.safe-horizon.org.

MONEY AND DIVORCE

CASE STUDY

Lorna Wendt met her future husband, Gary Wendt, at their small-town high school in Wisconsin. After attending the University of Wisconsin, they married in 1965. She worked as a music teacher while he attended Harvard Business School, and she later quit to raise their children while he climbed the corporate ladder. In 1997, Mr. Wendt was running the most profitable subsidiary of GE when he filed for divorce, offering his wife of three decades a paltry 10 percent of the hard marital assets. She was shocked: "When we started out with nothing, I was an equal partner, and at the end I was, too. In addition to 99 percent of the domestic workload, I was my husband's biggest supporter, married to the company but with no benefits."

What made the Wendt's divorce a newsmaker was the size of their wealth—at least $40 million in hard assets and up to $100 million in total—and that Mrs. Wendt stood up for herself and housewives across the country. Though about one-fifth of states were already awarding middle-class women half of their marital estates, Mrs. Wendt became the champion of true marital equality. She dared to challenge the judicial precedent that corporate wives weren't worth half the wealth the couple earned during the course of their marriage. "My case was never about the money," she argued. "It was about someone implying that I was a ten percent participant in my partnership. In reality, I always gave 100 percent, putting my career on hold to raise the children, manage the household and support him in his business endeavors." (She even hosted a holiday business party just days after she discovered her husband's secret plans to divorce her.)

In the end, the settlement awarded Mrs. Wendt $20 million, half of the hard assets (not half the couple's net assets). She then used her heightened profile to found the Equality in Marriage Institute, an organization dedicated to "promoting marriage as an emotional, legal and financial partnership of equals" (www.equalityinmarriage.org).

Nationally, divorce courts have a poor track record when it comes to treating women fairly in financial settlements. In general, a woman's standard of living falls by nearly a third after divorce while a man's actually improves by 10 percent. Add that to the fact that the divorce itself can seriously drain any individual or marital coffers and suddenly the financial consequences of divorce are awfully bleak. Hence, lawyer Stephen J. Jones's caution against running headfirst into divorce, "If you're unhappy now, imagine being unhappy and broke. It's a lot worse."

Many factors feed into the financial disparity between couples; according to one divorce researcher, "many women have sacrificed careers, and therefore their own pension, to raise their family and as a result are being unfairly punished." Another problem is that many women still go for the conventional assets—namely the house and cash—to the exclusion of retirement assets. Because distribution laws have begun to hurt the very people they are supposed to protect—women and children—it's important that you know how to proceed in this area, especially given the fickle result of Lorna Wendt's settlement, in which the judge proclaimed that "equity" does not necessarily mean "equal."

Talk Back/Fight Back

Of her now infamous divorce from Donald Trump, Ivana Trump said, "Don't get mad, get everything." While this may overstate what's real or desirable, the less-monied spouse in divorce cases—which usually means women—must take an aggressive approach to avoid being steamrolled:

- *Show YOURSELF the money.* Going into a divorce, it is critical that you have *all* the information on your family's financial situation. Before you even announce that you want a divorce, start making copies of bank statements, stock options, and insurance policies. Look for information on retirement assets, real estate, credit cards, and any safe deposit boxes. If you suspect your spouse is hiding assets, pay attention to receipts and paperwork around the house, you might be surprised at how much you can figure out on your own. And if you do not have an individual bank account, open one and begin squirreling away small denominations of money. You will need this for your own security and to retain a lawyer. As the thrice-divorced Johnny Carson once said only half-jokingly, "The difference between divorce and legal separation is that a legal separation gives a husband time to hide his money."

- *Balance your portfolio.* At the end of a marriage, many women want to keep what *Kiplinger's* magazine calls the "marriage museum": the house (after all, she may have worked hard on its upkeep and deco-ration). The problem is that stay-at-home mothers or wives who have given up earning power over time often lock up too much of their set-tlement in the house—which isn't liquid and often eats up any liquid funds with maintenance. Many find out too late that owning the house can be financially crippling. Make sure you are negotiating for a prac-tical settlement that balances cash, retirement assets, and any real estate. Ask yourself if your settlement works in the short-term and long-term: Will you have the cash you need immediately after the divorce and will your investments help you through your retirement?

- *Take care of the kids.* If you have children, calculate how much it will cost to continue to provide for your kids and to provide them with the lifestyle to which they are accustomed. Make sure you understand what your state's support guidelines look like and know how that compares to what it's going to take to keep them healthy and happy. This is also a good time to think about the major expenses of the future: Who will pay for day care? Summer camp? A used car? College?

- *Send the bills to your spouse.* One common divorce strategy is for the wealthier spouse to simply drag his or her feet, waiting for the legal costs to bankrupt the other spouse, forcing an unfair settlement. Talk to your lawyer about making your legal costs part of the settlement. Even mentioning this may make your spouse more likely to keep things on track and, more importantly, keep you in the money.

- *Hire a professional.* In the past, spouses have generally brought financial planners into the picture only after they've affixed that *ex* to their name. However, it's a very good idea to meet with a divorce financial planner at the beginning of the process to assist you with all of the above issues and more. Your lawyer or mediator will help you and your spouse come to a settlement, but they can't help you figure out exactly what you need to ask for. Financial planners can be expensive but, at the very least, be sure to hire someone—even just for an hour or two—to review your final settlement. This could pay dividends, literally, for the rest of your life. To find a professional in your area, contact the Association of Divorce Financial Planners at www.divorceandfinance.com or call them at (800) 270-1886.

CUSTODY

CASE STUDY

The scene was wrenching. On a sunny New York day in June 2004, Bridget Marks had to obey a court order to hand her four-year-old twin daughters over to their father, her ex-boyfriend John Aylsworth. The girls screamed for their mother as their father drove them away—without buckling them up because the car seats he had were too small.

Ms. Marks became pregnant while she was having an affair with the married Mr. Aylsworth and, despite pressure from him and his wife, she did not have an abortion. For the first few years after her twins were born, Mr. Aylsworth enjoyed informal visitation rights with the girls. He then sued for formal visitation and during that process the girls were diagnosed with vaginitis—an inflammation that can be caused by sexual activity. As a fit, responsible parent, Ms. Marks worried that the girls had been abused and filed a complaint with the court against Mr. Aylsworth.

Almost immediately, the system began to fail Ms. Marks and her daughters. Even though the diagnosis was entered into court and the girls' psychiatrist testified that it was 60-70 percent likely that the girls had been abused, the court disregarded the evidence and ended the official police investigation into the matter. To make matters worse, the judge ruled that Ms. Marks had coached her daughters into saying they had been abused and that she was incapable of fostering a good father-daughter relationship for the girls. The court took the girls away from Ms. Marks, punishing her in effect for trying to protect her daughters when there was significant evidence that they had been abused.

When Ms. Marks had to hand over the girls, television cameras filmed the girls crying for their mother and her emotional response to losing her children. Ms. Marks explained, "When a mother loses custody of her children, it's ugly, it's visceral but it's real. And I've had so many calls from women who say that's exactly what it looks like." Unfortunately, judges and the court of public opinion often prefer the calm, collected father to the distraught mother. "The more you act out, the more you're giving them exactly what they want," Ms. Marks said. " And then they'll just say, 'Oh look, see, she's crazy. She's delusional.' You have to maintain your cool."

A long ten months later, a New York appellate court reversed the custody decision and reunited Ms. Marks with her daughters.

According to another veteran of custody war, Patricia Duff, whose battle with businessman Ron Perelman made headlines in New York in the late '90s, "The system is archaic and confusing. Litigants are traumatized and ground down. Custody cases are a nightmare, and the system is a mess straight out of *Alice in Wonderland*. I wouldn't want anyone to go through what my daughter and I went through."

As with the rest of your divorce, the advantages of coming to a custody agreement on your own cannot be overstated. But it's very difficult to determine—whether by agreement or by litigation—what's in the "best interests of the child." As previously mentioned, family court judges have come to rely on the "expert" opinions of court-appointed forensic evaluators. These forensics often charge exorbitant fees and come in many packages—lawyer, psychologist, or social worker. Most states don't even have specific standard practices that forensics are supposed to use. It's all up to the individual "expert." Some use psychological tests, others long interviews with third parties, and others periods of observation. While all these tools might have value, very few states have any regulations or an appeals process for parents to pursue if they feel they've been wronged—in the findings or in the billing. It isn't uncommon for forensic fees to reach $40,000 or more. "They suck the life out of you, they suck the money out of you," argues well-known publisher Judith Regan, who paid in the hundreds of thousands of dollars. "And this is not sour grapes—I won."

Moreover, there have been cases of extensive cronyism among judges, lawyers, and forensics who go back to each other case after case. In New York, the indictment of a State Supreme Court Justice for accepting bribes to fix divorce and custody cases has brought about the guilty pleas or convictions of six people—all before the justice's trial has even begun. According to Andrew I. Schepard, director of the Center for Children, Families and the Law, "It's an industry and it's unregulated and it affects precious family rights. It would be lots better if this process were more transparent." Just think, one forensic might see a mother understandably distraught by the possibility of losing her children while another might see an unstable parent unsuitable to care for children.

Another pothole in custody law often comes in the states' meeting the federal requirements on guidelines for child support. State legislators are not generally family law experts and sometimes even well-intentioned laws can create backward results. For example, in New York, the law requires that a noncustodial parent must put up 17 percent of his or her salary for the care of 1 child, 25 percent for 2, 29 percent for 3, and so on. Some wealthier divorced spouses, who may not even want custody, find that it's cheaper to have custody and to be paid support than to leave the children with the less-monied spouse. This is obviously not the result anyone is looking for.

Talk Back/ Fight Back: Custody

Given that custody battles are often wars of accusations and rebuttals, it is crucial to come into the situation prepared. A corollary to the divorce truism that "whoever gets to the courthouse first wins" is that whichever parent does the legwork, gets custody. In the past, women may have had a distinct advantage in winning custody, but courts today are finding against women more regularly and are often doing so based on sexist prejudices, as the author documented in an early study of the problem as the NYC Consumer Affairs Commissioner in 1992. Over thirty states have similarly found—through official government studies—discrimination against women in the courts when it comes to divorce and custody battles. In order to avoid becoming a victim of this trend, follow these strategies:

- *Claim your kids.* Believing that they will automatically win custody of the children, many women don't do the necessary homework to keep custody. The first thing you should do is establish and document grounds for custody. With the advice of your lawyer, make a list of the positive reasons the children should stay with you—you're keeping the house they grew up in, they feel comforted by their school and community, you have more time to spend with them, or they spend more time with your parents, and so on. Also, make a list of reasons why your husband shouldn't have custody—he spends too much time at work, he doesn't have the supportive relationship with the kids that you do, he has a gambling problem, etc. Proving any and all of these things can be difficult, but with the help of your lawyer and a locally respected forensic psychologist, your chances of keeping custody are much greater. As Monica Getz, head of the National Coalition for Family Justice, says, "The system goes by proof, not truth."

- *Act defensively.* When making plans for post-divorce life that affect your children, use great care. A decision to move out of state, to put the kids in childcare, to further your own education, or to start a new relationship are all reasons that spouses sue for and win custody even when those choices actually improve the lives of the children. Despite the fact that the situation may be unfair, carry yourself at all times in a manner to which even the most conservative judges and jurists can't object.
- *Be calm.* While this strategy is mentioned above, it's worth reiterating here. Like Ms. Marks said, when mothers lose their children, it can be an ugly, emotional event that fathers and courts have used against mothers later. So, even though this is a very difficult situation, always conduct yourself in a professional but genuine manner—it will likely get you further with the judge than tears will.
- *Keep fighting.* While divorce proceedings themselves are rarely appealed and appended, it's much more common for custody battles to return to court again and again. Of course, you don't want your children to be hurt by the fighting between you and your spouse, but if you really believe that the children are better off with you, then keep fighting for custody

FINDING AND KEEPING A GOOD LAWYER

Divorce isn't just about your relationship with your spouse. It's about your relationship with your lawyer, the judge, any court-appointed forensics, and your children—and it's about how you negotiate the often delicate balance of these relationships. Since your lawyer will play a major role in this minefield of interactions, you need to find and hire the best advocate you can. Karen Winner, author of *Divorced from Justice: The Abuse of Women and Children by Divorce Lawyers and*

Judges, offers this warning: "You walk through the door of the lawyer's office like Little Red Riding Hood on the way to Grandma's house, only thinking of what you're bringing, not at questioning what you'll find. What you don't know about divorce lawyers can hurt you."

While most divorce lawyers are honorable professionals, some unethical lawyers have practically institutionalized ways to wrench money from soon-to-be divorcees, particularly from women. Divorce lawyers, who are subject to very few oversight regulations, are privy to many of the most intimate details of a client's life and thus can wield great manipulative power. For example, many ask at the first meeting how much money the woman and the marital estate have in order to gauge exactly how much he or she can wring out of the divorce. Retainer costs as high as $25,000 can lock a woman to her lawyer before she even has any real indication of what kind of lawyer he or she will be. Then throughout the divorce process, some lawyers will provide irregular, confusing bills that pad the costs of services for which a client has no way of accounting. For example, a client has little way of knowing how long consulting conversations took within the firm or knowing whether a partner farmed out his or her case to a newbie associate lawyer. Then, perhaps days before the settlement, that lawyer may present the client with an outrageous outstanding bill for thousands of dollars and demand he or she sign a promissory—that legally binds her to paying—or else the lawyer will quit. The client must then decide whether to kowtow to the lawyer's financial demands or to risk their settlement being neglected because the lawyer either quits or stops providing the best service possible. And if the client signs that promissory note, she may suffer a sharp decline in her standard of living, even if she has received a fair divorce settlement.

Talk Back/ Fight Back

When seeking a lawyer, avoid placing too much weight on the recommendations of friends or of local bar associations—both are too easily colored by friendships or business dealings. Look to a local divorce support group like the National Coalition for Family Justice for recommendations. Make sure any prospective lawyer specializes in divorce and family law. Since this is an intimate process that is going to affect you and your children for the rest of your lives, do not hire someone who has only passing experience with family law. You wouldn't ask a model airplane enthusiast to build an airplane to fly across the country, so don't do the same with lawyers. Once you have a candidate, then you can ask around about his or her reputation—and check with the local grievance board to see if any complaints have been filed. Finally, ask the lawyer for references. Even the best lawyers may be reluctant to do this, but he or she shouldn't have a problem with finding two or three satisfied clients willing to give you a call (they will likely have to call you due to attorney-client privileges).

Once you've begun your divorce, if you feel you're being represented poorly or are being overcharged, there are a couple of things you can do. First, start documenting everything—and demand specific documentation—for anything that seems suspect. Write down every action you know your lawyer is taking on your behalf, from phone calls to car services to actual legal documents. Then find the local bar grievance committee and file a report. While this won't likely get your money back, it can help in a number of ways: (1) it might straighten out your lawyer in the short run and (2) a filing will probably produce some action on the part of the disciplinary board—even if it's just to ask your lawyer about it—and that will help out if you do land in court against your lawyer. You can find out more about filing complaints and where to file them in your state at Lawyers.com, a reputable site by LexisNexis Martindale-Hubble (www.lawyers.com).

FIX IT: ENDING THE DIVORCE WAR

It has been nearly forty years since divorce law has seen any real, nationwide reform; even some states are in a matrimonial crisis. One of the most important ideas every state should adopt is a matrimonial client's bill of rights. In New York City, following the author's 1992 report noted above, the courts adopted rules of practice and statements of client's rights and responsibilities. Divorce lawyers are now required to give copies to any prospective client before a retainer is signed. These statements guarantee that clients are entitled to uncompromised attorney loyalty, to receive billing statements at least every sixty days, to know how many lawyers are working on their case, and to have any unused funds from the retainer returned at the end of the lawyer-client relationship.

Even though clients can be the best attorney watchdogs, states need to set more specific behavioral and billing standards for lawyers and other divorce professionals. In particular, courts need to examine and reveal relationships between lawyers, judges, and other professionals that might taint a divorce proceeding. Furthermore, court-appointed forensics should be held to uniform standards of observation and analysis. And in order to enforce these standards, states should establish a mediation or dispute process that allows victimized clients to pursue real compensation and relief. Also, court assignation of forensics or lawyers for children should be blind, to prevent cronyism playing into the lives of children.

Beyond regulating the billing in the divorce industry, courts should address the problem of wealthy spouses dragging out legal proceedings to force the other spouse to accept a one-sided and coerced settlement. One expert suggests that judges should "grant fair, timely counsel fees to non-monied spouses from monied-spouses." Another idea specifically for custody cases, in which never-ending cases only hurt children, is the requirement that judges make preliminary findings in cases within seventy-five days. The goal, according to Patricia Duff, is to make the system effective and efficient and not "a gravy train for lawyers and psychiatrists."

CHAPTER 9

THE RIGHTS OF SMALL
BUSINESS OWNERS

When small businesses get into trouble, they are free to go bankrupt,
unlike speculating, mismanaged, or corrupt big business that can go
to Washington for a complex bailout.
—Ralph Nader, acceptance statement for the
Association of State Green Parties Nomination
for President of the United States,
Denver, June 25, 2000

There are around 20 million small businesses in this country and
about 570,000 new ones are launched each year. These businesses
provide over half of private-sector jobs in the United States. But
much like any other role in life, the world of the small businessperson entails personal and professional hazards, causing roughly
550,000 businesses to close shop each year. Will zoning and regulation decisions bust your business? Where can you turn to get funds
when your nest egg gets cracked? How can you protect your product and brand name from imitators?

Laws covering small businesses are rarely straightforward. Even
determining what constitutes a small business can be complex. For
research purposes the U.S. Small Business Administration (SBA)
counts all independent businesses with fewer than 500 employees as
a "small business," but the awarding of government contracts uses different criteria for each industry. For instance, most construction companies are considered "small" if they are worth less than $28.5 mil-
lion, and most farmers are "small" only if they stay below $750,000
annually; but many financial institutions are "small" with up to $150

million in assets. Further complicating matters, some businesses are limited to fewer than 100 employees, while others can employ as many as 1,500 to get the government label of "small business."

And while big corporations have the means to lobby lawmakers for friendly rules and subsidies, that clout isn't possessed by the small businesses that make our economy run. Worse, big businesses can bully the small ones out of the marketplace and even out of government contracts meant specifically for them. In 2004 a SBA Office of Advocacy report found that $1.7 billion in government contracts earmarked for small businesses actually went to large firms like Hewlett-Packard, Oracle, Raytheon, and the Carlyle Group. Lloyd Chapman, founder of the American Small Business League, took a look into the government's small business database in 2002. "Within one hour, I found dozens of the biggest companies in the world," Chapman said. The SBA has committed itself to solving the problem, but like Chapman, small businesses would be wise to defend themselves.

KEY SMALL BUSINESS LAWS

Small Business Act In 1953 the *Small Business Act* created the Small Business Administration (SBA) to "aid, counsel, assist, and protect" small businesses. Since then, the agency has been responsible for providing loans to small businesses and backing private-sector loans, as well as providing disaster relief, general assistance, and a "fair proportion" of government contracts to small businesses. The SBA's mandate has grown over the years to include targeted assistance and financial aid to low-income applicants, women, minorities, and veterans. In 1976 Congress added the independent Office of Advocacy to the SBA to research and represent small business in legislation and rulemaking.

Regulatory Flexibility Act This law, enacted in 1980, forced rulemaking federal agencies to address the impact of regulation on small business before promulgating new rules. Any agency proposing a rule change that carries a significant economic impact on small entities has to submit an analysis to the SBA's Office of Advocacy in an attempt to simplify the compliance procedures and lessen the regulatory load. The SBA monitors agency compliance but has no authority to force agencies to change their procedures.

Small Business Regulatory Enforcement Act   Finding the *Regulatory Flexibility Act of 1980* too weak, Congress gave the SBA's Office of Advocacy new powers in 1996 with the *Small Business Regulatory Enforcement Act*. This law mandates that the EPA and OSHA create review panels before implementing regulations expected to have a significant impact on small businesses. The law also created an SBA Ombudsman to review regulations, and ten regional fairness boards, staffed by small businesspeople, to listen to the small business community and take their concerns to Congress and the executive branch. Furthermore, the law extended small businesses rights to (1) petition the agencies on regulatory matters and (2) the courts' power to relieve regulatory burdens and reduce penalties.

Other Laws   Naturally, there are countless other laws that small businesses will have to conform with, from federal and state tax codes to the *Uniform Commercial Code*. In fact, every law cited in this volume is bound to affect one business or another. The laws above are specifically designed to assist small businesses, but for more information on legal requirements regarding your firm, you can start at www.business.gov or visit a qualified legal advisor.

DEFENDING YOUR BUSINESS

Starting Off   Whether you are opening a small enterprise in the public square or a home-based business in your spare bedroom, you'll have to make some important decisions early.

The entrepreneurial spirit is practically second nature to us. Haven't we all floated to friends and family our ideas about what would make a good business? However, just because a suggestion of ours wins raves at dinner parties doesn't make it a no-brainer. Successful entrepreneurs scour the market for clues on how to proceed. Are there other businesses in the same sector? How will yours stand out against the competition? If you are building a product, what are the copyright and patent prospects? And most important, how do you know you'll find customers?

Starting any business is always risky, but with some research and planning you can minimize that risk. Begin by browsing the yellow pages and the Internet for businesses similar to your idea. Try to learn as much about them and their management as you can. See what works and what doesn't and start coming up with your own business plan. If your competition charges too much, you might see what you can do to keep costs down, or if the service or product is less than satisfactory, maybe the market will bear a higher price for something better.

Next, turn to trade magazines and government reports to get more in-depth information on the sector. A wide range of government research is available through the SBA's website at www.sba.gov and through other agencies that regulate industries. Contact the Better Business Bureau to see what the most common customer complaints are and try to address them in your business plan.

Make as many contacts in the industry as you can and try to learn from each one. Local business groups often have mentor programs and you can network with experienced business professionals through the nonprofit group SCORE by visiting www.score.org or by calling (800) 634-0245. In addition to providing free online counseling, they offer in-person help through nearly 400 chapters across the country.

As with other fields, the Internet makes it easier to network with other businesspeople. Online communities of entrepreneurs like Fast Company's Readers' Network, Company of Friends; Linkedin.com; and Ryze.com, to name a few, make it easy to brainstorm problems and get advice. Laura Allen did just that to find a new office for her company in Manhattan. "[The networks] provide an immediate community of people," says Allen, who used the sites to get leads for finding a bigger office near Union Square. Most online communities are free to join, but charge small fees for other services.

Finally, look to market research firms and the press. Much of the general research information will be available in trade publications, but you can pay to have specialized or custom market research done through a research firm.

CASE STUDY

Robert Byerley, from Dallas, Texas, got the research right when he decided to open an upscale dry cleaning business in his hometown. Byerley was inspired to go into the cleaning business when a local dry cleaner refused to replace or apologize for the iron-shaped mark burned into his designer duds. There and then the businessman decided he had found a market—a quality cleaning company that would stand behind its work.

But how to make it happen? Byerley knew there were numerous cleaners in town, but he also knew there were none that matched his idea of quality service. "I believed the things I wanted in a perfect dry-cleaner were incompatible with a discount operation," he told the *Wall Street Journal.* But Byerley also knew he would have to compete with the high-end chains.

To bring his plan to life, Byerley holed up for a week at the library, where he pored over trade publications and information from the government. He found that the cleaning industry brought in $16 billion a year, and was mostly run by family firms. A call to the Better Business Bureau revealed that the industry was riddled with complaints, the most popular being that "cleaners didn't stand behind what they did," according to Byerley. He discovered that new regulations would change the standards for handling and disposing of the chemical cleaning solvent in the coming years and decided that he could outfit his stores with equipment to exceed the new rules and gain an advantage in the marketplace.

Byerley brainstormed what he wanted his business to be. "I wanted a place people would be comfortable leaving their best clothes, a place that paired five-star service and quality with an establishment that didn't look like a dry cleaner." So he decided that he needed good locations with sharp-looking, free-standing shops, complete with a drive-through for pick-ups and drop-offs, televisions, and refreshments.

In 1996, Byerley opened his first dry cleaning store, Bibbentuckers, in a Dallas suburb. When business began to boom there, he opened stores in Dallas in 1997 and 1998. In 2004, his three stores recorded $8 million in revenue, and they continue to grow with little advertising.

GET ORGANIZED

Once you've hatched an idea, you'll have to determine your legal structure. There are a number of ways to define ownership and each variation has a number of benefits and potential downfalls.

Sole Proprietorship   The most common business structure is the sole proprietorship. Essentially, as a sole proprietor, there is no difference between you and your business. Your business cannot own property separately from you; there is no need to file taxes separately for the business; and there is no stock or other owners involved—though you can easily share ownership with your spouse. You can move funds freely between your business and your personal accounts (just remember to keep good records for tax purposes). The biggest drawback of the sole proprietorship is that you are personally liable for your business, which means that another party can sue you and be awarded your personal property for any lawsuits or debts that your business is found liable for. Many small businesses have little contact with the public so the personal risk is not great, but measure your risk carefully before taking this route. Meet with a business attorney if you're unsure. You might find that any liability risks your business has can be offset with a good insurance policy.

Partnership   If there are multiple owners (besides your spouse), the simplest legal structure is a partnership. A partnership is similar to a sole proprietorship, but the multiple owners are bound to each other by a partnership agreement. That agreement should clearly indicate the terms under which the partnership operates and how the profits and losses will be shared. It's not uncommon for partnerships to have terms that allow a partner to buy another partner's share of the business should he or she leave the partnership. Like a sole proprietorship, the owners are personally liable for the debts of the business.

Limited Liability Company   The limited liability company (LLC) is a newer form of business legal structure. The main benefit is that it limits your personal liability from your business without the complexity of incorporating. As with corporations, you can still be held liable for your personal actions as the owner, and for any debts you personally guarantee. With an LLC however, you can choose to file your taxes with your individual return or as a separate entity like a corporation. In short, an LLC can provide the tax benefits of a sole proprietorship with the legal protections of a corporation.

Corporation   Finally, for more complex business ventures, you might choose incorporation. Like LLCs, a corporation limits your liability because it is a separate entity from its owners. Private corporations are different from public corporations, whose shares are traded in a stock market. A corporation usually has to pay taxes as a separate entity while its shareholders pay taxes on the profits, but a small business can incorporate as an "S corporation" and just pay taxes on its share of the profits. The main difference between a corporation and an LLC is that an LLC has more freedom to determine the roles of the members/owners and how the profits and losses will be shared. In a corporation the shareholders are required to share the profits and losses in accordance with each person's stake in the company. Furthermore, corporations must adhere to strict formalities regarding their operation that many small businesses would find untenable.

While you may have a notion of what legal structure to go with, it's always a good idea to talk it over with a lawyer, accountant, or other tax professional before making a final decision—and in the case of incorporating, it's simply a must.

A NAME BY ANY OTHER...

Any business name that is not your own legal name has to be registered at the county and sometimes state level as a fictitious or DBA ("doing business as") name. Coming up with the perfect business or product name will not ensure a business success, but it can't hurt. A business name should be attention-grabbing while describing the type of products or services you provide. Just don't go ordering stationery the moment you dream up that perfect logo. It's a good idea to do a search to make sure your name doesn't run afoul of another company's trademark.

For businesses dealing with specialized services in a local capacity, you'll probably be fine just searching your county's and/or state's database to make sure there is no direct conflict. But in this era of online business, most businesses would be wise to do a more complete search to prevent trouble down the line. The costs of a trademark violation are simply not worth risking. The company with the trademark can hit you for profits and penalties while you watch all your investments in your name, advertising, logo, and customer base go south.

After you search your county and state business records, move on to looking for registered trademarks. You can check national registered trademarks through the U.S. Patent and Trademark Office, which has a helpful online database at uspto.gov/main/trademarks.htm. You should also find your state's agency that registers trademarks through the Secretary of State office or another government agency. If you have dreams to expand your product into a number of markets and grow your small business into a large one, you might want to invest in a search that covers unregistered trademarks, which still have common law protection. A trademark lawyer or search firm can conduct a thorough search, or advise you on how to proceed.

Once you've picked a safe name, you can register with your county or state for a small fee. For more insurance, consider filing your trademark with the U.S. Patent and Trademark Office, to protect your name in every state. You can apply online at www.uspto.gov/teas/index.html. You don't need an attorney to register, but a trademark specialist can be helpful. Once your business or product name is trademarked, it is your responsibility to defend it. You can sue any business or individual that infringes on your trademark.

Making a Name on the Web   Now that about half of U.S. small businesses have websites, according to a report by *Entrepreneur* magazine, it's a good idea to keep a list of possible website names when starting a business. A cursory search should tell you if someone already has registered your top choices. A number of online businesses, such as Register.com, deal with domain registration and can tell you if the URL you want is available and reserve it for a small subscription fee; and in recent years, the total cost of starting a website has fallen from $10,000 to $1,200. The report, "The Entreprenuer's Guide to Doing Business Online," offers helpful tips and can be downloaded at www.entrepreneur.com/downloads/paypalbusinessonlineguide.pdf.

LICENSE AND REGISTRATION, PLEASE

Dealing with the Feds   The federal government requires small businesses to register for an Employer Identification Number (EIN) through the IRS (corporations may be required to register additional forms). To do so, file Form SS-4, available at www.irs.gov. Sole proprietors can use their own Social Security number instead, but if you plan on hiring employees, an EIN may help to keep your business life separate from your personal life. Unless your business deals in drug manufacturing, alcohol, tobacco, firearms, transportation, or investment banking, you'll likely just deal with your local regulators for permits and licenses. Of course, if you have employees, you will also be compelled to comply with federal wage and safety laws, while other federal regulators such as the Environmental Protection Agency and Consumer Products Safety Commission may also have regulatory jurisdiction.

State and Local   Unless you do business in one of the few remaining states without income taxes, you'll have to register with the state's treasury department just as you did with the IRS. If you deal in retail sales, you will also need a license to collect sales tax. Retailers can also get a resale license to purchase goods tax free, otherwise you'll pay taxes twice, when you buy and when you sell.

You'll need to deal with your state and local governments to make sure that you get all the local permits and licenses you need and to comply with local regulations. This can be a harrowing part of starting a business, but states have tried to streamline the process. Each state has an office to help small business meet these requirements. You can find your state's small business development office by going to the SBA's website at www.sba.gov/hotlist/license.html.

Licenses generally cover professional qualifications for occupations ranging from lawyers and doctors to beauticians and barbers. Businesses may also need licenses to sell specific products, such as a license to sell liquor or a license to prepare food. Other permits can be required, such as one from the fire department to cover occupancy limits and fire safety. Further licenses or permits regulate any risks to the public or collect taxes for the local government. City and county requirements can be a little more difficult to ferret out, but a call to the city or county clerk's office should help, and local business groups such as your chamber of commerce or trade associations might also be of assistance.

Overburdened and Overregulated Regulations governing business are put in place to protect the public; indeed, this book highlights a number of them and argues for even stronger regulations in some instances. But some regulations only marginally advance a small public interest yet hamstring small businesses. Many of them are relics of the past, while others are just poorly written. As the New York Commissioner of Consumer Affairs, I enforced regulations that benefited the public while eliminating those that imposed burdens without benefits. (For example, did movie theaters really need to hire "matrons" to keep order?) So if you think a rule is unfair or overly burdensome, meet with the agency administrators to propose a change. (See the "Citizen Action" chapter for help with petitioning a government agency.)

Talk Back/Fight Back

The ombudsman's office of the SBA helps companies like Terminal Shipping Co. in Baltimore, which was penalized by U.S. Customs and Border Protection when a company representative filled out the wrong line on a form. "He was filling out the forms and all of a sudden they zapped him with $1,000," said the SBA ombudsman, Peter Sorum. After hearing from the SBA, the agency refunded the fine. You can make a confidential comment to the ombudsman, or find your regional fairness board, at www.sba.gov/ombudsman or by calling (888) REG-FAIR.

Zone Defense Zoning ordinances can affect even a home-based business—especially if you have large deliveries coming and going, employees parking on the street, attention-grabbing signs, and, above all, if you produce any type of pollution. A discreet home web business is likely to remain undiscovered, but it's always in your best interest to know your zoning status in case your business grows. It is rarely advisable to wait until complaints stack up and an investigation begins in order to comply with zoning laws. If your community thinks you're a bad neighbor, it will be difficult to appeal a zoning ruling. And if you're buying an existing business, don't assume you're out of the zoning and regulatory woods. The previous owners may have been granted exceptions or "grandfathered" out of new zoning requirements that you will have to adhere to.

CASE STUDY

Zoning and planning issues can get very political (and sometimes quite bizarre), as Jack Heckenkamp found out when he tried to open a coffee shop in the St. Charles area near St. Louis. The budding entrepreneur told the *St. Louis Post-Dispatch* that it had "always been a dream of mine to have a family-owned small business."

He looked at towns all around St. Charles County for the home of what would be called the St. Charles Coffee House and finally found a spot he liked in the adjacent city of St. Peters. But because the space was zoned for offices, Heckenkamp would have to ask the city for a variance. "I was told it would be a mere formality," he remembered.

But Heckenkamp was unaware of the grudge match between the city of St. Peters and its neighbor, St. Charles. St. Peters is the oldest and biggest city in St. Charles County, but that doesn't keep it from feuding with the neighboring city that bears the county's name. The city once even resorted to erecting a divider in the middle of a street to obstruct access to a Home Depot that it had lost to St. Charles. So when Heckenkamp went before the planning commission to ask for a variance to the zoning ordinance, he faced some hostile questioning.

"If you're going to have that in St. Peters, why are we calling it St. Charles Coffee House?" asked one of the commissioners. When he answered that he liked the name, the mayor shot back, "I would suggest you go to St. Charles and ask for this approval, huh?" Despite the hostility, Heckenkamp's variance was approved on a seven to two vote, proving that good sense can in fact prevail when you have a simple zoning need.

Talk Back/Fight Back

If your business is found in violation of a zoning ordinance, you have a few options. You could change your business operations to meet the law's requirements. But if that's not realistic, you can try petitioning your zoning board to change the ordinance. Or, in order to keep strict zoning laws from causing an undue hardship to small businesses, cities can make exceptions to their zoning ordinances. You might be able to win a "variance" or "conditional use" exception if you present your case to the zoning authorities.

Regardless of how you proceed, it's important to get the backing of your community. Try to win support of your neighbors and other businesses in the area. Bring a petition and get supporters to show up to the hearing if one is held. Consider the concerns of your neighbors and make some concessions that all of you can live with, if necessary.

Protecting Your Products If your business is based on a new product or invention, you can take steps to defend yourself from imitators by getting a patent. Patents come in three basic varieties. You can get a twenty-year "utility patent" for new products, manufacturing processes, and even improvements to those that already exist. A "design patent," which lasts fourteen years, covers the look of your product. There are also twenty-year patents for engineered plants that reproduce asexually. The patent process is expensive and takes anywhere from two to seven years, but fortunately there are some discounts for small businesses. And, while a patent lawyer or agent is advisable, you *can* go it alone if you please.

Your first step is to make sure your product qualifies for a patent. That means that it has to be "new, useful and nonobvious," which is to say it is unlike any other product on the market, and any that have previously been published or that have patents pending. You aren't required to do a search for other similar products, but it's generally a good idea to do so before you invest your time and money. You can search the U.S. Patent and Trademark Office website at www.uspto.gov, or head to a regional patent library. If you're overwhelmed by the project, you can hire a patent lawyer or search firm, which will usually cost between $750 and $1,000, according to Joanne Hayes-Rines, the publisher of *Inventors' Digest*.

The patent fees usually run about $1,000, but more complicated patents can easily go higher. On the other hand, small businesses, nonprofits, and individual inventors can get a number of the fees reduced by half. And some simple utility patents can be filed electronically at a base rate of $75.

The process gets more expensive if you hire a professional to shepherd your product through the application process. At approximately $2,000 and up, patent professionals will draw up your patent claim and draft artwork to ensure it has a good chance of winning an effective patent. Because a clumsily worded patent proposal may get turned down, or be too narrowly defined to stop future infringes from copying your product, it may be money well spent. Considering 83 percent of some 360,000 applications are rejected each year, you'll want to weigh your options carefully. Your chances of securing a patent increase on appeal, but so do the expenses.

Perhaps the best option for small businesses is to apply for a one-year provisional patent. There's no application required for provisional patents. You can just send a description and sketch of your product and pay the fee—which was $200 in 2005, but just $100 for small entities. This will give you the protection of using a "patent pending" label, and it also gives you a little time to check out your product's viability on the open market. If your product sizzles, you can go full steam ahead with a good patent lawyer, but if it fizzles you can cut your losses or proceed more carefully.

CHAPTER 10

CITIZEN ACTION

There is nothing beyond the reach of ordinary citizens doing the daily work of democracy, and no problem too great to tackle with the power of active citizenship.
— Joan Claybrook, President, Public Citizen

Our government *should* work for us and it's our right and responsibility to participate in our democracy. When the current system lets you down, it's within your power to change it. That certainly includes showing up on Election Day and casting your vote for the candidate who best represents your interests and values. But it means much, much more. Participating in community hearings on proposed local development, sitting on school boards, corresponding with your representatives on issues that matter to you, lobbying an entire legislative body on a bill you feel strongly about are others. Democracy means not that government must *do* what you—or even a majority—wants but it must *listen* to what you want.

Watching your government on TV can make it seem remote and inaccessible. Getting through to that "shining city upon a hill," as the puritan preacher John Winthrop imagined America in the seventeenth century, may actually feel more like Sisyphus pushing a rock up his own ancient hill. One gets the feeling that only $500-an-hour lobbyists have access to our elected representatives (and in the worst cases, that's far too close to the truth). But democracy is not caged within the halls of Washington, D.C. It's all around us. Government's power comes from the people, and when our democracy gets off track, it's our job to fix it. Corporate interests can often trump the public's interests in politics because the former can focus their substantial resources—lobbyists, lawyers, PACs, contributions—to fulfill their wish lists. Still, the people have something far more important than lobbyists' lucre—themselves!

To change the system, you have to know the system. Our government is a vast, multilayered organization, the hallmark of which is the separation of powers meant to achieve checks and balances. Knowing the right place to go to with your problem is the first step. The legislative branch makes the laws, so if you want to pass, change, or repeal a law, you need to go to Congress on the federal level, to your state legislature, or to your city and county officials.

The executive branch administers the law. While most of us would be hard-pressed to get a lunch with our president, governor, or mayor, the executive branch is far more open to you than you might expect, given you have the proper steely persistence. Executive branches at each level contain administrative agencies filled with career professionals who are supposed to be above the (often petty) politics that can stymie our elected officials. Because these organizations administer the laws that the legislatures write, it's here that the nitty-gritty policy work is done that affects our communities in broad ways, from the quality of our water, to worker and consumer safety, to public health, development, and zoning. When these agencies make rules, you have the right to weigh in by attending public hearings.

The judicial branch interprets the law and our Constitution. You should appeal to the courts if you have to sue a lawbreaker to vindicate your rights. The judicial branch is usually the final word on enforcement if you can't get a government agency to take action on your behalf. (For more on using the courts to defend yourself, see "The Rights of Clients" chapter.)

KEY LAWS FOR CITIZENS

U.S. Constitution The First Amendment to our Constitution states: "Congress shall make no law respecting an establishment of religion, or prohibiting the free exercise thereof; or abridging the freedom of speech, or of the press; or the right of the people peaceably to assemble, and to petition the government for a redress of grievances." Our rights to speak and organize are part of what make our democracy so brilliant and vibrant. Every great movement for justice, from the abolition of slavery to the Women's Rights Movement, has drawn inspiration from these words, as will future movements great and small. These rights are nothing less than the fundamental promise of our participatory democracy. They lay the groundwork for citizens to act when our government does not.

Federal Administrative Procedures Act   While our Constitution promises the right to petition, this law establishes how to do it. The 1946 *Administrative Procedures Act* imbued the process of administrative rulemaking with the great American tradition of citizen participation. The agencies of the executive branch are required to post notice of a rulemaking procedure and allow citizens to comment at public hearings. Any interested person has the right to petition to issue, amend, or repeal a rule. Additionally, each state has passed its own laws covering agency petitions.

Freedom of Information Act (FOIA)   This law, signed by President Johnson in 1966, effectively switched the burden of proof for requesting government records. Instead of having to prove to the government why you should be able to access records, the government now has to provide them or prove it is classified under one of the exceptions. The law applies to all executive departments and agencies but does not apply to elected officials like the President and Vice President, or Congress, or the Judiciary. All fifty states have added their own versions to cover state agencies. The *FOIA* has been amended many times, including the *Electronic Freedom of Information Improvement Act* in 1996, which, among other things, requires agencies to post most of their public data online.

Privacy Act of 1974   Much like the *FOIA*, the *Privacy Act* allows citizens to access files the government keeps about them and to correct any erroneous information. The law also dictates how the government can collect information about its citizens and prohibits, for example, information collected for one purpose to be used for another.

COMMUNITY ORGANIZING

Community groups are an important part of a functioning democracy. Because there's strength in solidarity, as with labor unions, when citizens join together they can draw attention to local problems and influence their elected officials. Being involved in a community group affirms Tip O'Neill's famous observation that "all politics is local." For instance, when the coalition ROAR (Raleigh Organizing for Action and Results) presented the city council of Raleigh, North Carolina, with a list of over 600 complaints from the city's neighborhoods in 2004, the officials responded by fixing 95 percent of them.

Joining Up There are thousands of groups around the country that represent the needs of different communities. It's easy to get involved on whatever level fits your lifestyle, from making donations, to volunteering, to becoming a leader and making a full-time commitment. By participating in neighborhood meetings, you can voice your concerns and motivate others to get involved. Making a leadership commitment will provide an opportunity to shape your government and neighborhood.

Finding a group shouldn't be too difficult. According to Richard Wood, a professor of Sociology at the University of New Mexico who tracks them, the presence of community groups has doubled in recent years. Churches have long been the most active organizers, but civic associations, political parties, and other groups also have organizations around the country and are adding more chapters. If you don't find a group that represents your needs, start one. There is a vast literature on community organizing and all you need to get started is a mission.

ACORN (Association of Community Organizations for Reform Now) is one of the largest of these groups. From its roots in Arkansas in 1970, the organization has grown to some 850 local neighborhood chapters in 75 cities across the country that represent the needs of low and moderate income individuals and families on issues like affordable housing, education, public safety, health care reform, living wages, and fair taxes. The organization also offers free tax help and credit counseling for those who need it. As a member-funded organization, the members decide which issues to tackle at the local level and they unite with other chapters to take on national and statewide issues. ACORN members go from forcing the city to put a crosswalk at a busy intersection one day, to negotiating community reinvestment with national banks the next. And they push government from inside and out by getting involved with legislation.

Simply knowing how to navigate government bureaucracies to gather information, petition, and lobby is no guarantee that you'll be able to make the changes that your community needs. When government inaction leaves your community behind, it's time to take direct action to solve your problem. According to Beth Butler, head organizer of ACORN in Louisiana, "Somebody has to fight every pinpoint in a zoning ordinance sometimes, but there are other issues that people in the community are much more concerned about."

Focusing on the processes of government without addressing the needs of the community can be a way of shooting yourself in the foot. "We deal with some of the civic associations in this town," said Butler. "They don't do direct actions and they lose all the time. Most of them really confine what they're willing to work on because they're so confounded by their own disempowerment."

CASE STUDY

Frenzella Johnson joined ACORN in New Orleans' Ninth Ward in 1981, when her young foster-child Cynthia was hit by a car on her way home from school. She was taken to the hospital for injuries but fortunately was not seriously hurt.

The street where it happened is actually a state highway where 18-wheelers from out of town would whiz by with no concern for the children walking home from school. That's because there were no school-crossing signs, crosswalks, or crossing guards.

Johnson found out about ACORN, became a member, and launched a campaign to make the neighborhood safer for her children. She went door to door getting signatures for a petition asking for the city to provide signs and crosswalks. Then ACORN members spoke to the principals of each of the five schools in the area and drew up a plan of action.

One day after school, the neighborhood parents and ACORN members all took to the streets to walk the elementary-age children home safely. "We blocked traffic from Alzar and North Claiborne and Alzar and North Robertson, all the way back to Canal Street," which Johnson estimates to be approximately two miles. And when the city failed to respond, Johnson and ACRON had a backup plan.

"We had our members call City Hall one by one. They open up at 9:00 and we had one member call at 9:01, another member call at 9:02, 9:03, 9:04, and so forth," Johnson recalled. "Nobody could call City Hall that particular day at all."

The result?

"We got what we needed," Johnson said. "They put crossing guards where there were none, and we reinstated all the crossing guards [in New Orleans] a year later."

Johnson has been a member of ACORN ever since and an employee beginning in 2002. Over the years, she has worked on campaigns to get lead out of schools, raise the minimum wage, and save the water board from privatization. To find an ACORN chapter near you, or to affiliate your group you can go to www.acorn.org, or call 877-55ACORN.

THE EXECUTIVE BRANCH

While the *right* to petition your government is enshrined in the Constitution, the *process* for doing so is governed by the *Federal Administrative Procedures Act* and by laws in each of the states. Government agencies oversee so much of our collective business that most issues can be addressed in some way by contacting the right agency. While anybody can bring a petition to an agency, you have the best chance of success if you make a strong and rational case backed by diverse groups and individuals from your community. This includes testifying at a planned public hearing or petitioning the government for a rule change or enforcement action. Such efforts are often the most cost-effective way to affect a policy change because it's less time-consuming than suing the government or lobbying an entire legislature.

Petitioning an Agency Most agencies operate as an arm of the executive branch, but some boards and commissions are independent. Several states have agencies led by elected officials, like the insurance commissioner in California, for example.

Regulatory agencies set rules and standards for industries to protect the public interest and ensure safety, such as the Food and Drug Administration (FDA) and the Consumer Product Safety Commission (CPSC). States have their own agencies to protect the public interest, which can often set rates to regulate the prices of certain goods and services. Public utility commissions, for example, regulate what you can be charged for gas, telephone, et cetera. Other agencies oversee licenses for professional services or business services, such as the 250-person New York Department of Consumer Affairs that the author once ran (1990–1993). Such offices have the power to revoke licenses, or have other means to enforce standards and discipline those who don't meet them. Some regulatory agencies are responsible for issuing permits to businesses to ensure safe operating standards. A permitting agency can issue controls for construction projects, waste disposal, and the use of toxic chemicals, for example. Work with your city and county planning commissions to get involved in setting high standards for your community and report violations when you believe they've occurred.

Service agencies oversee our government's social welfare and entitlement programs. These programs provide needed benefits to low-income families, seniors, veterans, and the disabled. Their policies directly affect the health and welfare of all Americans, but especially those in need. The Social Security Administration, for example, handles the benefits of every working American who pays Social Security taxes, but older Americans and the disabled on fixed incomes are particularly reliant on Social Security. Other programs at the federal, state, and local levels affect specific populations such as children and the indigent.

Support agencies handle the business of government by purchasing goods and managing contracts, property, and personnel. A government contract can mean jobs for the community, but we should also expect our government to do business with companies that work well with the community and its workers. If a government contractor degrades your environment or refuses to adhere to prevailing or living wage standards, in addition to appealing to a regulatory agency, you can petition the support agency in charge of the contract.

Procedures vary from agency to agency. Some may have detailed written instructions on how to file a petition, while others may offer very little information at all. It might be helpful to question the agency's legal department, but if you don't know which agency to go through, call your city's General Counsel's office to discuss the problem with them.

Get the rules early on in the process so you don't fail in your petition or complaint on a technicality. Tennessee and Wisconsin, for instance, require at least five individuals to sign a petition to a state agency. Many agencies are required to respond within a specific time period, usually between one and three months. A few agencies may deny your petition simply by not responding, but most are required to deny you in writing with a stated reason.

CASE STUDY

The Coalition to Save Waltham Hospital banded together in January 2002 when the owners announced they were closing the doors to the community hospital that had served Waltham, Massachusetts, for over a hundred years.

Dianne Koch, who had been a surgical nurse and materials manager at the hospital since 1977, became one of the coalition leaders. She described hearing the news of the proposed closure as analogous to finding out someone she loved had cancer. "You mourn, then you move on, thinking you can make their life good, what's remaining of it. Then it's, 'Wait, maybe we can fight. I'm not willing to accept this death.'" Living out the famous words of labor organizer Joe Hill, Koch didn't mourn, she organized!

Realizing that the support of the community was just as important as the support of the government, the Coalition held rallies at the hospital and at local schools, spoke at City Council meetings, and mailed 700 letters from supporters to its congressional delegation, and held meetings during lunch breaks. Because the hospital closing was scheduled to take place just ninety days after it had been announced, they had to hurriedly mobilize the community and convince the Massachusetts Department of Health that the hospital provided "essential services" that the community could not do without.

The Coalition scheduled time to testify at the public hearing before the Department of Health. They focused their testimony on the "essential services law," part of a health care reform package that passed the Massachusetts legislature in 2000. They presented evidence that the region had the state's highest rates of emergency diversion and that nearby hospitals could not readily absorb the 22,300 emergency visits Waltham handled each year. They showed that half of Waltham patients came from other towns, proving its importance to the entire region. By studying the hospital records, the coalition showed Medicare was substantially the biggest payer, affirming their claim that the closing would hurt the community's vulnerable seniors. They discovered that the hospital had the state's only eating disorder treatment program exclusively for women. This program, they argued, affected the health services for the entire state. The hospital staff also worked with a local church specially serving the Latino population, to provide a monthly clinic at the church, which would disappear with the closing. By highlighting the diverse populations the hospital served, the Coalition broadened its appeal to more allies and bolstered its case for the hospital's essential services.

At the crucial hearing, the Coalition carefully chose its speakers to include a minister, a spokesman for the elderly, and a disability rights activist. They submitted over 300 form letters that they had collected from seniors in the community demanding the services be continued. After the hearing, the Department of Health found that the hospital's services were indeed essential and obligated the owners to submit a closure plan detailing how patients would get access to services. The Coalition was able to keep the hospital open for a year, but eventually loss of staff and patients forced it to close.

But keeping the hospital open that extra year allowed the Coalition to plan a community health center just a few miles from Waltham to meet the community's needs and a 24-hour urgent care facility that would replace the hospital's emergency room. Accommodations for free shuttle services to other area hospitals were made, and the capacity for those hospitals was expanded. None of these proposals were under consideration when the hospital owner had abruptly announced the closing a year earlier.

Preparing Your Petition   When you, ideally with others, petition an agency or testify at a public hearing, clearly and calmly explain the problem and your solution. Detail how the community is hurt, how you propose to solve the issue, and how the community will benefit from your solution. Cite the law that gives the agency the authority to make the change you request, or make a case that the agency is in the best position to solve the problem.

Support your arguments with solid facts and keep it free of any derogatory language or accusations against your opponents. Things that get people fired up at a rally may not be appropriate for sober testimony. Include your personal experiences and your interest in the cause, along with the testimony and experiences of the individuals and organizations that are most affected by the rule.

Finally, when writing your proposal, consider any unintended consequences your proposal might cause. Would it cost significant monies to administer? Does the solution to your community's problem negatively affect a neighboring community? Likewise, identify the groups that might oppose you, their reasons, and how you can anticipate, preempt, or resolve those problems. You might even be able to meet with potential opponents, while drafting a petition, to see if you can work together toward a cooperative agreement.

If the agency decides to make a rule change, it will likely be reviewed by another government entity before it becomes official. Federal agency rule changes are reviewed by either the Government Accountability Office or the Office of Budget and Management. State processes vary from gubernatorial veto power, to legislative review, to an independent commission. If you win your petition, keep an eye on the agency to make sure your proposal is implemented properly. If you are denied or frustrated, you may be able to file a lawsuit against the government, lobby for new legislation, or put an initiative on the ballot yourself. For a more complete guide on petitioning the government, see the Consumers Union publication, *Getting Action: How to Petition Government and Get Results*, available free online at www.consumersunion.org/other/g-action1.htm or by calling (415) 431-6747.

THE LEGISLATIVE BRANCH

Meet Your Representatives Locally, your city council members write and implement your local laws. On the federal level, we are all represented by our district Congressperson and our state's two Senators. Most states, like the federal government, have two legislative bodies (Nebraska has only one), which introduce and vote on state legislation.

Your representatives should be responsive to you and your community all year round; democracy doesn't end the day after an election. And while it may not always feel like it in today's divided political climate, your elected officials represent you whether you voted for them or not. And if you didn't vote for them, you'd better get used to working with (and against) her or him anyway—these days it's about as likely for an incumbent Congressperson to die in an election year than to lose. So when an issue or law is important to you, let them know. That helps them understand what kind of representation your community is looking for and holds them more accountable when they ask to be reelected.

But taking your concerns to the state and federal capitol is only part of your representative's job. He or she should also offer community and constituent services, to represent you at home as well as in the legislature. Congress has three major functions, the most obvious being to legislate and write laws. Amy Rutkin, chief of staff to Rep. Jerrold Nadler (D-NY), explains that "the lesser known responsibilities of Congress include community representation and constituent services." Nadler's office has a team dedicated to community related issues. They go out into the neighborhoods of New York City to attend meetings and forums in order to gauge the concerns of the community.

Constituent services, Rutkin says, is there to "help individual constituents handle the often difficult bureaucracy of government to navigate services like social security, housing or veterans affairs."

Nadler's office has case workers to handle thousands of individual needs. "If someone has a problem with immigration," for example, "they can call our office and access help immediately. We act as an ombudsman, to help get services out of the executive branch."

Each government office should be equipped to offer some degree of personalized, individual help when you or your community requires attention. Services differ depending on the representative and the local needs. When contacting your representative, call their local office rather than the Capitol, and ask for the "constituent services" or "community representation" staff. You may also be able to get an idea of the services offered by visiting their website.

Lobbying   It's become one of the dirtiest words in politics, and with good reason. In 2004, lobbyists spent $3 billion massaging the federal government, according to the Center for Public Integrity. And the sheer number of them ballooned to 34,750, more than twice the amount that stalked the halls of Washington in 2000. Meanwhile, the line between lobbying, campaign fundraising, and legislating—to say nothing of bribery—is being drawn in ever-fainter hues. One lobbyist reported to *The Hill* that a Senate staffer spotted him at the Capital Grille and brought over his dinner bill to have it paid. But that's just the tip of the iceberg; all-expense-paid vacations, houses, boats, and other unethical perks from lobbyists to representatives continue to make headlines. Politicians seem addicted to the lobbyists' steady flow of campaign cash. Another anonymous D.C. lobbyist explained in an interview, "When a major lobbyist seeks a meeting with a member, within a few weeks they'll get an invite to the member's next fundraiser. If he gives, he'll get another meeting, and if he doesn't he won't—and anyone who doesn't understand that shouldn't be hired as a lobbyist."

But lobbying itself is not the dirty word. The four letter word, in this case, is "cash." We all should have the opportunity to petition our representatives for a redress of grievances and argue for our interests, the business community no more or less than the rest of us.

But the infusion of business money into legislative campaigns and election coffers creates an unfair advantage for the few with much over the many with little, and turns our system of checks and balances into a system of checks, checks, and more checks. As a citizen lobbyist, you won't get meetings as easily as the money-players will. But money only pays for a campaign—voters are the ones who vote. By making a clear case to your representative, and to the voters he or she represents, you *can* successfully counter the problem that money shouts in Washington and in our state capitals.

CASE STUDY

It's usually easier to stop a bill than to pass one, especially if you have the support of the executive branch. Just ask Krist Novoselic, founding member with Kurt Cobain of the famous rock band Nirvana. He probably never thought he'd be a lobbyist, but that's what happened when the Washington state legislature passed a law in 1995 that would have regulated the speech of musicians.

The "Harmful to Minors" bill was a rehash of a law that had been thrown out by the state's high court a few years earlier. The new bill would have overruled the state's own anti-obscenity laws calling for judicial determination and instead forced retailers to make their own call about what materials were "harmful." It would have chilled free speech and placed an undue burden on small businesses. "It was an insult," Novoselic said. "After all the music industry had done for this state."

To make matters worse, the legislature had just overturned the governor's veto on another bill, making it politically treacherous for him to attempt another veto. Novoselic joined an alliance with the Washington Music Industry Coalition and the Recording Industry of America to lobby the legislature to get lawmakers to change their position so a veto could be sustained.

"I knew my situation as a well-known musician could open doors for me, so we decided to hit the legislature," Novoselic recalls in his memoir/manifesto *Of Grunge and Government*. "We walked the lobbies of the capitol and met with lawmakers, presenting the case for music in our state. We were propelled by a proactive message. We stood for freedom of speech, and also made the point that the music industry brought cultural and economic vitality to our region. We propagated our deeply held belief that our music community is an asset, not a liability." Novoselic's alliance convinced enough senators to protect the governor's veto and the veto was upheld.

Novoselic's experiences with government made him rethink his political philosophy. Having once embraced the antiestablishment ethos of punk-rock rhetoric, he came to realize "that our democracy could be inclusive." The former Nirvana grunge-rocker has stayed involved in Washington state and has championed electoral reform like instant run-off voting and proportional representation. Novoselic's former manager, activist Danny Goldberg, even quipped to *The New Yorker*, "He'll be governor of the state of Washington one day.... He's our Arnold."

The simplest lobbying campaigns are organized letter-writing projects that show how your community feels about a particular issue. The goal is to turn out as many letters, phone calls, and e-mails by your fellow citizens as you can, reflecting your organization's position. Especially with computers and the Internet greatly improving our capacity to access and distribute information, we can let legislators know how we feel faster than ever; but computers are no substitute for the people.

In his book *The Citizen's Guide to Lobbying Congress*, lobbyist Donald E. deKieffer warns against engaging in a battle of computer-generated form letters: "In sum, it is a waste of money to engage in a war of computers. Your form letters will be answered by form letters, and you can be absolutely sure the Hill's computers are better than yours." DeKieffer instead suggests you provide your supporters with a fact sheet containing your position, the status of the proposed legislation, arguments to support your position, and the action you urge the legislator to take. Armed with the research, encourage your supporters to write their own letters based on their own perspective. Unique letters stand a better chance of being read and making an impact on your representative's staff.

For big national or statewide issues that affect your community, see if there is a group already lobbying for your side. If you find a national or statewide group promoting your cause, see how you or your organization can get involved by helping motivate your community locally. There's no reason to duplicate an effort that already exists. And it's far better to be part of a coalition of many groups with a broad reach to pool your resources and research.

Regardless of how many allies you make outside of government, you're going to need some on the inside as well. Every cause needs outside advocates *and* insider champions arguing the case to colleagues in the corridors of power. The first step is making contact with your own representatives to win them over. But you'll likely need to convince more than your own representatives to pass a law.

Legislative chambers have committees that deal with specific issues and control the agenda. They can rewrite your bill, or simply put it aside and prevent a vote. If you're serious about passing a law, you need to have support in the committee that is responsible for your bill.

So find out which committee your bill will go to and focus on its members, looking into their political affiliations and how they've voted in the past. Project Vote Smart is a nonprofit, nonpartisan organization that follows elected officials and provides their contact information, their voting records, and their ratings from interest groups across the political spectrum. Go to www.projectvotesmart.com to access their extensive database. The indispensable *Almanac of American Politics,* available at book stores and libraries, can also guide you on how each official has voted on the issues. Design your arguments to their political leanings and their constituents. If you can, contact organizations and individuals in their districts and get them to speak out to support your cause.

Finally, about half of the states allow you to take lawmaking into your own hands by petitioning to put an initiative or state referendum on the ballot. Likewise, it's common for local governments to have initiative and referendum processes. Activists for economic justice around the country have taken advantage of these tools to improve the lives of workers. Over seventy-five cities have passed living wage ordinances, which require companies that win big municipal contracts or tax breaks to pay their workers fair wages, usually well above the meager federal minimum wage. The movement has also had victories at the statewide level. In 2004, for example, Florida passed a minimum wage increase and other states are addressing wages and health care issues through ballot initiatives. For help passing a living wage law, see ACORN's *Living Wage Campaigns: An Activist's Guide to Building the Movement for Economic Justice* by visiting www.livingwagecampaign.org, or you can download portions of it at www.laborstudies.wayne.edu/Resources/guide2002.pdf.

RESEARCH YOUR COURSE

Building a Body of Evidence   Whatever your tactics, you'll need to research your cause to build support. Whether you are filing a petition with an agency, fighting legislation, lobbying for a new law, or otherwise trying to change the system, you'll always have to answer the same questions to prove that your position is right. What is the problem? Whom does it affect? How will your proposal make it better? Who benefits from your proposal? Are there any side-effects or consequences to your proposal? What, if anything, will it cost? How will it be paid for? And as you proceed with your proposal, the questions will only get tougher.

Start by identifying similar legislative models or grassroots movements from elsewhere and study their successes and failures. Contact the leaders of those movements to learn from them directly. Think tanks and policy institutes can provide a great deal of data and model legislation, but you may have to do additional research to adapt it to the specifics of your locality.

Find people and organizations who can help you with your research. Academics at local colleges may have done work on your issue. The faculty of economics departments, urban development, political science, or labor studies are good people to contact. A local law school might offer pro bono services for causes like yours, and legal services providers might offer free services if your proposal helps low-income families.

Try to bolster your case with figures and documents from the government whenever you can. The federal government makes most of its public data available online. You can start by going to www.firstgov.gov, the "U.S. Government's Official Web Portal." That site offers links to every federal agency and department, state, city, and county website and offers vital tools and links for statistical data. State and local agencies make an ever-increasing amount of data available online as well. But you can't always expect the data you need to be published. Many government records are never released to the public, and the federal Information Security Oversight Office revealed that government secrecy is on the rise. From 2001 to 2005, the number of classified documents doubled to over 15.6 million and documents are being declassified exponentially slower than they were in the '90s.

Free Information The *Freedom of Information Act* was passed in 1966 to give citizens more access to government documents. Likewise, the *Privacy Act of 1974* allows you access to records the government has about you. As noted above, the federal government must provide the information or prove that the information falls under one of the nine exemptions offered under the act.

The nine exemptions an agency can claim to deny a *FOIA* request are:

1. Requests involving issues of national security.
2. Requests involving internal agency personnel rules.
3. Requests involving information specifically exempt by other laws.
4. Requests involving confidential business information, or "trade secrets."
5. Requests involving internal governmental communications.
6. Requests involving personal privacy.
7. Requests involving law enforcement records.
8. Requests involving financial institutions.
9. Requests involving geological data.

The law applies to all of the executive cabinet departments and agencies, military departments, government corporations, independent regulatory agencies, and all other agencies of the executive branch. It does not apply to elected offices like the president and vice president, congress, or the judiciary. All agencies are required to develop a guide that is easy to read and easily accessed on its website and by other means, and to create an office to handle *FOIA* requests. The guide should make clear what type of records the agency keeps, how they can be accessed through *FOIA* requests, what legal restrictions the agency has to deny access to records, and how the agency determines whether the record qualifies for release under the *FOIA*.

The Department of Justice acts as the executor of the *FOIA* through its Office of Information and Privacy. Its website, in addition to providing information on its own *FOIA* procedures, offers detailed information on how to navigate the various government agencies and use *FOIA* provisions. The Department of Justice, however, has not always been the most ardent defender of individuals seeking records through the *FOIA*. A Congressional Committee on

Government Reform report admonished then Attorney General John Ashcroft's instructions from October 2001 that the government should withhold information whenever there is a "sound legal basis," encouraging instead that the executive branch should withhold information "only in those cases where the agency reasonably foresees that disclosure would be harmful to an interest protected by the exemption." Nevertheless, much discretion is given to the agencies for determining what information will eventually be made public. You have the option to appeal the agencies' decision, and if that doesn't work, you can take it to court. If you win, you can recover court costs and attorney's fees.

To make your request as specific as possible, find out everything you can about the information you're looking for. Your request can be denied if you don't describe the information accurately. The key is to understand what records the agency keeps and how they keep them. Check out the agency's "electronic reading room" in the *FOIA* portion of its website and see how the agency indexes its records. If you're still not sure, a call to the agency's *FOIA* officer might do the trick. Additionally, the *United States Government Manual*, available at libraries, has information on each agency. Remember to be specific. Agencies do not have to assemble any new records or interpret data in their records to satisfy your request, so try to figure out exactly what record might exist and describe it to the best of your ability. You don't have to know what the exact document is called, but you must be able to "reasonably describe" the information you're looking for.

The agency can charge for the time it takes to search for the records, review whether they can be released, and for copying charges. Each agency sets its own policy, but with search fees ranging from $11 to $28 per hour, and computer time running as high as $270 per hour, fees for information can get quite expensive. This adds more incentive to keep the request as specific and simple as you can. Fortunately, you can ask for a fee reduction or waiver. There are reductions for the media, researchers, academics, and other noncommercial users. Additionally, the law provides for a fee waiver if the request "is in the public interest because it is likely to contribute to public understanding of the operations or activities of the government and is not primarily in the commercial interests of the requester."

Making Your Request The law allows for an expedited request if you can show a "compelling need." Agencies are supposed to respond within twenty days, though they are commonly granted more time and little can be done if the deadline is ignored. For more information on making a request, the Reporters Committee for the Freedom of the Press has more information including a letter generator that allows you to plug in your information to build a *FOIA* request. Each state has its own freedom of information law, sometimes called a public records law. Look into your state's law to get a closer look at your local government. The Congressional Committee on Government Reform published *A Citizen's Guide on Using the Freedom of Information Act and The Privacy Act of 1974 to Request Government Records* in 2003, which can be requested from the U.S. Government Printing Office or accessed online, and the Federal Citizen Information Center can further answer your FOIA questions.

Ultimately, you have a good chance to see your request granted. Out of the 4 million requests made in 2004, 92 percent were granted in full and 3 percent were granted in part. But some agencies are more willing to share their information than others. The more guarded agencies like the CIA, State Department, and the National Science Foundation all approved fewer than 20 percent of *FOIA* requests.

* * *

Citizens have been protesting against and influencing their governments for thousands of years, in democracies and dictatorships alike. In Romania in 1988, when 100 people rallied against the Communist dictator Nicolae Ceauşescu, they were killed. Later, when 100,000 rallied against his brutalities and failures, *he* was killed.

A democracy manages to do this without bloodshed so long as citizens have a fair shot at being heard. America in 2006 is a seriously flawed democracy, largely because of the authoritarian impulses of both Bush and Co. and the far religious (f)right—which is a large topic and the basis of my forthcoming book, *Losing Our Democracy*. But a long-standing American habit of "fighting City Hall," as well as extraordinary new technologies such as the Internet, have enabled numerous groups to continue to talk back and fight back—and win.

Take the Patriot Act. After 9/11, it was not so much debated as stampeded into law, with only Russ Feingold (D-WI) objecting in the Senate. But by the time the law had to be reenacted in late 2005, some 400 communities and 7 states had passed grassroots resolutions opposing the law's infringements on civil liberties. And MoveOn and its nearly three million members had the ability to generate a huge letter-writing campaign—snail mail and e-mail—to influence the national and congressional debate. So in December 2005, not 1 but 47 senators raised serious objections to parts of the act that they believed betrayed the values of America. And President Bush had to agree to a compromise law.

For the highest value in America is democracy itself, which no foreign terrorist or native alarmist can take from us.

ACKNOWLEDGMENTS

The ambitious goal of *Defend Yourself!*—to cover nearly all the key areas of our lives—would have been an impossible task without the following individuals, who selflessly provided their time and expertise to our effort:

Sheila Adkins, associate director of public affairs for the Council of Better Business Bureaus; Beth Butler (executive director, Louisiana), Frenzella Johnson (activist, Louisiana), and Bertha Lewis (executive director, New York), of ACORN; Lovely Dhillon, executive director of Law School Consortium Project; Gene Eisner, labor attorney; Neil Getnick, chairman of Taxpayers Against Fraud and expert in false claims law; Monica Getz, president and founder of the National Coalition for Family Justice; Stephen J. Jones, attorney, National Coalition for Family Justice; Gene Karpinsky, executive director of U.S. PIRG; Barry Krane, divorce financial planner, National Coalition for Family Justice; Nomi Prins, senior fellow at Demos; Amy Rutkin, chief of staff to Congressman Jerrold Nadler; Thomas D. Shanahan, attorney, New York; Jon Sheldon, attorney at the National Consumer Law Center; and the dedicated attorneys at the U.S. Equal Employment Opportunity Center.

This book also belongs to the following generous individuals and institutions who saw the value of *Defend Yourself!* before even one word was written:

Paul Beirne; Steven Gluckstern; Francis and Isabelle Greenburger; Jane and Sidney Harman; Anne Hess and Craig Kaplan; Fred Hochberg; William Little Jr.; Jeffrey and Tondra Lynford; George and Dorothy Ring; Jane Rosenthal and Craig Hatkoff; Bernard and Irene Schwartz; Sam Simon; Michael Sonnenfeldt; Joseph Warren and Hermine Warren, The Dorothy Perlow Fund at the New York Community Trust; OPEIU and Michael Goodwin; Retail, Wholesale and Department Store Union and Stuart Appelbaum; SEIU Local 32BJ and Michael Fishman; UNITE HERE! and Bruce Raynor; and United Federation of Teachers and Randi Weingarten.

Last, we are indebted to the consumer and public interest advocates who continue to make the world safer and more just through their work. We are especially grateful for the work of organizations such as:

AARP; ACLU and the NYCLU; ACORN; AFL-CIO; Community Catalyst; Consumer Federation of America; *Consumer Reports* and its parent company, Consumers Union; Council of Better Business Bureaus; Economic Policy Institute; Families USA; HALT; Kaiser Family Foundation; National Coalition for Family Justice; National Consumer Law Center; National Employment Law Project; Nolo Press; Public Citizen; and U.S. PIRG and the state PIRGs.

Notes

CHAPTER 1: THE RIGHTS OF PATIENTS

pg 1: **John Nelson:** Julie Appleby, "High Court Blocks Some Patient Lawsuits," *USA Today*, June 21, 2004.

pg 1: **Americans' lack of health care:** Families USA, "One in Three: Non-Elderly Americans Without Health Insurance, 2002–2003," June 2004, at http://www.familiesusa.org/site/DocServer/82million_uninsured_report.pdf?do cID=3641.

pg 1: **Families USA finding on workers' premiums:** Families USA press release, "New Report Shows Health Care Is Far Less Affordable Than It Was Four Years Ago," September 28, 2004, at http://www.familiesusa.org/site/DocServer/Are_You_Better_Off_Press_Release _English.pdf?docID=4821.

pg 1: **HMO profit increase:** David Sirota, "The Big Squeeze," *The American Prospect*, September 2004.

pg 1: **18,000 Americans die each year due to lack of health care:** Institute of Medicine press release, "IOM Report Calls for Universal Health Coverage by 2010," January 14, 2004, at http://www4.nas.edu/news.nsf/6a3520dc2dbfc2ad85256ca8005c1381/8db6d11 af9b5cc4285256e1b004cade1?OpenDocument.

pg 3: **Supreme Court weakens some patient rights laws:** Linda Greenhouse, "Justices Limit Ability to Sue Health Plans," *New York Times,* June 22, 2004.

pg 3: **Medicare Parts A & B:** The official U.S. Government Site for People with Medicare, "The Original Medicare Plan," January 13, 2005, at http://www.medicare.gov/Choices/Original.asp.

pg 3: **Medigap:** The official U.S. Government Site for People with Medicare, "Medicare Plan Choices," December 9, 2004, at http://www.medicare.gov/Choices/Overview.asp.

pg 5: **a choice of health plans:** "CR, HMO or PPO: Picking a Managed Care Plan," *Consumer Reports*, October 2003.

pg 5: **HMO vs. PPO:** "HMO or PPO: Picking a Managed Care Plan,"

Consumer Reports, October 2003, at http://www.consumerreports.org/main/
detailv2.jsp?CONTENT%3C%3Ecnt_id=329183&FOLDER%3C%3Efolder_id
=162687.

pg 6: **Debra Moran story:** Jamie Court, "In Critical Condition: Holding
HMOs Accountable for Their Egregious Conduct," *Chicago Tribune*, June 22,
1998; Judy Press, "HMO Arbitration Case Heads to Top Court, *Chicago Tribune*,
January 13, 2002; Carmen Greco Jr., "Fight 'Wasn't Just About Me Anymore'
Woman Says," *Chicago Daily Herald*, January 21, 2002; Jan Crawford Greenburg,
"Ruling Affirms Right to Appeal HMO Decision," *Chicago Tribune*, June 21, 2002.

pg 7: **Kaiser Family Foundation study on internal reviews:** Peter Landers,
Amy Dockser, and Marcus Most, "Battling Denials Is Hard, But Persistent
Patients Often Prevail on Appeal," *Wall Street Journal*, October 6, 2002.

pg 8: **Health plan disputes:** Trudy Lieberman, Elizabeth Peppe, and Janet
Lundy, "A Consumer Guide to Handling Disputes with Your Employer or
Private Health Plan," January 2003. This study by the Kaiser Family Foundation,
Consumers Union, and the Center for Health Choices has information on how
to file an appeal in each state that offers external review, and additional information on the internal review process. You can find the report at
http://www.kff.org/consumerguide/.

pg 8: **Texas independent review process study:** Consumers Union
Southwest Regional Office, Public Policy Series, "Independent Review
Organizations: Consumers Gain Needed Care When Unaffiliated Medical
Experts Review Health Plan Denials," May 2002.

pg 10: **risk pools:** "The Perils of Buying Your Own Policy: Part Two," *Consumer
Reports*, September 2002; Kaiser Family Foundation, www.StateHealthFacts.org,
"State Sponsored High Risk Insurance Pools, 2002," at http://www.statehealth-
facts.org/cgi-bin/healthfacts.cgi?action=compare&category=Health+Coverage+
%26+Uninsured&link_category=Managed+Care+%26+Health+Insurance&link
_subcategory=State+Sponsored+High+Risk+Pools&link_topic=High+Risk+
Pools; Kaiser Family Foundation, www.StateHealthFacts.org, "State Sponsored
High Risk Pool Enrollment, 2001–2002," http://www.statehealthfacts.org/cgi-
bin/healthfacts.cgi?action=compare&category=Health+Coverage+%26+Uninsu
red&link_category=Managed+Care+%26+Health+Insurance&link_subcategory=
State+Sponsored+High+Risk+Pools&link_topic=High+Risk+Pool+Enrollment.

pg 10: **Medical Information Bureau:** Health Privacy Project, "What You Can
Do to Protect Your Privacy," at http://www.healthprivacy.org/usr_doc/
WhattoDo.pdf; Also see the Medical Information Bureau at www.mib.com.

pg 11: **"The Patient Care Partnership"**: American Hospital Association, "The Patient Care Partnership: Understanding Expectations, Rights and Responsibilities," 2003, at http://www.aha.org/aha/ptcommunication/content/pcp_english_030730.pdf.

pg 12: **Institute of Medicine on hospital deaths due to medical errors:** Aparna H. Kumar, "World Health Organization Targets Medical Mistakes," *Associated Press*, October 27, 2004.

pg 12: **Agency for Healthcare Research and Quality study:** Agency for Healthcare Research and Quality, "20 Tips to Help Prevent Medical Errors," AHRQ Publication No. 00-PO38, February 2000, at http://www.ahrq.gov/consumer/20tips.htm.

pg 13: **Pat Palmer:** Pat Palmer, Martha Ellis, and Christopher Slone, *The Medical Bill Survival Guide*, Warner Books, 2000.

pg 13: **reviewing your medical bill:** "Decoding Your Hospital Bills: You Can Fix Costly Errors," *Consumer Reports*, January 2003.

pg 13: **Nora Johnson:** "Preventive Care for the Pocketbook," *Washington Post*, June 27, 2004.

pg 14: **financial assistance for hospitals:** Community Catalyst, "Not There When You Need It: The Search for Free Hospital Care," October 2003, at http://www.communitycatalyst.org/resource.php?doc_id=267; Kaiser Commission on Medicaid and the Uninsured, "The Uninsured: A Primer," December 2003, at http://www.kff.org/uninsured/upload/29345_1.pdf.

pg 15: **Daisy Makeupson and Trey Daly story:** from Community Catalyst, Inc., "Not There When You Need It: The Search for Free Hospital Care," October 2003, at http://www.communitycatalyst.org/resource.php?doc_id=267.

pg 15: **"*badger them so they don't come back*"**: Daren Fonda, "Sick of Hospital Bills," *Time*, September 27, 2004.

pg 16: **K. B. Forbes story:** Donald Bartlett and James Steel, *Critical Condition: How Health Care in America Became Big Business—And Bad Medicine*, 2004, 16–24; Steve Neal, "Price-Gouging Hospitals Sticking It to Uninsured, Immigrants," *Chicago Sun-Times*, June 4, 2003; "HCA: Discounts for Uninsured Reaching Half of Eligible Patients," *American Health Line*, June 23, 2004; Consejo de Los Latinos Unidos News Release, "Victory for the Uninsured from HHS!," February 19, 2004.

pg 17: **Health and Human Services regulation:** Paul Barr, "Surviving a No-Win Situation; CMS, HHS Offer Guidelines, Direction on How to Bill Uninsured Patients," *Modern Healthcare,* November 8, 2004.

pg 18: **AHA billing guidelines:** American Hospital Association, "Hospital Billing and Collection Practices: Statement of Principles and Guidelines," at http://www.hospitalconnect.com/aha/key_issues/bcp/content/guidelinesfinal-web.pdf.

pg 18: **$200 billion on prescription drugs:** "Prescription for change," *The Economist,* June 16, 2005.

pg 19: **seniors make up 42 percent of drug spending:** Families USA, "Out of Bounds: Rising Prescription Drug Prices for Seniors," July 2003.

pg 19: **Seniors skipping prescription doses:** Dana Gelb Safran, et al., "Prescripition Drug Coverage and Seniors: How Well Are States Closing the Gap?" *Health Affairs,* July 31, 2002, at http://content.healthaffairs.org/cgi/content/full/hlthaff.w2.253v1/DC1?maxtoshow=&HITS=10&hits=10&RESULT-FORMAT=&author1=safran&fulltext=senior&andorexactfulltext=and&searchid=1121396040502_519&stored_search=&FIRSTINDEX=0&resourcetype=1&journalcode=healthaff.

pg 19: **Medicare drug benefit estimate:** Families USA, "Medicare Roadshow," Spring 2004.

pg 19: **Elizabeth Riems:** Christopher Carey, "Sky-High Drug Prices Create Unlikely Outlaws," *Knight Ridder/Tribune News Service,* October 4, 2004.

pg 20: **prescription price-matching:** "Save Money on Prescription Drugs," *Consumer Reports,* May 2001.

pg 20: **generics, "me too" and drug trial:** Marcia Angell, *The Truth About Drug Companies,* Random House, 2004, pp. 16, 96.

pg 21: **pill splitting:** "Save Money on Prescription Drugs," *Consumer Reports,* May 2001.

pg 23: **Vioxx:** Alex Berenson, Gardiner Harris, Barry Meier, and Andrew Pollack, "Despite Warnings, Drug Giant Took Long Path to Vioxx Recall, *New York Times,* November 14, 2004; Gardiner Harris, "FDA Failing in Drug Safety, Official Asserts," *New York Times,* November 19, 2004.

pg 23: **Vioxx ads:** National Institute for Health Care Management, "Prescription Drugs and Mass Media Advertising, 2000," November 2001, at http://www.nihcm.org/DTCbrief2001.pdf.

pg 24: **FDA drug ad review:** "Free Reign For Drug Ads," *Consumer Reports*, February 2003.

pg 24: **Universal health care:** Institute of Medicine press release, "IOM Report Calls for Universal Health Coverage by 2010," January 14, 2004, at http://www4.nas.edu/news.nsf/6a3520dc2dbfc2ad85256ca8005c1381/8db6d11 af9b5cc4285256e1b004cade1?OpenDocument.

pg 25: **universal health coverage poll:** Chris Silva, "Health Care for the Uninsured Shaping Up to Be an Election-Year Issue on Hill," *AHA News*, January 26, 2004, at http://www.ahanews.com/ahanews/hospitalconnect/ search/article.jsp?dcrpath=AHA/AHANewsArticle/data/AHA_News_040126_ HealthCare&domain=AHANEWS.

pg 25: **Bush administration backsliding on health care:** Jonathan Weisman and Jeffrey H. Birnbaum, "Bush Plans Tax Code Overhaul; Changes Would Favor Investment," *Washington Post*, November 18, 2004.

pg 26: **Ron Pollack:** Ron Pollack, "Making Health Care Affordable and Accessible," *What We Stand For*, New York, Newmarket Press, 2004, pp. 118, 130.

pg 27: **pharmaceutical interests lobbying:** Public Citizen Congress Watch, "The Medicare Drug War," June 2004.

pg 27: **Medicare "doughnut-hole":** Families USA, "Medicare Roadshow," Spring 2004.

pg 28: **JAMA editorial:** Phil B. Fontanarosa, M.D., Drummond Rennie, M.D., Catherine D. DeAngelis, M.D., MPH, JAMA, "Postmarketing Surveillance— Lack of Vigilance, Lack of Trust," December 1, 2004.

pg 28: **Dr. Alastair Wood:** Denise Grady, "Medical Journal Calls for a New Drug Watchdog," *New York Times*, November 23, 2004.

pg 28: *USA Today* **study:** Dennis Cauchon, "FDA Advisers Tied to Industry," *USA Today*, September 25, 2000.

pg 28: **money devoted more on drug approvals than monitoring:**

Gardiner Harris, "At FDA, Strong Drug Ties and Less Monitoring," *New York Times*, December 6, 2004.

CHAPTER 2: THE RIGHTS OF CLIENTS

pg 30: **Jimmy Carter**: Deborah L. Rhode, *Access to Justice*, Oxford University Press, 2004, p. 79.

pg 30: **American Bar Association survey:** Gary M. Stern, "Polishing the Image," *National Law Journal*, September 16, 2002.

pg 30: **can't afford a lawyer:** American Bar Association, *Agenda for Access: the American People and Civil Justice—Final Report on the Implications of Comprehensive Legal Needs Study*, 1996.

pg 30: **"equal justice under law":** Deborah L. Rhode, *Access to Justice*, Oxford University Press, 2004, p. 23.

pg 31: **Arbitration Act:** Reynolds Holding, "Millions Are Losing Their Legal Rights: Supreme Court Forces Disputes from Court to Arbitration—a System with No Laws," *San Francisco Chronicle*, October 7, 2001.

pg 33: **Kevin Schmerling story:** Jeff Gelles, "Consumer Watch: What Auto Industry Should Really Fix," *Philadelphia Inquirer*, July 6, 2001; Jeff Gelles, "Consumer Watch: Auto Service Goodwill Goes Both Ways," *Philidelphia Inquirer*, July 23, 2003; Jeff Gelles, "Consumer Watch: A Victory in Court for Angry Car Owner," *Philadelphia Inquirer*, April 7, 2004.

pg 35: **California small claims court study:** Thomas M. Gordon, "California Small Claims Court Study," HALT Small Claims Court Project, August 9, 2002.

pg 37: *Hartford Courant* **finding:** Jeffrey B. Cohen, "A Little Fight over Small Debt," *Hartford Courant*, December 12, 2004.

pg 38: **Jon Sheldon:** Kevin McCarthy interview with Jon Sheldon, May 10, 2005.

pg 38: **employee arbitration systems study:** Deborah L. Rhode, *Access to Justice*, Oxford University Press, 2004, p. 42.

pg 39: **mediation:** Roselle L. Wissler, "The Effectiveness of Court-Connected Dispute Resolution in Civil Cases," *Conflict Resolution Quarterly*, Fall-Winter 2004.

pg 41: **Florida pro se divorce cases:** Laurie Cunningham, "Splitting up; Divorcing Couples Can Now Use Lawyers for Piecework Tasks, but Some Attorneys Fear New Rules Will Create Liability," *Broward Daily Business Review*, December 18, 2003.

pg 44: **Statement of Client Rights:** New York State Unified Court System, "Statement of Client Rights," at http://www.courts.state.ny.us/litigants/ clientsrights.shtml.

pg 44: **one million U.S. lawyers and growing:** ABA Market Research Department, "National Lawyer Population by State," 2004, at http://www.abanet.org/barserv/statebars2004.pdf.

pg 44: **William Hornsby:** Kate Coscarelli, "How to Hire a Lawyer," *Newhouse News Service*, April 8, 2005.

pg 46: **federally funded legal service facing impediments and budget cuts:** T. R. Goldman, "In for a Fight, Legal Aid, Courts Dig in to Battle Bush Budget Cuts That Would Kill Some Popular Programs," *Broward Daily Business Review*, February 16, 2005, at http://www.lsc.gov/pressr/EXSUM.pdf; Brennan Center for Justice, "Struggling to Meet the Need: Communities Confront Gaps in Federal Legal Aid," March 2003.

pg 46: **Legal Aid Society of Salt Lake City:** Elizabeth Neff, "Legal Aid Shifts from Free to a Fee," *Salt Lake Tribune*, April 10, 2005.

pg 48: **Marvin and Margaret Farley story:** "Law Schools and 'Low Bono': Consortium Helps Solo Practitioners, Small-Firm Alumni Offers Affordable Help to Clients in Crisis," by Cynthia L. Cooper, *Equal Justice Magazine*, Fall 2002.

pg 48: **Lovely Dhillon:** Interview with Lovely Dhillon, May 14, 2005.

pg 48: **Law School Consortium campuses:** Univ of CA, Berkeley—Boalt Hall | CUNY | Golden Gate | Univ of MD | Univ of MI | Univ of NM | NY Law School | Northeastern | Univ of the Pacific—McGeorge | Rutgers | Univ of San Francisco | Santa Clara Univ | Syracuse | Univ of TN | T. Cooley | Touro

pg 53: **Michele Youngblood story:** Errol Louis, "Don't Deepen Wounds: Court Reforms Would Make Life Even Harder for the Injured," *New York Daily News*, July 13, 2004; Joseph P. Fried, "Waiting to Settle a Lawsuit? Be Wary of Cash Advances," *New York Times*, April 4, 2005.

pg 54: **Legal Grind:** Deborah L. Rhode, *Access to Justice*, Oxford University Press, 2004, p. 100.

pg 54: **We the People:** Ameet Sachdev, "Lawyers Draw Line to Protect Their Turf," *Chicago Tribune*, June 27, 2004.

pg 54: **ABA lobbied the federal government:** Adam Liptak, "US Opposes Proposal to Limit Who May Give Legal Advice," *New York Times*, February 3, 2003.

pg 54: **FTC and Department of Justice balked:** Ameet Sachdev, "Lawyers Draw Line to Protect Their Turf," *Chicago Tribune*, June 27, 2004.

pg 55: *Stanford Law Review* **study:** Kristin Weber, "Reject Curbs to Affordable Legal Services," *Broward Daily Business Review*, April 12, 2004.

pg 55: **Steven Lubet:** Adam Liptak, "U.S. Opposes Proposal to Limit Who May Give Legal Advice," *New York Times*, February 3, 2003.

pg 55: **HALT review of lawyer discipline systems:** HALT, "HALT'S 2002 Lawyer Discipline Report Card," at http://www.halt.org/reform_projects/lawyer_accountability/pdf/RC_White_Paper.pdf.

pg 58: **client compensation funds survey:** Mark Hansen, "Steady Course: Consistent Results Are Sign of Success for Client Security Funds, ABA Survey Shows," *ABA Journal*, March 2003.

pg 60: **qui tam and** *False Claims Act***:** Neil V. Getnick and Lesley Ann Skillen, "The Fundamentals of Qui Tam," International Association of Defense Counsel, meeting papers, February 2003; at http://www.quitamhelp.com/static/articles/articles.html.

pg 62: **Sarah Campbell:** Brennan Center for Justice, "Struggling to Meet the Need: Communities Confront Gaps in Federal Legal Aid," March 2003; at http://www.brennancenter.org/resources/atj/atj8.pdf.

pg 62: **Deborah Rhode on legal aid:** Deborah L. Rhode, *Access to Justice,* New York, Oxford University Press, p. 188.

CHAPTER 3: THE RIGHTS OF EMPLOYEES

pg 63: **"employment at will" doctrine:** Kathleen C. McGowan, "Unequal Opportunity in At-Will Employment," *St. John's Law Review,* Winter 1998.

pg 63: **percentage of workers represented by unions:** Lawrence Mishel and Matthew Walters, Economic Policy Institute Briefing Paper, "How Unions Help All Workers," August 2003.

pg 65: **Alaska, California, and Nevada all have statutes** that allow employees to receive overtime after eight hours in one day. Colorado allows overtime to kick in after twelve hours in a day. Additionally, California and Kentucky provide overtime for workers on their seventh consecutive working day. Barbara Kate Repa, *Your Rights in the Workplace*, 6th ed., 2002.

pg 66: **shaving time:** Steven Greenhouse, "Altering of Worker Time Cards Spurs Growing Number of Suits," *New York Times*, April 4, 2004.

pg 66: **Drew Pooters suing Family Dollar:** Kathleen Schalch, "Workers Who Don't Get Paid Overtime," *All Things Considered*, NPR, August 19, 2004.

pg 68: **"details of any hazardous chemicals or other materials…":** U.S. Department of Labor, Occupational Safety and Health Administration, *Worker Rights Under the Occupational Safety and Health Act of 1970*, at http://www.osha.gov/as/opa/worker/rights.html.

pg 71: **Tyler Pipe and OSHA:** The information about OSHA and workplace safety in reference to Tyler Pipe and its parent company McWane Inc. comes from David Barstow and Lowell Bergman's excellent *New York Times* series "Dangerous Business," from January 2003 and their subsequent follow-ups. Additional material on OSHA regulations comes from the David Barstow, et al., series "When Workers Die," also in the *New York Times* in December 2003. The citations are: David Barstow and Lowell Bergman, "Dangerous Business: At a Texas Foundry, An Indifference to Life," *New York Times*, January 8, 2003; David Barstow and Lowell Bergman, "Dangerous Business: A Family's Fortune, a Legacy of Blood and Tears," *New York Times*, January 9, 2003; David Barstow and Lowell Bergman, "Dangerous Business: Deaths on the Job, Slaps on the Wrist," *New York Times,* January 10, 2003; David Barstow and Lowell Bergman, "2 at Hazardous Foundries Tell of Events Costing One His Legs," *New York Times*, January 16, 2003; David Barstow and Lowell Bergman, "OSHA to Address Persistent Violators of Job Safety Rules," *New York Times*, March 11, 2003; David Barstow and Lowell Bergman, "Pipe Maker Is Fined Over Safety Violations," *New York Times*, April 15, 2003; David Barstow, Remy Gerstein, Robin Stein, and Tom Torok, "When Workers Die: US Rarely Seeks Charges for Deaths in Workplace," *New York Times*, December 22, 2003.

pg 72: **OSHA inspection criteria:** U.S. Department of Labor, Occupational Safety and Health Administration, *Worker Rights Under the Occupational Safety and Health Act of 1970*, at http://www.osha.gov/as/opa/worker/rights.html.

pg 72: **imminent workplace danger criteria:** U.S. Department of Labor, Occupational Safety and Health Administration, *Refusing to Work Because Conditions Are Dangerous*, at http://www.osha.gov/as/opa/worker/refuse.html.

pg 74: **defamation suit against the *New York Times*:** Cynthia Cotts, "Behind the Pulitzer," *Village Voice*, April 20, 2004.

pg 75: **2003 Gallup Poll:** Marie Evan, "Race Matters," *Black Enterprise*, February, 2004.

pg 75: **Alfred and Ruth Blumrosen study:** The study can be found at http://eeo1.com. For a general discussion, see also Reed Abelson, "Study Finds Bias on the Job Is Still Common," *New York Times*, July 24, 2002; Ben Hammer, "Labor of Love: Law Professors' Study Provides New Weapons in Fighting Job Discrimination," *Black Issues in Higher Education*, June 5, 2003; Susan Williams, "Analysts Find Bias Evidence in EEO-1 Reports," *Social Issues Reporter*, October 2002.

pg 75: **MIT study:** The study is available at http://econ-www.mit.edu/faculty/download_pdf.php?id=971. For a general discussion of the results see, Marie Evan, "Race Matters," *Black Enterprise*, February 2004.

pg 75: **9/11 backlash discrimination:** EEOC press release, "Backlash Employment Discrimination Charges Since 9/11/2001, Against Individuals Who Are, or Are Perceived to Be, Muslim, Arab, Afghani, Middle Eastern or South Asian," September 11, 2004; EEOC press release, "EEOC Litigation Settlements April 2004," June 16, 2004.

pg 76: **Bilan Nur story:** *EEOC v. Alamo Rental Car LLC, ANC Rental Corporation*, was filed on April 30, 2004. The details of the suit were provided by EEOC lawyers involved in the case.

pg 76: **Zia Ayub story:** Shelley Murphy, "Museum Eyed in Firing of Muslim," *Boston Globe*, October 1, 2002; EEOC press release, "EEOC files post-9/11 religion and national origin termination lawsuit against Worcester Art Museum," September 30, 2002.

pg 76: **Zia Ayub settlement:** "Museum Settles Discrimination Lawsuit," *Associated Press*, October 25, 2004.

pg 76: **El Raheb settlement:** "EEOC Litigation Settlements," press release, March 2005; at http://eeoc.gov/litigation/settlements03-05.html.

pg 77: **EEOC sexual harassment definition:** EEOC, "Sexual Harassment," March 2, 2005, at http://www.eeoc.gov/types/sexual_harassment.html.

pg 78: **increase in discrimination charges:** "Women at Work: Looking Behind the Numbers 40 Years After the Civil Rights Act of 1964," National Partnership for Women and Families, July 2004, http://www.nationalpartnership.org/portals/p3/library/NewsCoverage/WashingtonPostWomenDiscriminatedAgainst.pdf.

pg 78: **Morgan Stanley sex discrimination lawsuit:** Brooke A. Masters, "Wall Street Sex-Bias Case Settled; Morgan Stanley Agrees to Pay $54 Million," *Washington Post,* July 13, 2004; Brooke A. Masters and Amy Joyce, "Wall Street Women Take Suit to Court; Morgan Stanley Case Could Set Precedents," *Washington Post,* July 7, 2004.

pg 78: **"lose their jobs if they complain":** "Many Tales of Sex Bias Go Untold," *Buffalo News,* July 19, 2004.

pg 79: **Wal-Mart sex discrimination lawsuit:** Cora Daniels, "Wal-Mart's Women Problem," *Fortune,* July 12, 2004; David Streitfeld, "It's Berkeley vs. Bentonville as Lawyers Take On Wal-Mart," *Los Angeles Times,* June 28, 2004.

pg 79: **Louis Harris and Associates survey:** Nikki Katz, "Sexual Harassment Statistics in the Workplace and in Education," at http://womensissues.about.com/cs/sexdiscrimination/a/sexharassstats.htm.

pg 80: **Jane Doe story:** EEOC press release, "EEOC Litigation Settlements May 2004," August 18, 2004, at http://eeoc.gov/litigation/settlements/settlement05.04.html.

pg 83: **alternative base period:** The states that have implemented an alternative base period for unemployment insurance include Connecticut, District of Columbia, Georgia, Maine, Massachusetts, Michigan, New Hampshire, New Jersey, New Mexico, New York, North Carolina, Ohio, Oklahoma, Rhode Island, Vermont, Virginia, Washington, and Wisconsin. For more information, see the National Employment Law Project's "What is an 'Alternative Base Period' and Why Does My State Need One?" April 2003, at http://www.nelp.org/ui/state/access/apbfactsheet041003.cfm.

pg 84: **independent contractors denied unemployment benefits:** National Employment Law Project press release, "New Report Finds That Workers Are Wrongly Denied over $1 Billion a Year in Unemployment Benefits," December

4, 2003. The full report is available at http://www.nelp.org/docUploads/WholeTruth%2Epdf.

pg 85: **union stats:** AFL-CIO , "Join a Union: Fast Facts," 2005; at http://www.aflcio.org/issues/factsstats/upload/joinaunion.pdf.

pg 86: **Federick T. Golder:** Federick T. Golder, *Uncivil Rights: The Better Way of Resolving Conflicts at Work,* Lyra Enterprises, Marblehead, 2000.

pg 86: *Minimum wage statistics:* Jeff Chapman and Michael Ettlinger, "The Who and Why of the Minimum Wage: Raising the Wage Floor Is an Essential Part of a Strategy to Support Working Families," *Economic Policy Institute,* August 6, 2004, at http://www.epinet.org/content.cfm/issuebrief201.

pg 86: **OSHA given new powers:** David Barstow and Lowell Bergman, "OSHA to Address Persistent Violators of Job Safety Rules," *New York Times,* March 11, 2003.

pg 87: **Margaret Seminario:** David Barstow and Lowell Bergman, "OSHA to Address Persistent Violators of Job Safety Rules," *New York Times,* March 11, 2003.

pg 87: **Seminario's analysis of OSHA:** Interview with Margaret Seminario, *Multinational Monitor,* June, 1, 2003.

pg 87: **Patrick Tyson:** David Barstow and Lowell Bergman, "OSHA to Address Persistent Violators of Job Safety Rules," *New York Times,* March 11, 2003.

pg 88: **ergonomic regulations:** AFL-CIO, "Bush Administration Ergonomics Plan Fails to Protect Workers from Crippling Injuries," April 2002, at http://www.aflcio.org/yourjobeconomy/safety/ergo/upload/ergo_plan.pdf; interview with Margaret Seminario, *Multinational Monitor,* June, 1, 2003.

pg 88: **20 percent of EEOC cases resolved successfully:** Carrie Mason-Draffen, "An Age of Discrimination?" *Newsday,* March 23, 2003.

pg 88: **threatened to temporarily shut down the agency:** Richard Goldstein, "The Myth of Progress," *Village Voice,* March 18, 2003.

pg 89: **Alfred and Ruth Blumrosen proposal:** The study can be found at http://eeo1.com. For a general discussion, see Reed Abelson, "Study Finds Bias on the Job Is Still Common," *New York Times,* July 24, 2002; Ben Hammer, "Labor of

Love: Law Professors' Study Provides New Weapons in Fighting Job Discrimination," *Black Issues in Higher Education,* June 5, 2003; Susan Williams, "Analysts Find Bias Evidence in EEO-1 Reports," *Social Issues Reporter,* October 2002.

pg 89: **FAIRNESS Act:** Among the Supreme Court decisions FAIRNESS seeks to address are *Alexander v. Sandoval, 532 U.S. 275 (2001),* which limits a person's right to challenge the state in discriminatory application of federally funded programs; *Barnes v. Gorman, 536 U.S. 181 (2002),* which blocks persons with disabilities from seeking punitive damages for illegal exclusion from federally funded programs; *Gebser v. Lago Vista Independent School District, 524 U.S. 274 (1998),* which, in effect, protects schools from responsibility for a student's harassment unless the school can be proven to have acted with "deliberate indifference"; *Kimel v. Florida Board of Regents, 528 U.S. 62 (2000),* which blocks state workers' right to sue under the *Age Discrimination in Employment Act;* and *Circuit City Stores v. Adams, 532 U.S. 105 (2001),* which allows employers to force employees to sign arbitration agreements that forfeit their right to sue for discrimination or unfair labor practices, among others. For more information, see People for the American Way's website at http://www.pfaw.org/pfaw/general/default.aspx?oid=14832.

CHAPTER 4: THE RIGHTS OF CONSUMERS OF PRODUCTS

pg 90: **John F. Kennedy:** David Bollier, *Citizen Action and Other Big Ideas: A History of Ralph Nader and the Modern Consumer Movement,* 1991, at http://www.nader.org/history/bollier_chapter_2.html.

pg 90: *Consumer Reports* **estimate on ads:** *Consumer Reports,* "21st Century Consumer," January 2001, at http://www.consumerreports.org/main/detailv2.jsp?CONTENT%3C%3Ecnt_id=18759&FOLDER%3C%3Efolder_id=18151.

pg 93: *Consumer Product Safety Act:* U.S. Consumer Product Safety Commission, "A Small Business Guide to the U.S. Consumer Product Safety Commission," at http://www.cpsc.gov/businfo/smbusgde.html.

pg 95: **Priscilla Broomell story:** Jeff Gelles, "Consumer Watch: Return It, Sure, But There's a Cost," *Philadelphia Inquirer,* February 21, 2004.

pg 97: **warranty statutes:** Federal Trade Commission, "A Businessperson's Guide to Federal Warranty Law," at http://www.ftc.gov/bcp/conline/pubs/buspubs/warranty.htm.

pg 97: They are Alabama, Connecticut, Kansas, Maine, Maryland, Massachusetts, Minnesota, Mississippi, New Hampshire, Vermont, Washington, West Virginia, and the District of Columbia.

pg 99: **extended warranties:** *Consumer Reports*, "Extended Warranties: Say Yes, Sometimes," January 2005.

pg 101: *"restricted area":* Sharon Harvey Rosenberg, "Two Wrongs Won't Make It Right," *Miami Herald*, March 6, 2004.

pg 102: **Sheila Adkins:** Interview with Sheila Adkins, April 18, 2005.

pg 104: **Angie Gallant story:** Tim Talley, "Military Wife Leads Charge for New 'Lemon Law,'" *Associated Press*, March 6, 2005; Marie Price, "Lemon Law Leaves One Woman with Bitter Taste," *Tulsa World*, February 27, 2005; Marie Price, "House Roundup: BA Woman Leads Drive for Change," *Tulsa World*, March 12, 2005.

pg 108: **Linda and Boaz story:** E. Marla Felcher, *It's No Accident: How Corporations Sell Dangerous Baby Products*, Common Courage Press, 2001.

pg 110: **unsafe toys:** Joyce McDonald, EPHA, "Toy-Related Deaths and Injuries, Calendar Year 2003," US Consumer Product Safety Commission Memo, September 27, 2004.

pg 110: **nursery products:** Joyce McDonald, Division of Hazard Analysis, "Nursery Products-Related Injuries and Deaths to Children Under Age 5," US Consumer Product Safety Commission Memo, November 22, 2004.

pg 110: **child-safe toys:** "What You Can Do Before You Buy," *Consumer Reports*, November 2004.

pg 112: **Ralph Nader on the NHTSA:** Jeff Plungis, "Agency Created to End Highway 'Slaughter': But Effectiveness Undermined by Lax Enforcement Efforts," *Detroit News*, March 3, 2002.

pg 113: **David Pittle:** "The Trouble with Recalls," *Consumer Reports*, August 2004.

pg 113: **Graco Children's Products:** Edward Iwata and Jayne O'Donnell, "Graco Fined $4M for Lack of 'Timely' Reporting Defects Caused Danger for Kids," *USA Today*, March 23, 2005.

pg 113: **CPSC staff and budget cuts and lax oversight**; "Hazard in Aisle 5," *Consumer Reports*, November 2004.

pg 114: **recall faults:** "The Trouble with Recalls," *Consumer Reports*, August 2004.

CHAPTER 5: THE RIGHTS OF CONSUMERS OF FINANCIAL SERVICES

pg 115: **Elizabeth Warren:** Interview with Elizabeth Warren, *Frontline: Secret History of the Credit Card*, November 23, 2004, at http://www.pbs.org/wgbh/pages/frontline/shows/credit/interviews/warren.html.

pg 115: **Federal Reserve on cards over checks:** Griff Witte, "Debit Cards Give Plastic Edge over Paper," *Washington Post*, December 7, 2004.

pg 115: **average household's consumer debt:** Patrick McGeehan, "Soaring Interest Is Compounding Credit Card Woes for Millions," *New York Times*, November 21, 2004; Testimony of Tamara Draut, Director of the Economic Opportunity Program, Demos "Before The Subcommittee on Financial Institutions and Consumer Credit Regarding Financial Services Issues: A Consumer's Perspective," September 15, 2004, at http://financialservices.house.gov/media/pdf/091504td.pdf; Robin Stein, "The Ascendancy of the Credit Card Industry," *Frontline: Secret History of the Credit Card*, November 23, 2004, at http://www.pbs.org/wgbh/pages/frontline/shows/credit/more/rise.html.

pg 115: **Americans owed $804 billion to credit card companies:** Federal Reserve Statistical Release, G.19, Consumer Debt, February 2005, at http://www.federalreserve.gov/releases/g19/hist/cc_hist_sa.html.

pg 116: **annual American financial services fees:** "Financial Services, Don't Get Taken by Hidden Fees," *Consumer Reports*, May 2005.

pg 116: **US PIRG on credit report mistakes:** National Association of State PIRGs, "Mistakes Do Happen: A Look at Errors in Consumer Credit Reports," June 2004, at http://uspirg.org/reports/MistakesDoHappen2004.pdf.

pg 116: **credit-reporting agencies' secret consumer histories:** Malgorzata Wozniaka and Snigda Sen, "Credit Scores: What You Should Know About Your Own," *Frontline: Secret History of the Credit Card*, November 23, 2004, at http://www.pbs.org/wgbh/pages/frontline/shows/credit/more/scores.html.

pg 119: **Steve Strachan story:** Patrick McGeehan, "The Plastic Trap: Soaring

Interest Compounds Credit Card Pain for Millions," *New York Times*, November 21, 2004.

pg 120: **Providian:** David Leonhardt, "Credit Card Issuer Will Repay Millions to Some Customers," *New York Times*, June 29, 2000.

pg 121: **finance charge computation methods:** Federal Reserve Board, "Consumer Handbook to Protection Laws," July 24, 2001, at http://www.federalreserve.gov/pubs/consumerhdbk/cost.htm.

pg 122: **$50 credit card late fee and credit card monthly minimums:** "8 Things a Credit Card User Should Know," *Frontline: Secret History of the Credit Card*, November 23, 2004, at http://www.pbs.org/wgbh/pages/frontline/shows/credit/eight/.

pg 122: **penalty fee profits:** Patrick McGeehan, "The Plastic Trap: Soaring Interest Compounds Credit Card Pain for Millions," *New York Times*, November 21, 2004.

pg 122: **Direct Merchants Bank:** Lucy Lazarony, "Tough, New Penalties on Credit Cards," *Bankrate.com,* April 25, 2003, at http://www.bankrate.com/brm/news/cc/20030425a1.asp.

pg 123: **credit card applications; 60 percent of cardholders will never pay off their debt:** "Credit Card Industry Sent a Record Level of Marketing in US," *Wall Street Journal,* April 9, 2002; Andrew Becker, "The Battle over 'Share of Wallet,'" *Frontline: Secret History of the Credit Card*, November 23, 2004, at http://www.pbs.org/wgbh/pages/frontline/shows/credit/more/battle.html.

pg 123: **credit card users who keep a revolving balance:** Bradley Dakake, "Deflate Your Rate: How to Lower Your Credit Card APR," State PIRG Consumer Team, March 2002, at http://truthaboutcredit.org/deflateyourrate3_02.pdf.

pg 124: **minimum payment:** "8 Things a Credit Card User Should Know," *Frontline: Secret History of the Credit Card,* November 23, 2004. Available online at http://www.pbs.org/wgbh/pages/frontline/shows/credit/eight/

pg 124: **US PRIRG on credit report mistakes:** National Association of State PIRGs, "Mistakes Do Happen: A Look at Errors in Consumer Credit Reports, June 2004, at http://uspirg.org/reports/pages/MistakesDoHappen2004.pdf.

pg 127: **Know Your Rights; filing a complaint with the FTC:** Federal

Trade Commission, "Credit and Your Consumer Rights," March 2005, at http://www.ftc.gov/bcp/conline/pubs/credit/crdright.htm.

pg 127: **Federal Reserve finding on creditors withholding credit limits:** Robert B. Avery, Paul S. Calem, and Glenn B. Canner, "Credit Report Accuracy and Access to Credit," *Federal Reserve Bulletin,* Summer 2004, at http://www.federalreserve.gov/pubs/bulletin/2004/summer04_credit.pdf.

pg 128: **Reviewing your credit report:** Consumers Union press release, "Consumers in Western States Can Get Free Credit Reports Starting December 1, 2004," November 24, 2004.

pg 129: *Consumer Reports* **on billing errors:** "Credit Cards: What's Wrong with this Bill?" *Consumer Reports,* February 2004.

pg 131: **directory of federal agencies for creditor violations:** Federal Reserve Board, "Consumer Handbook to Credit Protection Laws: Directory of Federal Agencies," at http://www.federalreserve.gov/pubs/consumerhdbk/directory.htm.

pg 133: **bigger vs. smaller banks:** "Should You Supersize Your Bank Now?" *Consumer Reports,* July 2004.

pg 134: *Check 21* **may increase bounced check fees:** Consumer Federation of America & National Consumer Law Center, "Bounce Protection: How Banks Turn Rubber into Gold by Enticing Consumers to Write Bad Checks: An Examination of Bounce Protection Plans," January 27, 2003.

pg 135: **"substitute check" rights:** National Consumer Law Center, "New Check 21 Act Effective October 28, 2004; Banks No Longer Will Return Original Cancelled Checks," at http://www.consumerlaw.org/initiatives/check21.shtml.

pg 138: **Nancy Watrous Story:** Betty Lin Fischer, "Error Can Take Time to Correct," *Akron Beacon Journal,* December 26, 2004.

pg 139: **Elizabeth Warren:** Congressional Record, *Bankruptcy Abuse Prevention and Consumer Protection Act of 2005,* April 14, 2005; at http://www.govtrack.us/congress/record.xpd?id=109-h20050414-27&bill=s109-256.

pg 140: **Steve Dunn story:** Betty Adams, "Maine Man's Fight Against Identity Theft a Slow One," *Portland Press Herald,* May 10, 2004.

pg 141: **FTC report on identity theft:** Federal Trade Commission, "Identity Theft Survey Report," September 2003, at http://www.ftc.gov/os/2003/09/

synovatereport.pdf. See also, US PIRG and Consumers Union, "The Clean Credit and Identity Theft Protection Act: Model State Laws," November 2004, at http://www.pirg.org/consumer/credit/PIRGCUCleanAct9mar05.doc.

pg 141: **time and money spent clearing names targeted by identity theft:** Peter Brownfeld, "Identity Theft Worries Consumer Advocates," Fox News, February 10, 2004, at http://www.foxnews.com/story/ 0,2933,110923,00.html.

pg 142: **preventing identity theft:** Federal Trade Commission, "Avoiding Credit and Charge Card Fraud," August 1997, at http://www.ftc.gov/bcp/con-line/pubs/credit/cards.htm.

pg 144: **responding to ID theft:** Privacy Rights Clearinghouse and CalPIRG, "Identity Theft: What to do if it happens to you," April 2003, at http://www.idtheftcenter.org/Factsheet17A.pdf.

pg 146: **debt counseling services:** Consumer Federation of America and National Consumer Law Center, "Credit Counseling in Crisis: The Impact on Consumers of Funding Cuts, Higher Fees and Aggressive New Market Entrants," April 2003.

pg 149: **credit card legislation:** Consumers Union, "Current Congressional Proposals on Credit Cards," 2005; at http://www.consumersunion.org/yourwal-let/creditcard.htm.

pg 150: **examples of corporate data breeches:** *Wall Street Journal Online,* "Without a Trace," September 19, 2005; at http://online.wsj.com/documents/ info-idtheft0504.html.

pg 150: **Beth Givens:** Dionne Searcey, "Information Security: Consumer Alert," *Wall Street Journal,* July 18, 2005.

pg 150: **Database Security Breach Notification Act:** Joe Simitian, "U.S. No Help in Quest for Database Security Law," *San Jose Mercury News,* September 30, 2005.

CHAPTER 6: THE RIGHTS OF TAXPAYERS

pg 151: **Rossotti quotation:** Charles Rossotti, *Many Unhappy Returns: One Man's Quest to Turn Around the Most Unpopular Organization in America* (Cambridge, Mass.: Harvard Business School Press, 2005), p. 242. For further discussion, see David Cay Johnston, "A Tax Net That Catches Only Minnows," *New York Times*, March 6, 2005.

pg 151: **Rockefeller background:** Peter Dobkin Hall, "Happy Returns," *New York Times*, April 15, 2005.

pg 151: **125 million filed:** Internal Revenue Service, "2005 Filing Season Statistics," at http://www.irs.gov/pub/irs-soi/04ifss15.txt.

pg 151: **Oliver Wendell Holmes Jr.:** Internal Revenue Service, "Tax Quotes," at http://www.irs.gov/newsroom/article/0,,id=110483,00.html.

pg 151: **more than $300 billion a year:** National Taxpayer Advocate, "2004 Annual Report to Congress," December 31, 2004, at http://www.irs.gov/pub/irs-utl/ntafy2004annualreport.pdf.

pg 151: **39 percent cheat on taxes:** NBC News poll conducted by Blum & Weprin Associates, April 3-5, 2005, at http://www.pollingreport.com/budget.htm.

pg 152: **Half were wrong or incomplete:** National Taxpayer Advocate, "2004 Annual Report to Congress," December 31, 2004, at http://www.irs.gov/pub/irs-utl/ntafy2004annualreport.pdf.

pg 152: **IRS not studying trends:** Report of the Treasury Inspector General of the Tax Administration, "Analysis of Notice Error Trends May Identify Systemic and Procedural Causes for Erroneous Notices and Refunds," July 2002, at http://www.treas.gov/tigta/auditreports/2002reports/200230095fr.html.

pg 152: **38 percent received erroneous information:** GAO, "Report to the Chairman, Subcommittee on Oversight, Committee on Ways and Means, House of Representatives," November 2004, GAO-05-67.

pg 152: **IRS received 6 million calls:** National Taxpayer Advocate, "2004 Annual Report to Congress," December 31, 2004, at http://www.irs.gov/pub/irs-utl/ntafy2004annualreport.pdf; For further discussion: Daniel Pilla, *The IRS Problem Solver*, ReganBooks, 2004, pp. 16-20.

pg 152: **Taxation with representation:** Gerald Barzan, "Tax Quotes," IRS, at http://www.irs.gov/newsroom/article/0"id=110483,00.html.

pg 153: **Background on *Sixteenth Amendment*:** "Taxation," Microsoft Encarta Online Encyclopedia 2005, at http://encarta.msn.com.

pg 153: **Background on 1988** *Taxpayer Bills of Rights:* "Congress has Leveled the Playing Field for Contests with the Tax Man," *U.S. News & World Report,* March 27,1989; John J. Cross III, "Taxpayer Bill of Rights," *ABA Journal,* June 1989.

pg 154: **Background on 1996 Taxpayer Bill of Rights:** Neely, Green, Fargarson, Brooke & Summers, "Taxpayer Bill of Rights—The Sequel," *Findlaw,* July 1997, at http://library.findlaw.com/1997/Jul/1/127322.html.

pg 154: **Background on IRS Restructuring Bill:** George G. Jones and Mark A. Luscombe, "Tax Rights Worth Bringing to Your Client's Attention," *Accounting Today,* September 7, 1998; Peter Baker, "Clinton Signs IRS Overhaul into Law," *Washington Post,* July 23, 1998; Albert B. Crenshaw, "Moving a Mountain of Paper Taxes the IRS," *Washington Post,* April 12, 1998; "1998: Internal Revenue Service Reform Bill Signed into Law," Microsoft Encarta Online Encyclopedia 2005, at http://encarta.msn.com.

pg 156: **FDR Story:** Franklin D. Roosevelt, letter to IRS commissioner, 1938, Tax History Project, at http://www.taxhistoryproject.org.

pg 156: **Jane Smith story:** Interviews with Elsa Strayer and Jane Johnston, AARP Tax-Aide volunteers, November 2005. Mrs. Smith's name was changed to protect her privacy.

pg 158: **67 million returns were e-filed:** IRS, "2005 Filing Season Statistics," at http://www.irs.gov/pub/irs-soi/04ifss15.txt.

pg 160: **Background on Prater example:** Elaine Silvestrini, "Prosecuting Tax Schemes Reaches Across Bay Area," *Tampa Tribune,* April 16, 2003; John Hielscher, "Tax Trickery," *Sarasota Herald Tribune,* March 15, 2004; Office of the Attorney General of the State of Texas press release, "Attorney General Abbott Wins Agreed Judgement with Florida Owner of Tax Service Scam," March 25, 2003, at http://www.oag.state.tx.us/oagnews/release.php?id=109.

pg 161: **900 percent:** General Accounting Office, "Tax Administration: Most taxpayers believe they benefit from paid preparers, but oversight is a challenge for IRS," GAO-04-70, at http://www.gao.gov/cgi-bin/getrpt?GAO-04-70.

pg 161: **Statistics on audited filers:** "Audits on Wealthy Rise," *CNN/Money,* March 12, 2004, at http://money.cnn.com/2004/03/11/pf/taxes/audits_2003/index.htm.

pg 162: **"Provide sufficient information":** Daniel Pilla, *The IRS Problem Solver,* ReganBooks, 2004, p. 162.

pg 162: **Eliot Kaplan:** Joan Raymond, "A Kinder, Gentler Face for the IRS," *Newsweek,* April 16, 2001.

pg 164: **"This is notice...":** Daniel Pilla, *The IRS Problem Solver,* ReganBooks, 2004, p. 22.

pg 164: **Risch story:** Marc Schulhof, "How to Beat the Odds When the IRS Comes Calling," *Kiplinger's,* October 1999.

pg 165: **Jeffrey Levine:** Jill Andresky Fraser, "IRS Agent Jones Is on Line One,..." *Inc. Magazine,* April 1997.

pg 166: **Jeff Schnepper:** Jeff Schnepper, "Don't panic if the IRS sends you a letter," *MSN Money,* at http://moneycentral.msn.com/content/Taxes/Avoidanaudit/P34119.asp.

pg 168: **Wesleys story:** Albert B. Crenshaw, "A Struggling IRS Collects Its Fair Share of Problems," *Washington Post,* April 14, 1997, at http://www.washington-post.com/wp-srv/politics/special/tax/stories/irs041497.htm.

pg 172: **Mark W. Everson:** David Cay Johnston, "A Tax Net That Catches Only Minnows," *New York Times,* March 6, 2005.

pg 172: **Tax gap at hundreds of *billions* of dollars:** IRS, "New IRS Study Provides Preliminary Tax Gap Estimate," IR-2005-38, March, 29, 2005.

pg 172: **2005 IRS budget:** David Cay Johnston, "A Tax Net That Catches Only Minnows," *New York Times,* March 6, 2005.

pg 172: **Background on $450 million tax cheat and IRS enforcement procedures:** David Cay Johnston, "A Tax Net That Catches Only Minnows," *New York Times,* March 6, 2005.

pg 173: **Advocate finds customer service problems:** National Taxpayer Advocate, "National Taxpayer Advocate 2004 Annual Report to Congress Executive Summary," December 3, 2004, at http://www.irs.gov/pub/irs-utl/2004arcexecutivesummary.doc.

pg 173: **Nader quotation:** Ralph Nader, *The Good Fight,* New York, ReganBooks, 2004, p. 91.

pg 173: **Center for American Progress numbers:** Cassandra Butts and Christian Weller, "Tax Day: Average Americans Lose Out with Bush Tax Cuts," Center for American Progress, April 13, 2004, at http://www.americanprogress.org.

pg 174: **"...time to make the argument":** Robert Borosage and Celinda Lake, "Talking Taxes," *The American Prospect,* June 2005.

CHAPTER 7: THE RIGHTS OF SHAREHOLDERS

pg 174: **Carl Icahn:** Deborah Solomon, "Fighting for a Fair Share," *New York Times,* June 5, 2005.

pg 174: **James Kilpatrick:** James J. Kilpatrick, "Bloody Monday Comes to the Blue Ridge but Gently," *Chicago Sun Times,* October 22, 1987.

pg 175: **Stock ownership statistics:** Investment Company Institute & Securities Industry Association Report, "Equity Ownership in America," 2002, at http://www.sia.com/research/pdf/equity_owners02.pdf.

pg 175: **Middle-class stock ownership statistics:** Edward Wolff, "Recent Trends in Living Standards in the United States," New York University and the Jerome Levy Economics Institute, May 2002, pp. 17-18, at http://www.econ.nyu.edu/user/wolffe/; further discussion: Nomi Prins, *Other People's Money: The Corporate Mugging of America,* The New Press, 2004, p. 5.

pg 175: **Enron and corporate pension plans:** Louis Uchitelle, "The Rich Are Different. They Know When to Leave," *New York Times,* January 20, 2002.

pg 176: **Sen. Joseph Lieberman:** Press conference statement on the Government Affairs Committee hearings on the collapse of Enron, January 2, 2002, at http://hsgac.senate.gov/010201statement.htm.

pg 176: **Background on *Securities Acts of 1933 and 1934,* on *Investment Company and Investment Advisers Acts of 1940,* and on the *Sarbanes-Oxley Act of 2002*:** SEC, "The Investor's Advocate: How the SEC Protects Investors and Maintains Market Integrity," at http://www.sec.gov/about/whatwedo.shtml; SIA, "Primer on Securities: Basic Laws," at http://www.sia.com/capitol_hill/html/securities101.html; Conference of State Bank Supervisors, "Executive Summary of the Sarbanes-Oxley Act of 2002," at http://www.csbs.org/government/legislative/misc/2002_sarbanes-oxley_summary.htm.

pg 178: **Enron, Tyco, and WorldCom information:** Jonathan Weil, "Basic Principle of Accounting Tripped Enron," *Wall Street Journal*, November 12, 2001; David Armstrong and Laurie P. Cohen, "Tyco Is Pressing for Repayment of Loans, Bonuses," *Wall Street Journal*, September 17, 2002; Dionne Searcey et al., "Ebbers is sentenced to 25 years for $11 billion WorldCom fraud," *Wall Street Journal*, July 14, 2005.

pg 178: **"to protect investors...":** Public Law 107-204, "Sarbanes-Oxley Act of 2002," at http://thomas.loc.gov.

pg 179: **Nomi Prins:** Nomi Prins, *Other People's Money: The Corporate Mugging of America*, The New Press, 2004, p. 260.

pg 179: **Sarbanes-Oxley statistics:** Nomi Prins, *Other People's Money: The Corporate Mugging of America*, The New Press, 2004, p. 263.

pg 180: **Berhardine Timmerscheidt story:** Coleman Law Firm press release, "RE: Tampa NASD arbitration panel awards retired Palm Harbor Hairdresser $158,571 for the Mishandling of her Brokerage Account," undated, at http://colemanlaw.com/AwardsSettlements60.htm; Coleman Law Firm website, NASD Dispute Resolution for Case Number: 02-06934, undated, at http://colemanlaw.com/Awardssettlements60print.htm.

pg 180: **"I don't have the money...":** Helen Huntley, "Collecting from Broker Is Hard Part," *St. Petersburg Times*, May 23, 2004, at http://www.sptimes.com/2004/05/23/Columns/Collecting_from_broke.shtml.

pg 180: **"case...should unsettle any investor":** Helen Huntley, "Collecting from Broker is Hard Part," *St. Petersburg Times*, May 23, 2004, at http://www.sptimes.com/2004/05/23/Columns/Collecting_from_broke.shtml.

pg 180: **Broker use and approval statistics:** SIA & WirthlinWorldwide, "Annual SIA Investor Survey: Attitudes Toward the Securities Industry," November 4, 2004, p. 16, at http://www.sia.com/publications/pdf/2004investor-survey.pdf.

pg 181: **Suze Orman:** Suze Orman, *Young, Fabulous & Broke*, Riverhead Books, 2005, p. 220.

pg 181: **Background on choosing a broker:** NASD, "Invest Wisely: Selecting Your Broker," at http://www.nasd.com/web/idcplg?IdcService=SS_GET_PAGE&nodeId=472&ssSourceNodeId=469.

pg 182: **Background on NASD's BrokerCheck program:** NASD Brochure, "Providing Investors with Information on the Professional Background of Brokers and Firms," 2005, at http://www.nasd.com/web/groups/corp_comm/documents/home_page/nasdw_009888.pdf.

pg 183: **NASD fraud statistics:** NASD, "Investors' Best Practices: Common Investor Problems and How to Avoid Them," at http://www.nasd.com/web/idcplg?IdcService=SS_GET_PAGE&ssDocName=NASDW_005843.

pg 183: **Background on types of fraud:** Larry D. Soderquist, *Investor's Rights Handbook*, Practicing Law Institute,1993, pp. 199-205, 208, 211; NASD, "Invest Wisely: Selecting Your Broker," at http://www.nasd.com/web/idcplg?IdcService=SS_GET_PAGE&ssDocName=NASDW_005842.

pg 184: **Gene Murdock story:** Mark Gimein, "When Stock Tips Go Bad, Is the Broker to Blame?," *New York Times*, June 5, 2005.

pg 184: **"a piece of junk":** Steve Fishman, "Inside Eliot's Army," *New York*, January 10, 2005.

pg 184: **Gary and Lisa Friedman story:** Bloomberg News Service, "Merrill fined for faulty picks," *Newsday*, March 1, 2005; Jenny Anderson, "Merrill to pay Florida couple $1 million," *New York Times*, March 1, 2005; Jeff Ostrowski, "Merrill Lynch ordered to pay couple $1 million," *Palm Beach Post*, March 1, 2005.

pg 184: **Background on fighting your broker:** Larry D. Soderquist, *Investor's Rights Handbook*, Practicing Law Institute, 1993, pp. 219-225; NASD, "Invest Wisely: Selecting Your Broker," at http://www.nasd.com/web/idcplg?IdcService=SS_GET_PAGE&nodeId=472&ssSourceNodeId=469; NASD, "Investors' Best Practices: Common Investor Problems and How to Avoid Them," at http://www.nasd.com/web/idcplg?IdcService=SS_GET_PAGE&ssDocName=NASDW_005843; SEC, "SEC Center for Complaints and Enforcement Tips," webpage, at http://www.sec.gov/complaint.shtml.

pg 185: **Larry D. Soderquist:** Larry D. Soderquist, *Investor's Rights Handbook*, Practicing Law Institute, 1993, p. 220.

pg 185: **Background on clinics:** Colleen Debaise, "Arbitration Clinics Offer Service for Small Investors," *Wall Street Journal*, April 20, 2005.

pg 187: **Christopher Bebel:** Lauren Foster, "Investors Flock to the Courts," *Financial Times*, July 24, 2003.

pg 187: **Arbitration statistics:** NASD, "Dispute Resolution Statistics," updated June 15, 2005, at http://www.nasd.com/web/idcplg?IdcService= SS_GET_PAGE&nodeId=516&ssSourceNodeId=12. **Common Types of Fraud:** NASD, "Dispute Resolution Statistics," updated June 15, 2005, at http://www.nasd.com/web/idcplg?IdcService=SS_GET_PAGE&nodeId= 516&ssSourceNodeId=12.

pg 188: *Wall Street* **credits:** Stanley Weiser & Oliver Stone, 20th Century Fox, 1987.

pg 189: **2002 corporate scandal polling statisitics:** Peter Hart and Robert Teeter, NBC News/*Wall Street Journal* Poll, July 19-21, 2002.

pg 189: **Carol Bowie:**Gretchen Morgenson, "An Emboldened Investor Class Is Not Likely to Go Away Soon," *New York Times*, March 3, 2004.

pg 189: **Social screening statistics:** Stacy Teicher, "A Quick History of Values-Based Investing," *Christian Science Monitor*, February 9, 2004, at http://www.csmonitor.com/2004/0209/p20s01-wmgn.html.

pg 189: **Robert Monk:** Marc Gunther, "More Than a Wallet: Social Investors Move to the Mainstream," *National Catholic Reporter*, March 11, 2005.

pg 190: **Enron Annual Report:** Nomi Prins, *Other People's Money: The Corporate Mugging of America*, The New Press, 2004, p. 143.

pg 190: **Background on annual reports:** Adolph Lurie, *How to Read Annual Reports...Intelligently*, Prentice-Hall, 1983, pp. 15, 57-58.

pg 191: **Richard Scrushy, according to Malcolm McVay:** Graphic, "Decision Nears Testimony by the Ex-HealthSouth Chief," *New York Times*, April 7, 2005.

pg 192: **Eliot Spitzer story:** Steve Fishman, "Inside Eliot's Army," *New York*, January 10, 2005; Ameet Sachdev, "Marsh & McLennon to pay $850 million in settlement," *Chicago Tribune*, February 1, 2005.

pg 193: **Bruce Carton and class action statistics:** Krysten Crawford, "The $12 billion (and counting) payback," *CNNMoney*, June 15, 2005, at http://money.cnn.com/2005/06/15/news/fortune500/settlement_pool/.

pg 196: **Coca-Cola and ICCR story:** ICCR press release, "Coke applauded by religious shareholder for first step on HIV/AIDS in Africa," March 9, 2004, at http://www.iccr.org/news/press_releases/pr_coke3.9.04b.htm; ICCR, "2003-

2004 Annual Report," September 17, 2004, at http://www.iccr.org/news/annu-alreport.php; you can read Coca-Cola's report, "Our HIV/AIDS Initiative in Africa," at http://www2.coca-cola.com/ourcompany/hiv_report.html.

pg 197: **"Campaign GM" and apartheid:** Marc Gunther, "More Than a Wallet: Social Investors Move to the Mainstream," *National Catholic Reporter*, March 11, 2005; Stacy Teicher, "A Quick History of Values-Based Investing," *Christian Science Monitor*, February 9, 2004, at http://www.csmonitor.com/2004/0209/p20s01-wmgn.html.

pg 197: **Shareholder victories in 2003 and 2004:** G. Jeffrey MacDonald, "A record year for shareholder activism," *Christian Science Monitor*, June 28, 2004, at http://www.csmonitor.com/2004/0628/p14s01-wmgn.html.

pg 199: **Background on filing resolutions:** Securities Lawyer's Deskbook website, "Rule 14a-8—Proposals of Securities Holders," University of Cincinnati College of Law, at http://www.law.uc.edu/CCL/34ActRls/rule14a-8.html; G. Jeffrey MacDonald, "A Record Year for Shareholder Activism," *Christian Science Monitor*, June 28, 2004, at http://www.csmonitor.com/2004/0628/p14s01-wmgn.html; Jennifer Kramer, "Step by Step Guide to Filing a Shareowner Resolution," Shareowner Action Center, Social Funds.com, at http://www.socialfunds.com/sa/resolution.cgi.

pg 200: **Gretchen Morgenson:** Gretchen Morgenson, "Pathmark Vote Tests Wider Issues of Shareholder Control," *New York Times*, June 9, 2005.

pg 200: **Shareholders are learning by trial and error:** G. Jeffrey MacDonald, "A Record Year for Shareholder Activism," *Christian Science Monitor*, June 28, 2004, at http://www.csmonitor.com/2004/0628/p14s01-wmgn.html.

pg 200: **Arianna Huffington:** Arianna Huffington, "No More Pigs at the Trough," *The Nation*, February 3, 2003, at http://www.thenation.com/doc.mhtml?i=20030203&s=huffington.

pg 200: **Background on corporate and securities reforms:** Arianna Huffington, "No More Pigs at the Trough," *The Nation*, February 3, 2003, at http://www.thenation.com/doc.mhtml?i=20030203&s=huffington; Nomi Prins, *Other People's Money: The Corporate Mugging of America,* The New Press, 2004, p. 273.

pg 201: **William Gavin:** Adrienne Carter with Amy Borrus, "What if Companies Fessed up?," *BusinessWeek*, January 24, 2005, at http://www.business-week.com/magazine/content/05_04/b3917104.htm.

pg 201: **Nomi Prins:** Nomi Prins, *Other People's Money: The Corporate Mugging of America,* The New Press, 2004, p. 273.

pg 201: **Robert Monks:** Marc Gunther, "More Than a Wallet: Social Investors Move to the Mainstream," *National Catholic Reporter,* March 11, 2005.

CHAPTER 8: THE RIGHTS OF SPOUSES

pg 203: **Smith and Abrahms:** Gayle Rosenwald Smith and Sally Abrahms, *What Every Woman Should Know About Divorce and Custody,* Perigree, 1998, p. 9.

pg 203: **$30 billion:** Leah Hoffman, "To Have and to Hold On To," *Forbes.com,* February 24, 2005, at http://www.forbes.com/home/2005/02/24/ cx_lh_0224legaldivorce.html?boxes=custom.

pg 203: **$15,000 to $30,000:** Leah Hoffman, "To Have and to Hold On To," *Forbes.com,* February 24, 2005, at http://www.forbes.com/home/2005/02/24/ cx_lh_0224legaldivorce.html?boxes=custom.

pg 204: **5 to 10 percent:** Georgia East, "More Women Seeking Prenuptial Agreements," *Kansas City Star,* October 1, 2005, at http://www.kansascity.com/ mld/kansascity/living/12785148.htm.

pg 204: **Background for key laws**: American Bar Association *Factbook,* "Facts about Women and the Law," 1998, at http://www.abanet.org/media/fact-books/womenlaw.pdf.

pg 204: **Reno background:** "When Divorce, not gambling, reigned in Reno," *Smithsonian Magazine,* June 1996, at http://www.smithsonianmag.si.edu/smith-sonian/issues96/jun96/divorce.html.

pg 205: **Fault/ No-fault background:** Leslie Eaton, "A New Push to Loosen New York's Divorce Law," *New York Times,* November 30, 2004; New York State Bar Association, "Divorce & Separation in New York State," pamphlet, 2003.

pg 206: **Background on property and alimony:** Barry Krane, CFP, at National Coalition for Family Justice, "The Legal, Financial, and Emotional Issues of Divorce," seminar, Westchester, NY, September 24, 2005; New York State Bar Association, "Divorce & Separation in New York State," pamphlet, 2003.

pg 207: **Custody background:** Leslie Eaton, "For Arbiters in Custody Battles, Wide Power and Little Scrutiny," *New York Times,* May 23, 2004.

pg 207: **Child support background:** Laura Morgan, "Child Support Guidelines," *Findlaw*, 1999, at http://profs.lp.findlaw.com/child/child_2.html.

pg 208: **Background on annulment and legal separation:** "Annulment and Separation FAQ," Nolo.com, Oct. 18, 2005, at http://www.nolo.com/article.cfm/ObjectID/7D19D2CA-2D7F-4268-B9D401FE97EFB36D/catID/995EE405-21AA-4B4A-97CBABD905A37E1B/118/246/222/FAQ/.

pg 208: **Background on types of divorce:** Leah Hoffman, "To Have and to Hold On To," *Forbes.com*, February 24, 2005, at http://www.forbes.com/home/2005/02/24/cx_lh_0224legaldivorce.html?boxes=custom; National Coalition for Family Justice, "The Legal, Financial and Emotional Issues of Divorce," Seminar, Westchester, NY, September 24, 2005.

pg 209: **Background on Whites:** Mark K. Solheim, "A Civil Divorce," *Kiplinger's*, July 2005.

pg 210: **"Pox on you both":** Suzanne K. Bracker to Leslie Eaton, "A New Push to Loosen New York's Divorce Law," *New York Times*, November 30, 2004.

pg 211: **Scott Reeves:** Scott Reeves, "Covering Your Assets in a Divorce," *Forbes.com*, September 23, 2005, at http://www.forbes.com/personalfinance/2005/09/22/divorce-finances-legal-cx_sr_0923divorce.html?boxes=custom.

pg 211: **Bradley A. Pistotnik:** Bradley A. Pistotnik, *Divorce War!*, Adams Media Corporation, 1996, pp. 4–5.

pg 212: **Thirty percent:** "Domestic Violence and Abusive Relationships," Safe Horizons, at http://www.safehorizon.org/page.php?nav=snb&page=domesticvi-olence.

pg 212: **4 million women:** "Abuse in America," The National Domestic Violence Hotline at http://www.ndvh.org/educate/abuse_in_america.html.

pg 213: **Lorna Wendt story and quotations:** Matthew Benjamin, "Lorna Wendt," *U.S. News and World Report*, March 28, 2005, at http://www.usnews.com/usnews/biztech/articles/050328/28eewhere.htm; "Lorna Wendt, Founder," biography from Equality in Marriage website, at http://www.equalityinmarriage.org/lorna.html; David Whitman and Elise Ackerman, "Lifestyles of the Rich and Divorcing," *U.S. News & World Report*, December 15, 1997; Elisabeth Bumiller, "One Word from a Corporate Ex-Wife: Half," *The New York Times*, January 6, 1998.

pg 214: **Standard of living facts:** American Bar Association *Factbook*, "Facts about Women and the Law," 1998, at http://www.abanet.org/media/fact-books/womenlaw.pdf.

pg 214: **Stephen J. Jones:** Stephen J. Jones, at National Coalition for Family Justice, "The Legal, Financial and Emotional Issues of Divorce," seminar, Westchester, NY, September 24, 2005.

pg 214: **"Women are increasingly...":** Nigel Spencer as reported in "Female Divorcees Face Funding Crisis," *Money Marketing*, September 1, 2005, p. 20.

pg 216: **Background on Finance Talk Back/Fight Back:** Barry Krane, CFP, at National Coalition for Family Justice, "The Legal, Financial and Emotional Issues of Divorce," seminar, Westchester, NY, September 24, 2005.

pg 217: **Bridget Marks story:** Bob Port, "Double Despair," *New York Daily News*, June 2, 2004; "Every Mom's Nightmare," segment on September 9, 2005, episode of *A Current Affair*, more information at http://www.acurrentaffair.com/showdetail.php?eid=155; interview with Tom Shanahan, attorney for Bridget Marks, December 10, 2005.

pg 217: **Patricia Duff:** Aly Sujo, "Custody Chaos," *New York Post*, October 15, 2004.

pg 217: **Judith Regan:** William Sherman and Bob Port, "These Folks Spell Divorce M-O-N-E-Y," *New York Daily News*, May 29, 2004.

pg 218: **New York divorce-fixing:** Jim Hinch, "Garson Case Fireworks," *New York Post*, September 23, 2005, at http://www.nypost.com/news/regional-news/53860.htm.

pg 218: **Andrew Schepard:** Leslie Eaton, "For Arbiters in Custody Battles, Wide Power and Little Scrutiny," *New York Times*, May 23, 2004.

pg 218: **NYS child support percentages:** New York State Division of Child Support Enforcement, "Custodial Parent Information," at https://www.newyorkchildsupport/custodial_parent_info.html.

pg 219: **Thirty states have found discrimination:** Gayle Rosenwald Smith and Sally Abrahms, *What Every Woman Should Know About Divorce and Custody*, Perigree, 1998, p. 9.

pg 219: **Claiming your kids:** Bradley A. Pistotnik, *Divorce War!*, Adams Media Corporation, 1996, chapter 8.

pg 219: **Monica Getz:** Karen Winner, *Divorced from Justice*, ReganBooks, 1996, p. 214.

pg 221: **Karen Winner:** Karen Winner, *Divorced from Justice*, ReganBooks, 1996, pp. 3-4.

pg 223: **"fair, timely counsel fees":** New York City Department of Consumer Affairs, "Women in Divorce: Laywers, Ethics, Fees & Fairness," study, March 1992.

pg 223: **Seventy-five-day requirement and Patricia Duff:** Richard Schwartz, "Look Out, Divorce Court," *New York Daily News*, October 11, 2004.

CHAPTER 9: THE RIGHTS OF SMALL BUSINESS OWNERS

pg 224: **Ralph Nader:** Ralph Nader, acceptance statement for the Association of State Green Parties Nomination for President of the United States, Denver, June 25, 2000, at http://www.4president.org/speeches/nader2000acceptance.htm.

pg 224: **small business statistics:** SBA Office of Advocacy, "Small Business by the Numbers," June 2004.

pg 225: **government contracts to small businesses:** U.S. SBA, "Small Business Size Standards Matched to North American Industry Classification System Effective June 21," 2004, http://www.sba.gov/size/sizetable2002.html#fn8.

pg 225: **Lloyd Chapman:** Ilana Debare, "Fight for the Little Guy: Petaluma Man Wrests Federal Contracts from Big Business," *San Francisco Chronicle*, June 22, 2005.

pg 228: **Laura Allen:** Jeremy Quittner, "Need for Connection Fuels Online Business Networks," *Crain's New York Business*, April 5, 2004.

pg 229: **Robert Byerley Story:** Ann Zimmerman, "Small Business (A Special Report); Do the Research: To Understand the Market—and the Competition—for Your Idea, You'll Have to Delve Beyond the Obvious," *Wall Street Journal*, May 5, 2005.

pg 232: **online businesses:** Rieva Lesonsky, "The Entrepreneur's Guide to Doing Business Online," sponsored by *Entrepreneur Magazine* and PayPal, January 2005.

pg 234: **Peter Sorum:** Andrea Cecil, "National Ombudsman Office is Well-Kept SBA Secret," *Baltimore Daily Record*, October 31, 2003.

pg 234: **Jack Heckenkamp Story:** John Sonderegger, "Talk of Charleytown: Request to Open St. Peters Coffeehouse Is Grounds for City Officials to Boil Over," *St. Louis Post-Dispatch,* August 22, 2003.

pg 237: **Joanne Hayes-Rines on patents:** Raymund Flandez, "Now What...; Get a Patent: Do You Need One? Will You Get One? Is It Worth It?" *Wall Street Journal*, May 9, 2005.

CHAPTER 10: CITIZEN ACTION

pg 238: **Joan Claybrook:** *Public Citizen News,* Vol. 21, No. 1, 2001, at http://www.citizen.org/documents/pcnews30ann.pdf.

pg 241: **ROAR; Richard Wood:** Yonat Shimron, "Local Coalitions Find Their Voices; Officials Hear Call for Reform," *Raleigh News and Observer,* June 21, 2004.

pg 242: **Beth Butler:** interview with Beth Butler, July 1, 2005.

pg 243: **Frenzella Johnson story:** Interview with Frenzella Johnson, July 1, 2005.

pg 246: **petitioning government agencies:** Harry Snyder, Carl Oshiro, and Ruth Holton, *Getting Action: How to Petition the Government and Get Results,* 2002 at http:www.consumersunion.org/other/g-action/.htm.

pg 246: **Dianne Koch story:** Emily Sweeney, "Life Goes On at Threatened Hospital: Staff Works to Heal Patients and Keep Institution Open," *Boston Globe,* January 31, 2002.

pg 247: **Coalition to Save Waltham Hospital:** Alex Sugarman-Brozan and Laurie Martinelli, *Holding On: Fighting to Preserve Essential Services at a Community Hospital,* October 2003 at http://www.communitycatalyst.org/resource.php?doc_id=227%3Cbr%20/%3E.

pg 250: **Amy Rutkin:** Interview with Amy Rutkin, June 28, 2005.

pg 250: **$3 billion lobbying federal government:** Jeffrey H. Birnbaum, "Officials Fail to Track Lobbying, Report Says," *Washington Post,* April 8, 2005.

pg 250: **34,750 lobbyists, doubled from 2000:** Jeffrey H. Birnbaum, "The Road to Riches Is Called K Street," *Washington Post,* June 22, 2005.

pg 250: **Capital Grille bill:** Jonathan E. Kaplan, "K Street Grumbles About Entitlement Culture," *The Hill,* June 23, 2005.

pg 250: **"anyone who doesn't understand that shouldn't be hired as a lobbyist:"** Mark Green, *Selling Out,* ReganBooks, 2002, p. 14.

pg 251: **Krist Novoselic story:** Krist Novoselic, *Of Grunge and Government,* RDV Books, 2004, pp. 37-9.

pg 251: **Novoselic: "It was an insult...:"** Nicole Brodeur, "Novoselic's New Sound Is Political," *Seattle Times,* October 28, 2003.

pg 252: **Danny Goldberg:** Nick Paumgarten, "Post-punk," *New Yorker,* October 18, 2004.

pg 252: **Donald E. deKieffer on lobbying:** Donald E. deKeiffer, *Citizen's Guide to Lobbying Congress,* Chicago Review Press, 1997, pp. 54-6.

pg 255: **government secrecy:** Scott Shane, "Increase in the Number of Documents Classified by the Government," *New York Times,* July 3, 2005.

pg 257: **Committee on Government Reform report; fee waivers:** Committee on Government Reform, *A Citizen's Guide on Using the Freedom of Information Act and the Privacy Act of 1974 to Request Government Records,* 2003.

pg 257: **Cost of *FOIA* request:** Reporters Committee for the Freedom of the Press, *How to Use The Federal FOI Act,* 2004, at http://www.rcfp.org/foiact/index.html.

INDEX

About the Author

Mark Green, President of the New Democracy Project, was New York City's Consumer Affairs Commissioner from 1990 to 1993 and elected Public Advocate from 1994 to 2001. He is the author or editor of 19 previous books, including *The Consumer Bible, What We Stand For*, and two *New York Times* bestsellers—*Who Runs Congress?* (1972) and *The Book on Bush: How George W. (Mis)leads America* (with Eric Alterman, 2004).